VOICE *of* REASON

V*of*OICE
REASON

Why the Left and Right Are Wrong

RONN OWENS

WILEY

John Wiley & Sons, Inc.

Published by John Wiley & Sons, Inc., Hoboken, New Jersey.
Published simultaneously in Canada.

For general information on our other products and services please contact our
Customer Care Department within the United States at (800) 762-2974, outside the
United States at (317) 572-3993 or fax (317) 572-4002.   \

Wiley also publishes its books in a variety of electronic formats. Some content that
appears in print may not be available in electronic books. For more information
about Wiley products, visit our web site at www.wiley.com.

Library of Congress Cataloging-in-Publication Data:

Owens, Ronn.
    Voice of reason : why the Left and Right are wrong /Ronn Owens.
       p. cm.
    ISBN 0-471-48282-X (cloth : alk. paper)
    1. Political participation—United States.   2. Political
culture—United States.   3. Right and left (Political science.   I.
Title.
JK1764.O93 2004
306.2′0973—dc22

                                                              2003025144

For Jan, Sarah, and Laura

Contents

Forewords

(Left) `◄ ONE WAY`　　　　　　　　　`ONE WAY ►` **(Right)**

I must confess: I don't hate George W. Bush. Sure, his policies suck. He's rolled up the biggest deficit in history. And, under false pretenses, he rolled us into an unnecessary war in Iraq for which we're going to pay the price for a long time.

Nevertheless, I still don't hate George W. Bush. He doesn't know any better. But I do hate Ronn Owens. For a very good reason: Because I'm jealous!

But I also love Ronn Owens. For a very good reason: Because he's so damned good.

Like you, I'm a political junkie and a talk radio fanatic. Wherever I travel in the country, I always tune into local

I've been fortunate to count Ronn Owens as a friend for a number of years, despite our political differences. I also have a lot of respect for him as a broadcaster. He is the quintessential host, not because he is intelligent—which he is—or because he is funny and articulate—which he also is—but because he cares about what his listeners think. He respects and appreciates his audience and values their opinions regardless of how much he may disagree with their particular position on any given topic.

And Ronn's listeners know how he feels about them. They know that, every time he gets behind the microphone, he will tell them what he thinks, but he talk radio. Because I want to know what's going on, what the hot issues of the day are—and what ordinary Americans think about them. To find that out, there's no better forum than talk radio.

The only problem is most talk radio hosts sound the same. Since most station managers are afraid to hire a liberal, most talk show hosts are right-wingers. And you can predict exactly what they're going to say. Either, like the oh-so-predictable Rush Limbaugh, they blame everything from Mad Cow Disease to the poor performance of NFL quarterbacks on liberals. Or, like the ever-so-pompous Bill O'Reilly, they sound like they're just reading the daily talking points of the Republican National Committee. "Isn't George Bush wonderful? And here's why." Listening to them, I just want to throw up.

Unfortunately, there's not *one* liberal talk show host syndicated nationwide (so much for complaints about the so-called "liberal media"). But if there were one liberal voice on the dial, I must admit, he or she would probably sound as slanted to the left as most other

will never preach to them or denigrate. He shares his opinions (and he has a lot of them, like all great hosts), but he's always willing to share his audience's likes and dislikes with equal grace and interest. They know he never minces words when it comes to any issue, whether it's Gray Davis' recall, Arnold Schwarzenegger's election, or Brad Pitt's views on U.S. foreign policy.

Ronn also has a strong, intuitive sense of right and wrong, and what should be right and wrong in today's volatile world. I don't always agree with his position on an issue—like his support for a single national identity card—but I always believe that Ronn is telling me what he honestly believes, whether we agree or disagree.

For example, Ronn believes the truth lies in the middle, and it really lies on the conservative right. Ronn will know the truth once he has experienced a Hannity Epiphany. As my listeners know, the truth is only known once you've been "Hannitized" and Ronn needs a little "Hannitization." The left may be sincere, but they're sincerely wrong. I am amazed that so many liberals still don't talk shows are now to the right. The only difference is, they'd be reading the talking points of the Democratic, not the Republican, National Committee.

And then, thoroughly fed up with the lack of voices on the left and the redundancy of voices on the right, I come home to the Bay Area. I tune into KGO and Ronn Owens and get a big smile on my face. How stimulating! How refreshing! And how maddening!

That's why I love and hate Ronn Owens at the same time. Because I've been listening to him forever. And yet, honest to God, I still never know ahead of time where he's going to come down on any particular issue. I love that. When I turn the dial, I'm looking for somebody who thinks for himself. I want somebody who's an independent thinker. Somebody who looks at every issue fresh and asks: Does this make sense or not? In other words, I relish the possibility of being surprised.

Alone among a population of echo chambers, Ronn Owens has that rare ability to think for himself. Even though he's been doing it for 25 years, he doesn't take a knee-jerk response to any issue. Unlike

get it. Far too many liberals see no connection between values, education, the moral health of our nation, and America's security and prosperity.

The truth lies in the beliefs of the conservative right. At heart, American conservatives like myself are believers in the Constitution. We believe that the principles embodied in the Constitution are enduring, and that to whatever extent we deviate from them we put our liberties at risk. Our views are consistent because we believe in absolute truths and in the essential soundness, even righteousness of the Founder's vision of government. The conservative vision is that America returns to its founding principles because these principles are the pillars of freedom. Without them, America will not continue to be great; with them there is no limit to our future.

It's our differences that keep the great medium of talk radio interesting. *The Ronn Owens Program,* along with the leaders of our industry like Rush Limbaugh and Michael Reagan are some of the reasons talk radio has experienced such an exciting renaissance in recent years. Talk radio has most other talk show hosts, who are slaves to their political bias—"if George Bush (or Bill Clinton) is for it, I'm for it"—Ronn actually thinks before he leaps.

Now, granted, that may make for some bizarre opinions. In the wild California recall election, for example, I did not agree with how Ronn finally voted . . . but at least his point of view was not predictable. It demonstrated some original thinking. And, most importantly, it made for great debate—and weeks of great talk radio.

Same with President Bush. One day, I tune in and hear Ronn singing his praises for leading us into war in Iraq. I scream out loud at the radio. The next day, I hear him blasting Bush for running up the biggest deficit in history and destroying the American economy—and I'm a happy camper again. Which proves Ronn is right, at least half of the time.

I have also heard Ronn Owens do two other things you never hear from anyone else on talk radio, myself included: Admit he had changed his mind and admit he was wrong. It takes a big man to do

become the national town hall of the twenty-first century. More than the voting booth, the radio dial is where American democracy thrives. It's where people go to share their views and their values, their peeves and their passions about the large and small events that shape their daily lives. Talk radio is the one place where the American people can be heard on a daily basis, and be heard instantly by their neighbors, both down the street and across the nation. It's the one place in the real world where each person's opinion has an impact.

Ronn Owens makes people laugh, he makes them angry, and most of all, he makes them think. His listeners welcome him into their homes, automobiles, and offices, and they appreciate the fact that he likes them in return.

The only thing that I find exasperating about Ronn is that he makes what he does look effortless. Without the bells, whistles, and flash of some hosts, Ronn reaches his audience and makes friends without breaking a sweat. His radio show is a three-hour conversation among friends, five days a that. Bet you never heard Rush Limbaugh admit he was wrong. Because, he'll be the first to tell you, he never is.

For those of you not fortunate enough to live in the greater San Francisco Bay Area, there's only one problem: You can't find Ronn Owens on your radio dial. Weep no more. Read this book. And then tune into Ronn on the Internet at kgo.com. Pretty soon, you'll be as hooked on Ronn Owens as I am.

BILL PRESS
Political Analyst
MSNBC

week. He's the good guy next door who is always willing to listen and proffer good advice—and he has the wisdom to know when to speak up and when to listen. There's a reason Ronn Owens has been on the air in San Francisco for nearly three decades—he's an incredibly talented radio talk show host.

Thanks, Ronn.

SEAN HANNITY
Hannity & Colmes
Fox News Channel

Preface

If you've ever referred to Bill Clinton as "Slick Willie," or to George W. Bush as "Shrub," "Dubya," or "the fictitious President," this book is not for you.

Then again, maybe it is. Maybe you need it more than anyone else. Maybe you've become a victim of the disturbing polarization that has a stranglehold on the United States.

I'm not talking about a split between men and women, blacks and whites, the wealthy and the working class. I'm talking about politics today, and the ever-increasing gap going on right now between the far left and the far right.

Surveys show that 60 percent of the people in this country place themselves somewhere in the middle of the political spectrum, voting on the left on some issues, while voting on the right on others. They're the ones who in fact run this country and who determine its direction. They're the ones who decide who is elected president. They don't necessarily vote the party line, but instead look at each issue and evaluate each candidate on a case-by-case basis before casting their vote.

Yet, you'd never know that from watching Sunday morning TV forums, cable news programs, or listening to certain talk shows. Instead, you'd think there were only two kinds of Americans: fundamentalist conservatives and bleeding-heart liberals.

What's worse, both sides are so preoccupied with hating each other, they've become increasingly divided by the issues, suspicious of each other, and inflexible in their beliefs. You're either for or against not just an issue, but an entire ideology. If you supported the war in Iraq, you must love Bush. If you opposed it, then you're a Bush hater.

As a result, many Americans find themselves boxed in by what they *think* they should believe. Labor represents the working man, so we should always support labor. Business makes America work, so we should always help business. Democrats or Republicans (whichever the case may be) are on our side, so we should always give them our vote.

But where do you go if your political beliefs support some aspects of your party's philosophy, but not all of them?

Where do you go if you think toppling Saddam Hussein was morally right, yet denying a woman the right to an abortion is morally wrong?

Where do you find representation if you strongly believe we ought to legalize drugs in this country, but are equally passionate about the notion that gun possession is a constitutional right?

The key problem for me—and the key problem for the rest of us who have quietly listened and learned, even as the far left and the far right both continue to badger us (not to mention, each other)—is the word *always*. To me, to insist that one side is always right is to close the door on your own conclusions.

For over 28 years, I have been the host of the number one rated radio program in the greater San Francisco Bay Area. Day in and day out, I talk to the people who make the news: from presidents to prime ministers, from movie stars with political views to the police officer who brought us all together in the weeks after 9/11 when he sang "God Bless America" at Yankee Stadium during the 2001 World Series. I also talk to the people who are impacted by the news—ordinary people like you and me. I bring up the issues that are on our minds every single day. I get the dialogue going, listen to what you have to say, and tap into what you're thinking on any given topic, at any given moment.

I compete directly against Rush Limbaugh, and I consistently beat him—the only major market personality in the country to do so. I do this not with bombast, not with vitriol, but by looking at both sides of an issue calmly, fairly, openly, honestly, and with a healthy dose of common sense.

I know, I know, that's hard to believe—especially today, when it seems the only way a talk show host can succeed is by taking stands that are far to the right (and, to a lesser extent, far to the left) of the political spectrum.

I understand why they do it that way. It's easy. Everything is black and white for them. Agree with a host on the far right, and you're absolutely correct; disagree, and you're a moron, a fool, uninformed, or completely un-American. Disagree with a host on the far left, and you're either a tool for big business, a stooge for the rich, or a person with no intellect or feelings.

That's never been my style. I may not always agree with my listeners, but if a caller or a guest presents a view on a particular issue that is different from my own, and which makes complete sense . . . I'm willing to change my mind.

Again, that's an unusual characteristic for a radio talk show host. But when it comes to the way in which the vast majority of us come to form our opinions, it's hardly unusual at all.

If our opinions are always so rigid and inflexible, why do we have opinion polls, and why do the results of these polls so often fluctuate? How could former President George H. W. Bush go from having a 90 percent approval rating less than a year before the 1992 election to becoming a man who lost the White House to Bill Clinton?

Contrary to what the folks on the extreme left or extreme right would have us believe, you and I are eminently capable of making up our own minds without anyone telling us how we're supposed to think. We just haven't been heard from before.

There is no approach to politics today that really, truly speaks to us, one capable of presenting and discussing the issues that are important to this country in a way in which the majority of Americans—the 60 percent of us who are politically "in the middle"—can comfortably identify.

Until now. That's what this book is about. By eschewing the politics of the extremes, we can stem the polarization that's killing this country and find common ground between all Americans, left, right, and center. And we can do this together by approaching each issue with clear eyes, an open mind . . . and a *Voice of Reason*.

A Voice of Reason is a person who will listen to both sides before making up his mind. It's someone who isn't afraid to change his mind if the other side makes a point that is compelling, persuasive, and reasonable.

A Voice of Reason is capable of arguing a point of view intelligently without turning it into a personal issue, trying to put down the other person's thoughts or resorting to name calling. In other words, he's willing to consider an issue on its own merits.

A Voice of Reason is a voice that's calmer and far less shrill than the voices of the extremes.

Which isn't to say that a Voice of Reason cannot be passionate. He's just not that "my way or the highway," party-line passionate that you always hear ranting from the far left or extolling from the far right. Anyone who has listened to my show knows that a Voice of Reason can weigh both sides of an issue, take a stand, and still argue that position as passionately as anyone else.

That said, a Voice of Reason is also someone who understands the meaning of compromise. It's a person who understands that you can't always get everything you want, and that at the end of the day, you still have to work with people. It's a person who believes in a win-win philosophy, not a win-lose philosophy.

Most of all, a Voice of Reason is capable of arriving at his own conclusions, without being spoon-fed his answers by the party line. It's a person who isn't afraid to go against the grain sometimes.

Because let's face it. Politically speaking, if you want to be liked, the answer is real simple: You move to the extremes. Because when you're with the extremes, you never really have to think—all you have to do is go along. More to the point, because everyone around you feels the same way, you're going to find yourself praised, and you're going to find your opinions validated.

Whereas those of us who are in the middle, judging each issue on its own merits, often find—depending, of course, on what the issue is and how we happen to see it—that the people who were our friends suddenly become our enemies, and, conversely, the people who were our enemies suddenly become our friends.

Then again, there are times when the people who were our enemies simply refuse to come around, despite our willingness to meet them halfway and consider their point of view. Which means that in the long run, you can count on having fewer friend-ships—or, I should say, less validation for your ideas—if you hap-pen to be "in the middle."

Finally, a Voice of Reason is an approach to politics that has been sorely missing for the vast majority who consider themselves "in the middle." That's the approach we're going to take over the course of this book.

We'll try to figure out how this polarization started, how it be-came prevalent, what makes it so appealing and why it's become so increasingly destructive. We'll look at some of the wedge is-sues and what keeps them in the spotlight. And we'll try to come up with a dose of common sense that, hopefully, will steer every-one—politicians, pundits, and ordinary people alike—more to-ward the middle. Because that, again, is where the votes are. That's where the decisions in this country are made.

Being in the middle of the political spectrum does not mean that we do not care, or that we have no strong opinions. Far from it.

We care a great deal about this country. We just want to be able to think clearly, without restraints, and without preconceived notions, as we form our own opinions.

RONN OWENS

November 2003

Acknowledgments

My thanks to Matt Holt, my editor at John Wiley & Sons, who originally approached me about this project; Ed Robertson, for capturing my voice so well; Susan Schustak, my producer; Cathy Kennedy, my assistant; Mickey Luckoff, who brought me to San Francisco; and of course my wife, Jan Black Owens.

About the Author

Ronn Owens is the host of the number one-rated talk radio show in Northern California, *The Ronn Owens Program*, on KGO-AM in San Francisco. With over 500,000 listeners, Owens is the only major-market radio personality who consistently beats Rush Limbaugh in the ratings. *Talkers* magazine named Owens #13 on their list of the Top 25 Greatest Radio Talk Show Hosts of All Time. The first 12 on the list all host syndicated programs, making Owens the #1 local talk show host in radio history. Ronn is also the winner of the prestigious Marconi Radio Award for Major Market Personality for the Year, an honor bestowed on him by the National Association of Broadcasters in October 2003.

Political Pragmatism
Is No Oxymoron

Political debate in this country is clouded by labels. We label ourselves as Democrats or Republicans, liberals or conservatives, maybe even as ultra-liberals or arch-conservatives.

Once you attach a label to your political views, you tend to become stubborn. If you're a liberal, you presume conservatives are all wrong. If you're a conservative, all liberals are stupid. If you're a Democrat, you can't believe in fiscal responsibility that may involve spending cuts. If you're a Republican, you can't come out in support of gun control or a woman's right to choose. You get so entrenched in your own views that you lose the capacity to listen. You fail to see that the other side just might have a point.

Me? I hate labels. I find them constrictive.

People in the media often think of me as a *centrist*. I understand why. It's a label of convenience. Politically speaking, my views are "middle of the road." To most people, a centrist is someone who positions himself right down the middle all the way through.

If I had to choose a label for myself, I'd say I was a political pragmatist. I believe in consensus. I don't think countries should ever be governed along a strict party line, nor do I think people should ever reflexively vote the straight party line. I take each issue as it comes, judge it on its own merits, and make my decisions from there. In fairness, the more dispassionate you are about an issue, the easier it is to be open to both sides.

Philosophically, that translates into a person whose inclinations are liberal when it comes to social issues, but conservative on economic issues and foreign affairs. A true centrist always stays in the middle and approaches the issue from there, while a political pragmatist will very likely take stands on one side or the other. There are issues that are black and there are issues that are white. Put them all together, and you end up in the middle, philosophically . . . but your views don't always follow the same rigid pattern. Some would say your views don't follow any pattern at all.

I also find that most people who consider themselves politically "in the middle" tend to think like me. We're not strictly liberal, and we're not strictly conservative. And that drives the extremes nuts.

For example, I strongly believe that who you sleep with, or what you do in the bedroom, is really none of my business as long as you're both adults. Keep the government out of our private lives—which, on the surface, sounds like a basic, fundamental, traditionally conservative position. At the same time, I happen to think that if you're a gay couple committed to each other, you ought to be entitled to the same sort of union as any straight couple would. That idea, of course, skews very, very liberal.

You have a right to live your life in the way you choose to live it. Then again, so do I. You have the right to express your opinions, even if they're different than mine. But you don't have the right to impose your will on others. You don't have the right to block the entrance of an abortion clinic to espouse your pro-life agenda, or shut down the Golden Gate Bridge in the middle of the afternoon to protest the war in Iraq, or tie up Friday rush hour traffic on the busiest street downtown just to call attention to your cause, no matter what you advocate or how important you think your position may be. Your right to your opinions, and my right to mine, ends the minute those rights start to impair other people's ability to live their lives in the way *they* see fit.

A political pragmatist is apt to be very liberal, maybe even libertarian, on social issues. On economic or foreign affairs, though, we're far more conservative. And much of that comes from sharing the viewpoint, traditionally championed by conservatives, that the United States is a damn good country.

For those of us who are in the middle, part of our problem with the far left is the misguided, traditionally liberal belief that somehow we're the bad guys—that the United States imposes its will on other nations and that it's always our fault when things go wrong. Therefore, by implication, all other countries are better.

I don't want to sound like a flag waver, but what country could possibly be better than ours?

You want to live in Cuba? Sure, they may have medical care for all their citizens, but even that comes with a price: You can't speak your mind!

You want to look at the Scandinavian countries? No doubt, there's much that is desirable about their way of life, but look at their rate of taxation. It's worse than ours.

China? North Korea? Russia? Iran? Syria? Get serious!

Think about it objectively, and it's a slam dunk. There's no better place in the world to live than in the United States.

On the other hand, I'm not exactly comfortable with all those ultra-conservatives out there who look at America with blinders on. You know the type. They're the ones who think our country can do no wrong. They're the ones who will never admit that even the United States screws up once in a while, and that we're not as perfect as we'd like to think.

SOMETIMES, GRIDLOCK IN POLITICS CAN BE A GOOD THING

That said, a true centrist is always looking for compromise—and that *is* a fair reflection of the way I think.

I'm a big believer in the "half a loaf" theory. If you can't get everything you want, you try to get part of what you want.

That's why I've never understood why the Democrats nominated extreme liberals such as Michael Dukakis or George McGovern, or why the Republicans nominated an arch-conservative like Barry Goldwater. It doesn't make any sense. You push too far to the outside, and you won't get anything—or anywhere, for that matter.

Here in California, we saw this happening for the longest time with the Republican party. They nearly became extinct. Until Arnold Schwarzenegger was elected governor last year, every major state office in California was held by a Democrat. As it stands, the Democrats still have the majority in both the Senate and the State Assembly.

I thought that was terrible because it left no opportunity for political debate. It was as though we had a politburo in Sacramento: Once the assembly came up with an idea for a bill, they floated it, and then they passed it . . . and the Democratic governor would sign it.

You need to have some variety. You need to have some debate. There needs to be some kind of a check, just like we have a system of checks and balances with the three branches of government.

On the other hand, as strong as the Democrats are on a state level in California, they've made it easy for the Republicans to become increasingly strong on a national level. And I don't want that, either. I don't want the Republicans too strong. I don't want the Democrats too strong.

The problem is, my congressperson is Nancy Pelosi. On a personal level, I just think the world of Nancy Pelosi. I've known her for a long, long time. I respect her. I like her. She is the leader of the Democratic party in the House of Representatives. She also happens to be a classic "San Francisco liberal."

What do I mean by San Francisco liberal? Allow me to explain by briefly going over some of the recent positions taken by our intrepid Board of Supervisors.

Providing food and shelter to homeless people instead of cash is reactionary—that was their argument in the November 2002 election when "Care Not Cash" appeared on the ballot. For that matter, they also held that asking beggars not to aggressively panhandle anywhere in San Francisco is discriminatory and deprives them of the right to make a living.

One Supervisor not only got into a physical confrontation with then-Mayor Willie Brown, he also scuffled with police officers who were trying to enforce the law. Yet, he was handily re-elected in a crowded field. One year later (as if we needed an encore), this same Supervisor breached political protocol after his name came up to be temporary mayor while Brown was out of town. Not content with simply holding down the fort for a day, this hothead took it on himself to appoint two people to a powerful city commission and have them sworn into office behind the mayor's back.

And then there was a vote on whether to prohibit urinating in the streets. It lost. Big!!

I've lived and worked in San Francisco for over 28 years. On social issues, I'm as liberal/libertarian as anyone. Yet, compared to some of the clowns we have on the Board of Supervisors, I feel like Jesse Helms.

So you can understand that if you're a Democrat, having a San Francisco liberal as your House Whip is like throwing meat to hungry lions. Republicans will eat this up.

Ross Perot used "gridlock" as a pejorative. But I think gridlock in politics can be a good thing.

I want to have contention among my representatives in government. I want to see a battle between the two sides. If neither party is too strong, that leaves the door open for debate, for discourse, for a careful examination of all sides of the issues. If neither party is too strong, that lessens the odds of a "rubber stamp" approval of legislation without any real consideration of the issues at all.

Now some would say that the check for politicians is the election. To some degree, that's true. But look at the election. More often than not, people just aren't voting—at least, they're not showing up at the polls in large numbers, as was once the case. Those who do vote don't always do so intelligently. They're just as likely to vote on the basis of which ad they liked best as they are on the basis of the issues. In this respect, they're not so much voting for one side as they are voting against the other.

Think about most of the political ads we see these days. They hardly ever talk about why you ought to vote for Joe Candidate. Instead, they usually focus on how awful his opponent is. Why? Because that's what grabs our attention. It's the same reason why it's more interesting to watch the scene of a car crash than to watch traffic flow smoothly.

I DON'T WANT TO BE ON ANYBODY'S TEAM

California also has a new system where you can vote in either primary. That has to be one of the stupidest ideas I have ever heard.

Think about it. Logic says, "You're a Democrat, you vote for the Democratic nominee. You're a Republican, you vote for the Republican nominee." But here, you can be a registered Democrat and still participate in the Republican primary, and vice versa. Which means you could have right-wing Republicans stuffing the ballot box for the weakest Democratic candidate, and left-wing Democrats doing the same for an inferior Republican candidate, leaving us to choose between two weak prospects come November.

If you're going to have two political parties, you should only be able to participate in your own party's primary . . . and that's that. Same goes for political candidates. If you're running for political office, you shouldn't be able to manipulate the other party's primary election so as to virtually handpick your opponent in the general election—as our system in California currently allows.

Problem is, for those of us in the middle, it's getting harder to know what either of these parties stand for.

There was once a time when most people thought of Republicans as fiscally responsible. Yet, we've recently seen the Bush administration push through a $350 billion tax package that only serves to increase our deficit far more drastically than it was before. And these are the folks who supposedly hate spending!

So what do these parties really stand for? What's their point of view?

If we played a game of word association, and you said to me, "Republican party," I'd say, "against abortion rights," "not big on the environment," "ultra-conservative." I'd think of people like Tom de Lay, Bill Frist, Trent Lott, and Ann Coulter. If you said "Democratic party," I'd say "woman's right to choose," "more government is better government," "big on spending." I'd think of Al Sharpton, Jesse Jackson, Carol Mosely Braun, and Al Gore running far to the left in 2000.

These, of course, are two extremes. That's not the way it should be.

Maybe we're at a point in our society where political parties have outlived their usefulness. Maybe if we didn't feel that we had to be affiliated with one party or the other, we might actually get somewhere instead of being polarized like we are right now by the politics of the extremes.

There is something to be said about the two-party system in Great Britain. At least they're direct and honest about it: You have your liberals, and you have your conservatives.

Here in the United States, it's much, much harder to tell the difference. I mean, who's really a Democrat, Zell Miller or Ted Kennedy? Who's more of a Republican, Jesse Helms or Olympia Snow? Given their voting records, Olympia Snow ought be to a Democrat and Zell Miller a Republican. Yet, because they belong to one party or another, they have to follow the party line.

No wonder so many of us are in the middle of the spectrum. There are times when we may side with one political party or another, but it's often reluctantly (or at least, temporary). There's no formal "middle of the road" philosophy, no "voice of reason" center where we can feel comfortable. The Republicans are too far to the right for us. The Democrats veer too far to the left. No third party exists that really matches our point of view.

One of the major reasons why no third party exists is that there's no money behind it.

Sure, we've seen flashes of it. There was George Wallace and the American Independent party back in 1967. You had John Anderson and the Independent party in 1980. Perot and the Reform Party in 1992. The Libertarian party always seems to be on the cusp, but they can't quite get over the top. Then there's the Green party, which some would argue siphoned votes away from Al Gore in 2000 by running Ralph Nader as their candidate— effectively splitting the Democratic vote and enabling George Bush to win.

None of these parties have been able to capture the kind of money and attention that the two major parties have. And after all, monied interests tend to have strong beliefs one way or the other. For every major corporation pushing for pro-business legislation, you have just as many unions pushing for legislation favoring workers. By and large, it is these two extremes that dictate the agenda.

That leaves people like me, who don't always side one way or the other, smack in the middle. We'd much rather look at each issue on a case-by-case basis, and for that reason it's tough to pigeonhole us.

Now I realize a politically astute person might say, "Ronn, who are you fooling? Liberal on social issues, conservative on foreign affairs—you sound like a neo-con to me."

I disagree. A true neo-con is someone like William Kristol, the editor of *The Weekly Standard*. Now I have great respect for Bill. I've interviewed him many times. I think that when it comes to foreign affairs, we're very much on the same wave length. But when it comes to social issues, I'm not so sure. He doesn't seem too concerned about some of the more uncompromising stands of the GOP in their platform.

That's why I hate labels. I don't want to belong to any one "team." I don't want to feel obligated, or worse still, become complacent. And deep down, most people need the comfort of knowing they're affiliated with somebody. They need to feel some sense of validation of what they believe in right now.

At least, that's what you see with the extremes.

A MAJORITY WITHOUT A VOICE

We've reached a point in politics today where everything is becoming black or white, and ideas have become entrenched. Certainly, that's what you get when you listen to conservative talk radio, or when you watch certain cable news shows. Everyone's coming at it from a particular perspective—that perspective being, "Our way, *always,* is the right way to go." As a result, the majority of us who consider ourselves "middle of the road," who don't quite look at everything that simplistically, are quietly sitting in the background, frustrated, watching and waiting for our moment to speak.

I wouldn't call us a "silent majority"—that term is *so* Spiro Agnew-ish, and besides, you know how I feel about labels. But we are "silent" in the sense that, again, there isn't any one, unified platform that can effectively speak for the rest of us. Because contrary to what the far left or far right would like to believe, most people don't participate in extreme partisan debates. Most people do what I try to do, which is to look at each issue as it comes up, judge it on its own merits, and then make a decision.

Take George W. Bush, for example. Now here's a man I did not vote for in the 2000 election. Instead, I supported Al Gore—reluctantly, I might add, because I felt Al Gore made a huge mistake when he abandoned the Clinton "New Democrat" positions.

To me, Bill Clinton was an excellent president because he understood the importance of compromise. This was a man who figured out a way to work with Newt Gingrich when nobody thought it was possible: when the Republicans seized control of the House after the 1994 elections. Sure, Clinton may have been a "new Democrat" in that he governed slightly left of center. But he was also very much a political pragmatist. In a word, he was someone I could identify with.

So when Al Gore ran for president, I had hoped he would've run along that same platform. But he didn't. Al Gore's platform was far, far more to the left than Bill Clinton ever was. The further he distanced himself from Clinton, the more he lost sight of who he was. That was dramatically demonstrated in the debates. There were three debates, and there were three Al Gores: the tough one, the mild one, and the middle one. It was like the Three Bears

I still voted for Gore, mind you, because candidate George W. Bush was someone for whom I had a visceral dislike at the time. (No rationale behind it. I just didn't care for the guy.) Besides, I figured if it came down to choosing between someone who's more to the left and someone's who more to the right, go with the guy who's more to the left. That's just my basic inclination.

That said, I am a pragmatist. I may not have liked Bush as a candidate, but once he was inaugurated he became my president. I respect the office, and I respect the man.

Here's a guy who (from my perspective, anyway) really knew what he was doing in the area of foreign policy, who essentially said what a lot of us in the middle have been saying for years: that the United States has lost its position of respect in the world. That we had become a doormat in the eyes of quite a few countries, and that as a result we were no longer feared. And that in this turbulent world, if you have to choose between being liked and being feared, better to be feared. There has to be both a carrot and a stick if we want to make sure that countries act in a civil fashion.

So when Iraq came up, Bush took the situation and reacted to it decisively. And of course, the impact of our actions with Iraq went far beyond the borders of that country. The reason there's progress toward peace in the Middle East today is a direct corollary to what we did in Iraq. The reason why Syria is now cooperating with us, as well as why Iran finally finds itself under the microscope, is a result of the war in Iraq. Suddenly other countries are starting to think twice about ticking off the United States. Suddenly they're thinking, "Hey, maybe we shouldn't flaunt our ideas in front of them. There might be sanctions or other repercussions. Maybe we ought to be a just little more cautious whenever we deal with them in the future."

I think that's fabulous. The United States is more of a superpower now than it ever was under Bill Clinton. I think that's a wonderful, positive outcome.

Now, does that necessarily make me a Bush fan? Hardly. Almost every single domestic plan he has for this country, I oppose. I don't necessarily see his tax cut as a stimulus to the economy. I don't believe in "faith-based organizations"—I think there ought to be separation between church and state. I'm appalled at the lack of tolerance his Administration has shown when it comes to the rights of gay people. I don't understand how he (or any other President, for that matter) could possibly be against the idea of prescribing marijuana for medicinal purposes, especially if it could help alleviate the suffering of someone dying from AIDS, cancer, or other terrible diseases. I strongly oppose most of his judicial appointments, which are far to the right. I'm very, very strongly pro-choice, and George Bush is a president who's very strongly pro-life.

And as much as I backed the president on the war in Iraq, that doesn't entitle him to a free pass in that arena, either. In July 2003, when the controversy over the nature of the intelligence on which President Bush based his decision to invade Iraq first became public, I not only supported the House Investigation Committee's efforts to look into the matter, I strongly called for open hearings. Why would anyone be opposed to finding out the truth? As someone who strongly supported the war—and who took a lot of flak for that, I might add—that support becomes a little tenuous if you won't at least admit to me that something may have been wrong. Or that you know how to start what we did in Iraq (as Tom Friedman might put it), but have no idea how to finish it.

So if the election was to be held tomorrow, and I had to choose between President Bush and someone else, my answer would have to be, "Who's the someone else? Then I'll decide." Like most Americans, I think I'd want to consider that option and see how the rest of the field lines up before I make up my mind.

WHAT'S SO BAD ABOUT CHANGING YOUR MIND?

One of the worst things about extremist thinking is this ridiculous notion that changing your mind is a sign of weakness.

Let's say you're a politician. Twenty years ago, or whenever you started your career, maybe your views on abortion were far more conservative than they are today. For whatever reason, your beliefs on the matter started to change over the years. Once you were staunchly pro-life. Now you've evolved into a pro-choice advocate.

Unfortunately, the political environment today is such that if you dare change your views on anything, both sides will hold it against you. You're considered a traitor by your own party for switching ideologies, while the other side labels you a waffler, someone who "flip-flops" back and forth on any given issue.

Former CNN chairman Walter Isaacson made the same point about "flip-flopping" in an interview last year in *W Magazine*. Speaking specifically about Israeli Prime Minister Ariel Sharon, Isaacson said, "He flip-flopped. And that's the basis for the most common political attack ad. Usually when a leader changes his mind, he looks weak, which is why leaders are often so afraid to change their minds."

I think that's a terrible reality that puts politicians in a classic no-win situation. Stick to your guns for fear of being attacked, and your opponent will think you're rigid. Shift gears, or at least be willing to *consider* the other side, and you're somehow perceived as weak, unprincipled, wishy-washy, or worse.

The whole idea that changing your mind conveys weakness is not only stupid, it doesn't reflect reality. If it did, then we wouldn't need Gallup polls, surveys, approval ratings, or things like that.

People change their minds all the time. And thank God for that.

Before 9/11, George Bush's approval rating hovered at around 50 percent. In the days and weeks immediately following 9/11, that figure jumped to nearly 90 percent. In times of crisis, people clamor for leadership—any leadership. As a country, we were badly shaken by the events of that horrible day. We looked to the president for confidence, assurance, and guidance, and he more than rose to the occasion.

Same thing happened as far as the war in Iraq was concerned. Polls taken following the State of the Union Address, which the president delivered six weeks prior to the war, showed that Bush's overall approval rating registered at 59 percent—a 33 percent drop from the high he enjoyed in the months following 9/11. Nearly half of the people surveyed expressed disapproval for the way the president handled the economy, while two out of every five were dissatisfied with how he managed foreign policy.

Two months later, when the Iraqi regime toppled, Bush's approval rating shot back up to 70 percent.

This isn't just the case with the president. This happens with any elected official, on any level. Our opinion of how well they're doing their job constantly fluctuates, depending on the economy, on changing events, on the level of unemployment, on any given number of factors.

Military commanders change strategies all the time in the heat of battle. So do our security leaders. "It has been said that the most fatal illusion is the settled point of view," said Homeland Security Secretary Tom Ridge last year in a speech before the Commonwealth Club of San Francisco. "This is where danger finds easy sanctuary. This is why America's security must also be consistent with changing times."

Implicit in Ridge's remarks was the notion that in this age of suicide bombers, sleeper cells, and bioterrorist attacks, we can never assume that those who don't like us won't try to hurt us. We must be prepared for anything. For the sake of our safety and our way of life, we have to analyze each situation as it comes up and keep our options open.

Funny, but I don't remember anyone blasting Ridge for saying that.

If a quarterback doesn't like the defensive alignment he sees on the field, he calls an audible. Yet no one ever knocks him for that. As a matter of fact, most football analysts would give the quarterback credit for having the foresight to change his mind.

So why the double standard when it comes to politicians?

Changing your mind is no sign of weakness. Changing your mind shows that you've carefully weighed an issue from both angles and that you're open to saying, "You know something? Maybe the other side does have a point."

And if, after weighing both sides, you do find yourself siding with the "other camp," that doesn't make you a traitor. Not in my book, anyway. What that tells me is that you're someone who has looked at an issue carefully and intelligently and come to a decision *on your own,* as opposed to the way your party is "supposed to think."

In today's divisive political climate, that takes a lot of courage.

THE ROAD TO NOVEMBER IS THROUGH THE MIDDLE

I often think of what Vermont Senator Jim Jeffords said in 2001 when he switched over from the Republican party and became an Independent. "I didn't leave the Republican party," he explained. "The Republican party left me."

That's the dilemma facing any elected official when it comes to politics today. Doesn't matter whether you're running for senator, governor, or president of the United States—if you want the nomination, you have to win the primary.

How do you do that? By appealing to the fringes: the kind of "knock on doors, work the phone banks, stand outside subway stations at seven in the morning and pass out handbills" people who really are on the fringes of politics. To win the nomination, they're the ones you have to cater to, because they're the ones who are going to go out to the polls on a rainy day and vote, no matter what. Even if it's an "off-year" election, with only one or two initiatives on the ballot, these people will vote.

With the average person, that's not always the case. That person may just as easily vote or not vote in the primary or in an off-year election. So in this respect, once again the political parties are controlled by the extremes.

Now that you've won the nomination, how do you win in November? By moving to the center. Nothing earth-shattering about that—it's just common sense. You already have the Democratic vote sewn up. To get the Republican vote (or at least, enough of it to get yourself elected), somehow you have to move to the center. You have to find a way to appeal to the millions of people in middle America who may not (and in all probability, do not) agree with your party's liberal points of view.

Except you can't move too close to the center, lest the extremes—the people on the fringes who got you the nomination in the first place—accuse you of flip-flopping. Or worse, stay home on Election Day.

You know what? That's absurd. No matter which way you go, you wind up setting yourself up to be a hypocrite.

The reality is, if you want to win the White House, you need a candidate who's willing to say, "This is who I am. I'm not running strictly on the basis of what you or your party wants to hear on any given issue. I'm running on the basis of what I think is right."

Case in point: Bill Clinton, who ran as a "new Democrat" in 1992. "New Democrat" is just a euphemism for "not being a left-leaning Democrat."

Another case in point: Arnold Schwarzenegger, who won as a "new Republican" in the recall election last year. Schwarzenegger ran as a fiscal conservative, yet he also espoused views on abortion, gun control and gay rights that went against contemporary conservative doctrine.

EXTREMIST THINKING: KEEP IT SIMPLE AND CHANNEL YOUR ANGER

The problem with polarization is that it's too easy. You look at an issue, see how it plays liberal or conservative, then work backwards to see how it justifies your point. Then you offer simple solutions that have the broadest application possible.

Suppose you're a left wing radio talk show host. A congressman comes up with an idea for a bill that would award amnesty to any illegal aliens who manage to avoid detection from immigrant authorities for a period of five years. You really don't have to think it out. Your response is automatic: "Illegal immigrant, poor people, got to take care of them, got to help them, great idea, let's do it." Doesn't matter how much of a slap in the face this would be to your parents, my parents (who came to the United States in 1940), or any of the countless other people who had to abide by certain rules and certain laws when they first migrated to this country. Why should we give a free ride to illegal aliens, just because they managed to beat the system?

Because you're a left wing radio talk show host, that's why. Regardless of what you may personally believe, you have to spout the party line, lest *you* be accused of flip-flopping.

If you're a right wing host, your take on the issue is likewise automatic: you either blame everything on the liberals, or you pin it on the government. You look for an enemy, be it foreign or domestic, and you point the finger at "them." You hear talk of a bill proposing amnesty for illegal aliens, and it's, "What, are they nuts? We're Americans, dammit! It's our country! We must close off our borders! They broke the law, screw 'em! Send 'em back from where they came!"

There's no room for compassion. There's no reason for it—after all, you're a right wing radio talk show host. It's the same kind of reflexive response . . . only with arch conservatives, it's all about anger and where to direct it.

But that's exactly what extremist thinking does: it forces people to think backwards, not forward. Once you've attached yourself to a particular political philosophy, you simply work in reverse to justify your point of view. And you do that, of course, by ignoring anything that's on the other side, while latching onto everything that justifies your point.

And you call that freedom of expression?

What's the point of having political debate when you can't even consider the other side?

Political debate isn't just about winning. It's also about listening.

Maybe it's time we ought to think less about winning the argument and more about thinking it through. Maybe it's time we stop talking *at* each other and start talking *to* each other, so that we can at least consider the other side and work toward compromise and solutions.

Not too many talk show hosts can say this, but I'm open to having my mind changed. That's what has made me successful, and I think it's a quality that would make anybody reading this book successful as well. Here's why.

If you open your mind and listen to what other people have to say, you'll learn. Not only that, you'll find that when you talk about an issue—whatever that issue happens to be—the conclusion you've come up with is better, more intelligent, and more clearly thought-out than it would be if you were simply spouting the party line.

Why? Because you came up with the answer yourself. You thought it through, considered every angle, and *made your own choice,* instead of having someone else do it for you.

When you think about it, that's really what polarization hath wrought. That's really where the far left and far right both have it wrong. That's why, as we determine the future direction of this country, we must somehow find a way to bridge the gap between the extremes and bring us all closer to the middle.

And if we can't find common ground, then by all means let's create it!

9/11 and the
Great Divide

I may be based in San Francisco, but I operate on East Coast time. If you do the kind of news talk, issues-oriented show that I do, you really almost have to.

I'm on the air nine to noon weekdays on KGO-AM. A typical day for me starts around 4:30 A.M. I get up and go through all the different newspapers (I read about five a day) looking for interesting, topical items that I can discuss with listeners on that day's show. I'm somewhat old-fashioned when it comes to reading the paper: I still enjoy the tactile sensation of holding a newspaper in my hands. At the same time, though, I love my gadgets. There are certain web sites that I'll check out every day on my Mac, plus I get periodic news updates from CNN and CBS on my RIM Black-Berry. If a major story breaks during the morning, I do whatever any of you might do. I either turn on the radio or head straight for the television.

So at 5:46 A.M. Pacific time on the morning of September 11, 2001, I was already up and well into my routine when I heard the report that a plane had somehow flown directly into the World Trade Center. I turned on the TV and was shocked and frightened by the images of American Airlines Flight 11 slamming head on into the north tower. I was sick to my stomach and could barely believe my eyes when suddenly, to my complete horror, it happened all over again. Only this time it wasn't a replay. It was a live shot of United Flight 175 flying straight into the south tower of the World Trade Center. Before long, I would also see footage of a third plane, American Airlines Flight 77, which had just smashed into the Pentagon. And then finally, there was the report of United Flight 93 crashing in a field 80 miles southeast of Pittsburgh, Pennsylvania.

In the space of just a few minutes, terrorist hijackers had commandeered four commercial airliners carrying innocent people and used them as weapons of mass destruction. Their sole purpose was to inflict fear, death, and chaos upon the United States. Three of these planes were deliberately flown into buildings also filled with thousands of innocent people.

I can't imagine anyone who can honestly look at 9/11 without intense feelings of passion. I can't imagine anyone, liberal or conservative, who was not impacted by the horror of the planes hitting the buildings and of people leaping to their death . . . or by the relief we felt when we learned that thousands of people had miraculously escaped the Twin Towers before the buildings completely disintegrated . . . or by the heroic images of police officers and firefighters alike racing up floor after floor, looking for others to save . . . or by the images of rescue workers sifting tirelessly through the rubble at Ground Zero, searching for survivors they would never find . . . or by the painful sight of family members holding signs and placards with pictures of loved ones, hoping desperately that they might still be alive . . . or by the fear and vulnerability that overcame all of us as we realized the world as we once knew it was never going to be the same.

9/11 changed so much in this country. There's no getting around that. "Loss of innocence" was the phrase so many of us latched onto in our feelings and reactions to the events of that horrible day. We used it so often in our conversations, it practically became a cliché.

And yet there was no better way to put it. Our innocence *was* lost that day. That, and so much more.

For a lot of people in this country, the idea that anyone—no matter how violent their regime or extreme their political beliefs—would even think of inflicting such large scale death and destruction *on our own home shores* was simply incomprehensible. Sure, we had all studied history. We had lived through wars. But a nation going to war, or a soldier dying in the act of war, was one thing. Innocent people dying in their office building as they began their work day was another. It was a display of evil beyond the realm of anything any of us had ever seen before.

It's hard to say anything positive came from such a heinous act of violence . . . and yet some good did happen.

9/11 made us all reevaluate our priorities. Suddenly nothing seemed more important to us than the love of our families. Who can forget the profound role that cell phones would play on that day . . . the flurry of calls made to loved ones from aboard the planes or from inside the buildings, hoping desperately for one last chance to say goodbye . . . the countless other calls that some victims would make to themselves, in hopes that the message beep on their phones might somehow help rescue workers locate them among the rubble. Who among us couldn't help but wonder that but for the grace of God, it could have been *our* city targeted, *our* office building destroyed, *our* loved ones killed in the process . . . or that when we kissed our spouse and children and left for work that day, we may have never seen them again.

"Wake up call" was another phrase we often used in talking about 9/11. Certainly it stirred an appreciation for America that had probably been dormant in many of us for a long, long time. We may have known it intellectually, but far too often we were too caught up in our own little worlds to stop and realize what a truly good country we have.

Me, I prefer to think of it in more visceral terms. 9/11 was like a severe punch in the stomach that lands you in the hospital. Maybe you only get the wind knocked out of you. Maybe you're hurt so bad that you wind up in emergency surgery. You come out of it scared, shaken, woozy, and disoriented. At the same time, you're relieved because you know it could've been much worse. You look at your family and friends who are gathered around you, and you realize, "Hey, I'm lucky to be alive. I'm just glad that the people I love are safe and here with me."

9/11 certainly changed me. I know in my entire life I never felt as proud of this country and its people as I did after 9/11. That sense of patriotism has stayed with me, as it has with so many of us. Even today, there are times that when I think back to what happened, I find myself suddenly tearing up—and I'm not exactly an emotional guy. Not in that sense, anyway.

And in that spirit of solidarity, in the sense of recognizing the importance of protecting our country, our leaders, our family, and our friends from those who want to harm us, 9/11 also brought forth a new era of vigilance that many of us have embraced. This is our country and we want to keep it safe. We are even more united than perhaps we've ever been before. I would submit that's a good thing.

What disturbs me, though, is the politicization over 9/11 that we increasingly see today. On the one hand, the right wing plays it to death, latching onto our newfound patriotism every chance they get to justify domestic legislation that isn't necessarily in our country's best interest. On the other hand, the left wing practically ignores it. They are so unwilling to concede that the world today is safer now that Iran, Syria, and other countries know that the United States won't take any crap from anyone, you almost get the impression they forgot 9/11 even happened.

In that respect, 9/11 exemplifies the divisive nature of extreme politics more than anything else. For all its unifying powers, 9/11 drove the left and the right even further and further apart. That alone makes 9/11 a defining moment that underscores the need for a "voice of reason" philosophy.

FRANCIS GARY POWERS AND THE JOLT TO THE SYSTEM

How'd we ever get to be this way? Let's go back and take a look at four key moments in recent U.S. history that would eventually give birth to the political fringes.

The first watershed would have to be the U-2 affair that occurred in 1960 at the height of the Cold War. At that time, the former Soviet Union was head and shoulders above the rest of the world when it came to intelligence gathering networks. Satellite technology as such had not yet been perfected. In an effort to close the gap, the United States built a high-altitude long-range reconnaissance plane that would fly over Russia, ostensibly for "weather missions" but in reality to gather valuable information on Soviet military preparedness. The plane, known as the Lockheed U-2, flew several such covert operations between 1955 and 1960.

In May 1960, word of the U-2 was leaked to Russian intelligence. The plane was shot down and its pilot, Francis Gary Powers, was subsequently captured by the KGB. While military officials tried to negotiate Powers' release, President Eisenhower ordered NASA to issue a statement saying the plane had been conducting "weather research" and that mechanical problems had caused Powers to accidentally veer into restricted Soviet airspace. To prevent the true nature of the mission from becoming known to the public, no mention was ever made of the fact that the plane had been shot down. As part of the ruse, NASA doctored registration and markings of a second U-2 plane and showed these papers to the press. That plan backfired, however, after Soviet Premier Nikita Khrushchev told reporters that a U.S. plane had indeed been shot down and even displayed parts of the wreckage as evidence.

Today, the U-2 incident may not seem that riveting—and compared to other Cold War matters such as the Cuban missile crisis, perhaps it wasn't. From the standpoint of the roots of polarization, though, it's quite significant because it demonstrated for the first time that we could be manipulated or lied to as a country. Up to that point, Americans generally believed in their government. We had no reason not to. So it was a real jolt to the system to realize that our leaders would just turn around and lie to us. That in turn cast a cloak of suspicion that our government has never since been able to shake.

VIETNAM AND THE GENERATIONAL SPLIT

A few years later came Vietnam, which raised our newfound cynicism about government to an entirely new level.

In many ways, Vietnam was perhaps the most profound instance of polarization in our lifetime. The war was not only unpopular, it marked the first time in modern history where the American public was not entirely behind its troops. Up until that point, there was an unwritten rule that we always support our soldiers in times of war. That was the way it was throughout the conflicts in Korea, World War II, and World War I. No matter what our differences were at home, it was important for the morale of our troops that we kept a united front.

That all changed with Vietnam. Either you backed the war or you didn't. Everywhere you went, people had strong feelings one way or the other. Not only that, each side began using statistics to back up their arguments, just as we see today—and they would be just as unyielding, one way or the other, as is also evidenced today.

Vietnam erupted just as the entire counterculture movement was taking shape around the country. The civil rights movement was also in full swing, while women's liberation was not far behind. This was the early 1960s, when the notion of a *generation gap* first came into being. So it would come as no surprise to find that, by and large, opinions on Vietnam were also pretty much split along generational lines. We saw no better examples of that than the sit-ins and protests that took place on college campuses throughout the country. Men would burn their draft cards, seek refuge in Canada, become conscientious objectors, or find other ways to express their opposition.

Before long, these sentiments made their way into other areas of our culture. Footage of protestors yelling "Hell no, we won't go" became a staple of the evening news, along with footage of the war itself. Heavyweight boxing champ Muhammad Ali (then known as Cassius Clay) would be stripped of his title when he refused to serve in Vietnam, saying "I ain't got nothing against no Viet Cong." Director Robert Altman voiced his dissent by way of the movie *M*A*S*H,* a biting satire of war set against the background of Korea but with overt anti-Vietnam references. And as the 1960s gave way to the 1970s, we saw the generational divide play out each week on television in the heated political debates between arch-conservative Archie Bunker and his ultra-liberal son-in-law on *All in the Family*.

Not only was Vietnam generational, there was such growing cynicism of government in general, you could find advocates for any point of view, no matter how extreme it may have been. That made it a lot more respectable as you moved out toward the fringes, which in turn made extremist thinking more acceptable. Years later, that respectability would grow even more with the emergence of the Internet.

WATERGATE AND THE SLIPPERY SLOPE

The next major watershed moment was the Watergate scandal in 1972. If Vietnam fed on the cynicism that started with the U-2 incident, Watergate fueled it. Suddenly, the people who really distrusted government were starting to attract attention. That was never the case before. It used to be, if you genuinely believed that the government was conspiring against you, you were dismissed as some sort of kook. Now you were getting acceptance. How could you not? The networks were covering the Watergate hearings gavel to gavel when they began in the spring of 1973. The entire world was watching. Suddenly your ideas were playing out every day in living rooms across the globe.

With all due respect to the late Francis Gary Powers (who would be tried for espionage and serve two years in a Russian prison before the United States could broker his release), fudging about the U-2 was one thing. Fudging about Watergate was another. Sure, we may not have appreciated our government lying to us about spying on Russia, but at least Eisenhower could honestly say he was doing it in the interest of national security. (That doesn't necessarily justify the deception, but it does lessen the sting.) The shenanigans going on in the Oval Office under Richard Nixon were altogether different. After all, Nixon had just won a landslide reelection in 1972. His supporters were legion, and they honestly believed he had galvanized the country. Once people realized how badly he had betrayed their trust, they became very emotional about it.

The reaction to Watergate, like that of Vietnam, was like a heated tug-of-war. The players who lined up on both sides of the matter were very passionate about their views. Those feelings would inevitably pull people more toward one side or the other.

I was in Cleveland at the time of Watergate, hosting a talk show on WERE. That was also about the time when Baruch Korff first came onto the scene.

Korff was a Ukrainian rabbi who became a rabid Richard Nixon advocate after the president secured exit visas for Jews from the Soviet Union during the Yom Kippur War of 1973. When the Watergate scandal began to heat up, Korff founded the National Citizens Committee for Fairness to the Presidency to help fund Nixon's legal defense. That, plus an unabashed, unquivering loyalty for Nixon through thick and thin, made Korff a fixture in radio throughout the 1970s, even after the president resigned.

Korff was a master of the "slippery slope" argument—the kind you often see with extremist pundits today. You know what I'm talking about. You start with a simple, all-purpose statement, such as "Abortion equals murder," that you always return to in order to prove yourself right: "Yes, that nine-year-old rape victim who was impregnated by her assailant has had a terrible, traumatic ordeal. But she should still have to carry that child. Abortion is murder, murder is wrong, therefore abortion is wrong." (To be fair, a typical left-wing slippery slope argument would be "Abortion is always justified, even in the case of an abortion performed on a 13-year-old without parental consent.")

Korff could be downright nuts at times. He was utterly convinced, for example, that Deep Throat was none other than then-Nixon aide Diane Sawyer, even though most Washington observers tend to agree that the real identity of the infamous unknown informant was probably a man.

That doesn't take away the fact that from a radio talk show host's point of view, Rabbi Korff was always, *always* a great phone guest. You could count on him to defend Nixon come what may, even on matters that most people would agree were genuinely indefensible. He'd start with the premise, "Nixon is president, the president is always right, therefore Nixon is right," and just keep driving that point home no matter what, more often than not whipping himself into a frenzy along the way.

That's really how the extremes work. The more emotionally charged they become over an issue, the more likely they are to push you in one direction or the other. Conversely, the more dispassionate you can be about an issue, the more likely you are to consider it on its own merits and come to a decision about it without any political baggage attached.

THE INTERNET MAKES THE FRINGES RESPECTABLE

After Watergate, the next significant turning point for the fringes would have to be the rise of the Internet in the early 1990s.

For the extremes, the World Wide Web was an absolute dream come true. Suddenly the Baruch Korffs of the world didn't sound quite as wacky they did before. There's something about seeing even the most far out political views in print that almost gives them credence.

Not that we did a 180° or anything. It's just that as the Internet became increasingly mainstream, and web sites, web 'zines, and other online outlets continued to proliferate, radicals on both ends of the political spectrum saw what a perfect vehicle the Web was to express their opinions. The Web not only made them seem legitimate, it also gave them access. Suddenly it was quick, easy, and relatively inexpensive to project their ideas onto others—millions of others who shared their point of view, but who up to that point had no means of communicating it.

And that made the fringes credible. The Internet gave them an audience, who in turn found validation for their opinions . . . which in turn made the fringes respectable. No matter how disparate or extreme you are, whether you believe George W. Bush is even more dangerous than Saddam Hussein or consider the world a safer place now that Saddam's out of the picture, you're bound to find someone who agrees with you somewhere out there in cyberspace.

So if I were a right-wing conservative, I wouldn't expect Molly Ivins or Arianna Huffington to support my opinions. I'd go to Ann

Coulter, William Safire, Bill O'Reilly, or George Will. Conversely, were I a left-wing liberal and wanted validation, I wouldn't read Coulter, Safire, and the like. I'd look to Ivins, Arianna, Bob Herbert, or Robert Scheer.

Don't get me wrong. I'm a huge fan of the Internet. I probably spend an average of three hours a day online. I love the instant access to information. You don't have to wait until six o'clock to find out what happened today. You log on and boom, you have the news of the world whenever you want it from hundreds of different sources.

The problem I have with the Internet, as far as the roots of polarization is concerned, is that it's *too* easy. Almost as easy, in fact, as backward thinking itself.

Think about it. By making the matter of finding validation for your opinions as simple as "point and click," the Internet in many ways encourages the sort of reflexive thinking on which the far left and the far right equally rely. Just do what the pundits say or vote along the party line and you're all set.

You may not realize it, but that again is letting others decide for you.

I don't care if you're a liberal Democrat or a conservative Republication. When we forego our ability to form our own opinions, that can't be good for our country.

WE'VE BECOME A NATION OF INSTANT GRATIFICATION

One other negative about the Web, albeit a comparatively minor one, is that it's rife with errors.

I'm not talking about mistakes in spelling or grammar, although there are certainly plenty of those. I'm talking about the number of factual inaccuracies you often find on web sites for cable networks, local TV stations, and otherwise reliable news sources.

That, to be sure, speaks to the highly competitive nature of the industry and how it relates to news. In this day and age of high-speed access and 24-hour news channels, there's a constant battle for content. The Internet in that respect is like a huge beast that constantly needs to be fed in order to survive.

But in many ways the Web is also a reflection of who we are and how we live our lives.

Jim Bohannon is a talk show host who for years filled in for Larry King back when Larry did his overnight show on the Mutual radio network. In 1993, he finally inherited the program when Larry left radio to concentrate on his hugely popular CNN show, *Larry King Live.* Jim's been going strong on Mutual (now Westwood One) ever since.

Two weeks after the 2000 election, when the outcome of the Florida vote was still very much up in the air, Larry invited a bunch of radio talk show hosts to come on the show and hash out the issue. I was one of the guests on the panel, as was Jim Bohannon. At some point during the hour, Jim came up with a line that I have remembered ever since: "Americans are the only people in the world who can look at something that's in a microwave and actually say, *Faster, faster!*"

When you think about it that tells you everything you need to know about life in the twenty-first century. We've all grown so accustomed having instant access to information that we've collectively become like two-year-olds. We look for every short cut we can possibly find—and if we can't find the solution we're looking for right away, we instantly start to whine! That mentality carries over into the way we do our work, drive our cars, report the news, and as mentioned before, form our opinions.

In that respect, the Internet has also become a classic way of figuring out who's first, as well as who's most accurate. That is increasingly evident in the way in which television reports the news today.

This isn't new by any means. Given the choice, most television news shows would rather be first than be entirely correct. That notion stems not just from when TV news first became entertainment, but once TV news started making a profit for networks and local stations alike.

Back in the days of Walter Cronkite, Huntley-Brinkley, and Howard K. Smith, the most important goal of network news shows was being accurate. Once you're making money, though . . . sure, you still want to be accurate, but what you *really* care about (if you're a network executive, anyway) is the bottom line. You make money from big ratings, and you get big ratings because of reputation.

News organizations are always angling for the catchiest slogan, sound byte, or video byte they can find to trumpet their own success. "Give us 22 minutes, and we'll give you the world." "All news, all the time, on the air and online." "The more you listen, the more you know." And if a newspaper, radio station, or TV network has a reputation for delivering the top stories first, or landing more exclusive interviews than any other competitor, people will naturally read it more, listen more, or watch it more. People naturally gravitate toward No. 1.

I mentioned before how my BlackBerry comes with automatic news alerts from CNN and CBS. Invariably CNN is ahead of CBS, and invariably they're right.

I realize it's not popular to say this, but Matt Drudge is also often first. More often than not, he's also accurate. Consequently, *The Drudge Report* is one of the first places I check for major stories, along with CNN. Now if Drudge were to start screwing up . . . I'd still go to him, but he'd no longer be first. He'd be 5th, 6th, 10th, or 20th.

I can't help but think of that old *Seinfeld* episode where Jerry and the mother of the woman he's dating are jockeying for the No. 1 position on the girl's speed dial list. Once the mother realizes that Jerry has supplanted her from the top spot, she does everything she can to knock him out.

The same thing goes for the "rush to be first." News organizations are no different than any other competitive industry. They want us to turn to them first, and they'll use whatever technology is available to get our attention before the others get it first.

Unless we all of a sudden decide to grind our fast-paced lifestyle to a halt, that "rush to be first" mentality isn't ever going to change.

Besides, so long as the end result is such that we're able to know more than ever before even faster than before, why would we even want that to change?

Sure, there will be times when your organization may be the first to report a big story yet somehow get it wrong. But if you do, *so what?* That sort of thing is so rare, it's easily forgiven and (almost) instantly forgotten.

It's not as if we suddenly stopped watching the TV networks after they prematurely awarded Florida to Al Gore as a result of the famous Voter News Service gaff on Election Night 2000. Nor did the people in Chicago stop buying the *Tribune* after the paper ran the infamous "Dewey Defeats Truman" headline in 1948.

Common sense says that if a news source consistently botches a major story, its audience or readership will go eventually someplace else. Even so, if your reputation is solid, it'll still take a while before you finally lose it, rightly or wrongly. Either way, the marketplace will bear that out.

Beyond that, I don't see what else we can to do stop it.

Consider the Jayson Blair controversy of early 2003. Now you would think that if any paper would be "on top of it" as far as accuracy in reporting was concerned, it would be the *New York Times*.

There again, it all goes back to the "rush to be first." Watergate made *Washington Post* journalists Bob Woodward and Carl Bernstein the first newspaper personalities to become genuine celebrities. Consequently, every cub reporter wants to be the one who breaks the big story. Every TV journalist wants to be Dan Rather, who happened to be in Dallas on the day JFK was assassinated. That was his springboard to fame. He got noticed.

Everybody wants to be first with the news, and we can't wait for them to give it to us. There's nothing wrong with that. It's who we are.

The Internet has made us into a nation that thrives on instant gratification. All that hype about the impact the information superhighway would have on our lives turned out to be true. We've become so accustomed to having everything right away, we can't imagine it delivered any other way.

THE E-MAIL READ 'ROUND THE WORLD

That said, a great deal of what floats around in cyberspace is either invalid, unsubstantiated, or patently untrue. Yet, you'd be surprised how many of these things are accepted as fact simply because they're posted online.

This, as we know, is how e-mail scams, hoaxes, and urban legends propagate. And while some of this stuff is clearly fun, many of these items are deliberately worded with the kind of inflammatory language that extremists use to push people into one corner or another.

It doesn't matter whether you're on the left or the right. Once you've triggered a response, your actions are the same. It's as though you're Emmitt Smith running with the football. You look for whatever hole you can find on the other side, no matter how small, and blast your way through it as though that disproves everything else about their argument.

Then again, you get an e-mail about a subject that really touches a nerve, you may decide to forward it to your friends, who forward it to their friends, and so on. Then it becomes a lot like the old game of telephone. The more that e-mail is forwarded, the more altered it becomes, to the point where it often barely resembles the original message at all.

I know a little about this. Two days after September 11, I was doing my show when a caller and I got into a debate over how to deal with the Taliban. This, of course, came at a time when everything was heated and all of us were very much on edge. While I was still trying to sort through everything, I agreed with what President Bush said when he addressed the nation in the hours after the attacks—that countries that harbored terrorists would have to share the responsibility of their actions. Time and again the Taliban was asked to surrender Osama bin Laden to the United States. Time and again they refused. Consequently, I said on the air that if the Taliban continued to shelter bin Laden, Afghanistan would unfortunately have to bear the brunt of U.S. military activity. At that point, the caller flippantly suggested that we ought to "bomb Afghanistan back into the stone age."

Little did I know this would set off a chain of events that would forever link me with a man named Tamin Ansary.

Tamin Ansary is a San Francisco writer whose father was an Afghani politician. He himself was born in Afghanistan, so he knew the region exceptionally well. As it happened, Tamin was also listening to my show that day. Once he heard talk about "nuking"

Afghanistan, the words and the way the caller threw them out obviously hit close to home. So he wrote a letter expressing his views on the matter, e-mailed it to about 20 friends, and mentioned that he was responding to remarks he had heard on the radio on *The Ronn Owens Program*.

That e-mail would be read, forwarded, and re-transmitted repeatedly across cyberspace over the next 48 hours, making its way to probably a hundred million people in the process. It was eventually posted on over 50 web sites (including Salon), as well as picked up by countless newspapers and wire services throughout the world.

And because my name happened to be mentioned in the very first paragraph, I received a ton of responses myself, most of which were not very nice. Which is ironic, considering that philosophically Tamin and I were actually on the same page on this particular issue. While I never advocated savagery, barbarism, or leveling a nation of innocent people, I did suggest that our response to 9/11 had to be severe. Tamin made the same exact point in his e-mail and reiterated it on the air when I invited him on the show to talk about it a couple days later.

I mention the episode for two reasons. One, it reminded me how quickly things can spread on the Internet—or how radically a forwarded e-mail can change as it makes its way through cyberspace. In addition to seeing the caller's remarks erroneously attributed to me (bombing anyone "back into the stone age" is not a phrase in my vernacular), I also came across versions that changed Tamin's gender from male to female, or which referred to him as a Harvard Law student or a professor at Stanford when he was in fact neither.

More importantly, the reaction to Tamin's e-mail also exemplified the divide between the extremes when it comes to foreign affairs, and particularly our response to terrorism.

Ultra-liberal views on foreign affairs usually boil down to this: If there are two sides to a conflict, go with the underdog and assume they're in the right. It doesn't matter if the so-called "downtrodden" are ruled by a government that has subjugated the rights of its citizens for decades—they're still the underdog! They're not in power, they've been oppressed, ergo we must support them.

With arch-conservatives, it's more a matter of "Circle the wagons, we've done nothing wrong, the rest of the world hates us, so let's get them before they get us, even without conclusive evidence." That kind of approach doesn't make a lot of sense either.

By and large, those who jumped all over that e-mail (and, consequently, all over me) were 100 percent opposed to the idea of any U.S. retaliation whatsoever. It was a response to a clear-cut common sense issue that made no sense to me. It was also a harbinger of things to come in the aftermath of September 11.

9/11 STOPS US IN OUR TRACKS

If the U-2 incident was one of the first incidents to trigger the era of modern political cynicism, making people increasingly wary of the U.S. government, then 9/11 was the moment that turned it on its head.

For Baby Boomers who grew up protesting the war in Vietnam, 9/11 was that douse of cold water that made you stop and realize where we are as a country and how we got to be there.

All of a sudden, there was no other choice. We had to trust our government. Not only that, *we did.* And we did because we knew that as flawed as our government was, it still was a hell of a lot better than Al Qaida.

Sure, the era of good feelings would only last a few weeks. Deep down, we all knew it was just a matter of time before Democrats and Republicans resumed their partisan business as usual.

But there's a reason why people across the country suddenly started buying flags again and displaying them outside their house every day for an entire year—I did, and I'd never done that in my entire life. There's a reason why men and women began wearing flag pins on their lapels, or why we were all so moved when we heard Officer Daniel Rodriguez of the NYPD sing "God Bless America" at Yankee Stadium during the 2001 World Series.

It was a combination of realizing what a truly great country we had, while giving the finger to the enemy at the same time.

If the Internet helped speed us up, 9/11 definitely slowed us down. It made us all pull back and take a good hard look at our country. It made us all care more about politics, foreign affairs, our lifestyle, our loved ones, and the role of the United States in the world. The mood of the country was so incredibly raw. Everybody needed to heal.

In the world of radio, if you want to succeed as a talk show host, you need to think in terms of "What can I talk about today that people really care about?" For me, the answer to that question has always come down to the three words that matter most to the vast majority of listeners: *me, here, now.*

In the weeks following 9/11, I never had to worry about that. All of us were affected by it. All of us needed to talk it out. And that's exactly what we did.

In a way, though, 9/11 was the one day in my life I was *not* a talk show host—I was a news anchor. The reports on the attacks were still unfolding by the time I came on the air at 9:00 A.M. I was as angry and scared and uncertain as my listeners, yet I couldn't convey any of those feelings on the air. I still had a job to do.

9/11 was also a defining "voice of reason" moment when it came to George W. Bush and our response to terrorism. At least I felt that way. Bush may have been my president, but his record at that point generally consisted of domestic policies I did not support. Safe to say, I probably sided closer to the 50 percent who did not approve of his administration at the time than to the 50 percent who did.

That said, I strongly agreed with the president after 9/11 when he made "no distinction between the terrorists who committed these acts and those who harbor them." I also remember how strongly I felt about the speech he gave before the Joint Session of Congress on September 20, 2001. I said it to my wife Jan that evening as we watched it together, and I said it again on the air the following day: I thought it kicked ass.

I still didn't care much for the president's domestic agenda, but I absolutely supported his resolve to aggressively go after international terrorists.

Which brings us back to the question of polarization. Because as much as the horror of 9/11 brought us closer together, our response to the matter (and particularly, our military response) drove us even further apart.

SOUR GRAPES AND LIBERAL NAVEL-GAZING AT ITS WORST

As I mentioned before, while I tend to be liberal when it comes to social issues, I'm far more conservative on foreign affairs. So admittedly my views in regard to 9/11 are slightly skewed in that direction.

That said, I think it's fair to say that in some ways, liberals never had a chance. If you opposed the concept of harsh retaliation, if you were against the war in Afghanistan (or for that matter, the war in Iraq), the mood of this country post-9/11 created an environment that made it very difficult to express that point of view. There was a certain arrogance and intolerance that got swept up with the overwhelming patriotism many of us were feeling, some for the first time in our lives. No matter how valid your grounds for opposition may have been, they basically fell on deaf ears. Our country had just been attacked, and we wanted to do something about it.

At the same time, though, some extreme liberals just flat out didn't get it. That was plain to see in many of the comments they made in the wake of 9/11.

Here in the Bay Area, we saw this play out at one of the worst possible times: right in the middle of a memorial service honoring the victims who died on United Flight 93, the San Francisco-bound plane that crashed in Pennsylvania after its passengers heroically fought back against their hijackers. Many state and local politicians were in attendance that day, including Governor Gray Davis, Senator Dianne Feinstein, Senator Barbara Boxer, Representative Nancy Pelosi, and San Francisco Mayor Willie Brown. The ceremony, which took place at the Bill Graham Civic Auditorium in downtown San Francisco, was one of many held throughout the country on Monday, September 17, the national Day of Remembrance.

Among the dignitaries to address the crowd that day was Reverend Amos Brown, a Baptist minister who was also once a member of the San Francisco Board of Supervisors. Brown (no relation to the Mayor) spoke for bleeding hearts across the country when he said, "America, is there anything you did to set up this climate? What did you do—either intentionally or unintentionally—in the world order, in Central America and Africa where bombs are still blasting? What did you do in the global warming conference when you did not embrace the smaller nations?"

It was a scathing criticism of U.S. foreign policy that given the time and venue was incredibly ill-advised, not to mention completely wrong.

9/11 had happened just a few days before. The confidence of our country was still badly shaken. Not only that, family and friends of many who died on the planes and in the World Trade Center were seated on stage. It was not the time and definitely not the place to wag your finger at the United States, no matter how strongly you may happen to feel about the matter.

What Amos Brown did was comparable to asking an elderly robbery victim what she did to provoke the man who had just mugged her, or a young rape victim what she did to spur on her assailant when she's barely recovered from the trauma. That line of questioning is so inappropriate, it's absurd.

About the only thing that could make it worse is if Brown's comments were somehow validated.

Guess what? They were.

The auditorium was packed that day with left-wing peace activists. Once Amos gave them an opening, they went nuts. They cheered. They applauded.

Only in San Francisco.

Thankfully, the politicians in attendance had the good sense to be outraged. Gray Davis and Dianne Feinstein got up from their seats and left while Amos Brown was still speaking. Even über-liberal Nancy Pelosi cut right to the chase when she followed Brown to the podium: "With all due respect to some of the sentiments that were earlier expressed—some of which I agree with—

make no mistake: The act of terrorism on September 11 put those [who perpetrated it] outside the order of civilized behavior, and we *will not* take responsibility for that."

While it pleased me to hear Brown's comments so strongly denounced, I was still upset that he said them. To me, it was liberal navel-gazing at its worst.

Liberals who persist in their belief that "we must ask ourselves first and foremost how we got into this situation and how we can change the way in which the rest of the world perceives us" are naïve at best.

First of all, we have a right to have our own beliefs and our own foreign policy. And number two, nothing, *nothing* we could do would've been good enough for Al Qaida, or for any other faction in the world who despise us, and who would despise us no matter what we did. Their hatred for this country is inbred, constant, and feeds on itself.

I heard the far left voice the same kind of sentiment at the time we invaded Iraq. I didn't buy it then, either.

I hate to burst their bubble, folks. But the United States is the strongest, most prosperous, most successful country in the world. That, above anything else, is why people hate us.

Think about it. When you were in school, did you like the class president or the head cheerleader, or did you resent them? In sports, do you root for the Yankees or the Raiders or the Lakers, or do you love to see them fail? Truthfully, do most people admire Bill Gates or Steve Jobs or Larry Ellison for their innovation, or do they have a visceral dislike for them simply because they're rich and powerful? (Well, with Larry Ellison they may have a point.)

That same sort of bitterness was very much evident in the far left reaction to 9/11. It was sour grapes, pure and simple.

I'll bet we would have never heard from any of the liberal critics had Bill Clinton still been in the White House. Their comments smacked of little more than hatred for the Bush administration. How else can you account for it?

You don't go to a funeral and say to the widow, "Gee, Blanche, I'm sorry for your loss, but Harry owed me $3,000. Would you happen to have it on you?"

Common sense says there's a time and place for everything. You allow the grieving party time and space to heal and *then* you make your request.

I think liberals who used the Day of Remembrance to voice their own agenda did so mainly to get attention for themselves or for their cause. That certainly appeared to be the case with Amos Brown. Every major media outlet covered the story. His comments shook the entire Bay Area. For that reason, I decided to take him to task. We spent an hour talking about the issue on the air the following day.

I thought people such as Amos Brown were callous and unfeeling—and I said that to him on the program. I couldn't see how anyone with even an ounce of compassion could watch the images of innocent men and women jumping to their deaths from the World Trade Center and actually ask, "What did we do to bring this on ourselves?"

Amos Brown's remarks that day showed him to be utterly insensitive to the pain and loss suffered by the families and survivors that the memorial service was supposed to be honoring. Which is ironic considering that when Brown was a Supervisor, he was very much a champion of what I like to call "qualify of life" issues. By that I mean basic matters of everyday importance to people in large metropolitan areas, such as being able to work your way through traffic without panhandlers slamming a cup in your face and asking you for money. Having bus service you can actually rely on, instead of watching five buses race past your stop at once then waiting an hour for the next one to arrive. Enjoying the simple right to lead your life the way you want to without impediments that would prevent you from doing so.

DON'T SHOVE PATRIOTISM IN MY FACE

We talked before about the overwhelming surge of patriotism that swept this country in the wake of 9/11. No doubt, that brought out the best in liberals and conservatives alike. But it also brought out the worst.

For example, you might recall there was a minor flap over the growing number of TV news anchors who began wearing flag pins on the lapels of their blazers shortly after 9/11. Peter Jennings wore one. So did Tom Brokaw. The vast majority of us who were sitting at home and watching the networks never gave it a second thought. After all, many of us were suddenly wearing flag pins, too. It was a way of symbolizing pride and support for our country in the face of adversity.

Except that liberals cried foul, claiming that the presence of flag pins made the anchors look as though they were right-wing sympathizers. Their argument, of course, was based on the notion that conservatives often wrap themselves up in the flag, resorting to patriotism as a last resort to get their point across.

It was hardly an earth-shattering topic, but it was still perfect for talk radio.

A voice of reason would say, "What's wrong with that? News anchors are paid to be unflappable, but they were just as affected by the horror of 9/11 as you and me. Maybe they started wearing flag pins for the same reason a lot of us began displaying flags when we had never done that before . . . because we were all proud of our country, and we just wanted to show it." To me, it was another classic "time and place" scenario that showed once again how out of touch the far left was with what the rest of the country was feeling.

That said, there is a larger issue here where the left wing does have it right. There is a self-righteousness that comes with patriotism to which many conservatives are completely blind.

For my money, patriotism comes in two shapes. You can be loyal to this country and love it with all your heart without also living in a vacuum. You know that the United States is the best country going, but you also realize it's not perfect. Part of our duty as Americans is to be vigilant, to care about the future of this country so that we continue to grow and prosper, be just, and always reach our fullest potential.

That form of patriotism, I like and respect.

What I don't care for is the kind of "love it or leave it," "wearing a flag pin in your lapel and therefore believing that automatically entitles you to an advantage in every argument you come up with," self-righteous jingoism often exhibited by those on the far right of the political spectrum.

That's not patriotism as far I'm concerned. That's just an attempt to get a free pass.

You can be patriotic without being arrogant about it or shoving it in my face. Don't tell me, "Ronn, if you love this country, you would support the war in Vietnam"—or for that matter, "you would oppose the war in Iraq." Don't say that. You can disagree over policy and still be a true American. Isn't that what this country is supposed to be about?

Once you resort to loyalty as your bottom-line argument, patriotism loses it for me.

Here again is where I got into it with people on the right in the aftermath of 9/11.

I mentioned earlier that every day for the entire year following 9/11, my family had a flag flying in front of our house. Many other families on our street had flags out, and they were out there 24/7. Well, strictly speaking, flag etiquette says you can't do that. You can only have the flag out during certain hours of the day, you have to take it down at sunset, you have to fold it a certain way, and so forth.

My neighbors and I didn't do it that way.

Now does that suddenly make me unpatriotic, because I didn't do it strictly by the book? Maybe I'm patriotic because I put out the flag. Maybe I'm not because I didn't treat the flag "with the proper respect." I don't know, and I don't care.

Common sense would say that what counts is what comes from the heart.

There were flags out up and down our block because we all just wanted to look at a flag. Whenever I got up in the morning, I'd see the flag. When I went out to get the newspapers, I'd see the flag. When I left for the station or came home at the end of the day, I'd see the flag.

I'm sorry, but I happened to like that. It made me feel proud.

You may disagree, but I would submit to you that's far more patriotic than the person who puts up the flag and takes the down the flag every single day by rote while also believing this country can never do anything wrong.

A REASONABLE APPROACH TO TERRORISM . . . OR, THERE ARE TIMES WHEN RACIAL PROFILING MAKES A WHOLE LOT OF SENSE

I mentioned before how when it comes to individual rights, I tend to be very liberal. At the same time, I don't understand why we cannot agree on basic issues when it comes to terrorism. I don't understand how we can let reflexive actions take precedence over common sense.

Here again I go back to the response to the Tamin Ansary e-mail. By and large, those who jumped all over me when I suggested we take action against the Taliban tended to be liberals who refused to recognize the threat to this country that most conservatives saw, as well as those of us in the middle.

Now, in fairness, Afghanistan was never a threat to us—Al Qaida was. It wasn't as if the Afghani people were suddenly going to come over and fire into our streets. And as I readily conceded at the time (and again two years later, when it came to the war in Iraq), any military aggression taken by the United States will inevitably result in civilian casualties on their side as well as military casualties on ours.

Unfortunate, yes. Uncomfortable, yes. But whoever said war was antiseptic?

By the same token, liberals who opposed the invasion of October 2001 conveniently ignored the Taliban's deplorable treatment of women, just as they would later overlook all the years of brutal torture and degradation the Iraqi people endured under Saddam Hussein when they opposed the war in Iraq.

Talk about backward thinking. I mean, here you have this basic issue of gender equality, which is practically one of the founding tenets of modern liberalism today, and they completely threw it out the window!

It just shows once again how extremists focus on one particular point, then cherry pick areas that justify their point of view while conveniently disregarding all others.

Take profiling at airports, another topic that radical liberals unilaterally oppose without considering the larger issue.

The larger course, of course, would be terrorism. Our personal safety is at stake.

If you're seated on a plane, odds are those two guys from Libya with scowls on their faces are far more likely to hijack the plane than that little old Swedish woman seated next to you, or the seven-year-old boy across the aisle. Consequently, common sense says you should probably pay more attention, security-wise, to the Libyans than you would the Swedish woman or that youngster.

This isn't to say it could never happen. It's just that statistically speaking, there aren't that many elderly Swedes or seven-year-olds listed among known international terrorists.

That doesn't necessarily entitle anyone to a free pass. It does suggest, however, that we exercise a reasonable amount of vigilance when it comes to some people in certain situations. I have no problem with that idea at all. It's only common sense.

Common sense would remind us once again that there are people out there who plain don't like us. There are people out there who want to deprive us of our lives, and our way of life.

Obviously, some terrorists will succeed; 9/11 made that perfectly clear.

At the same time, we're not going to just sit quietly and let them have their way; 9/11 also made that clear.

Times have changed, folks. Our world has become a little more precarious in the days since 9/11. And while it's been said before, dangerous times do call for—well, perhaps not "dangerous" measures, but certainly serious ways of dealing with the equally serious issue of maintaining our personal safety.

That said, you'll still find radicals on either side of the gamut that simply refuse to agree on what needs to be done. On an issue such as profiling, extreme liberals will argue that singling out one group of people is racist and goes against our philosophy as a nation, therefore it's wrong. Extreme conservatives, on the other hand, will say profiling smacks of big government and marks the first step in the decay of our society. The individual will have fewer and fewer rights, while the government will be doing more and more things to make our lives difficult.

Which goes to show that in some respects, the far left and the far right aren't as different as you think. That's a topic for a whole other conversation, which we'll get into next.

If Both Extremes Are Equally Obnoxious, Then Why Is the Far Right Far More Appealing?

For years, the far left has been trying to find a high-profile radio talk show host who can compete with Rush Limbaugh on a national level. In fact, as recently as last year, both Al Gore and Al Franken were involved in efforts independent of each other to launch programming that hoped to provide a "liberal" alternative to conservative talk radio.

I'll give you two reasons why that will never work. Number one, right wingers have a sense of humor. Left wingers don't.

I realize that's a generalization. There are always exceptions. Certainly Al Franken has a sharp sense of humor. I've enjoyed his work since the nascent days of *Saturday Night Live*. Al is about as liberal as you can get. Then again, Al is a professional comedian.

Conversely, Bill O'Reilly of the Fox News Channel is about as conservative as you can get. I've yet to find evidence that Bill has any sense of humor.

On the whole, though, I would submit to you that my general observation holds true.

I've been in radio for over 35 years. I've interviewed countless people on both sides of the spectrum: actors, lawyers, lawmakers, pundits, politicians, presidents, world leaders and everyday ordinary citizens. You name it, I've talked to them. By and large, I have found that the more conservative a person's political views are, the more relaxed and outgoing he tends to be, which very often translates into warmth and a decent sense of humor. Conversely, the more liberal a person's views, the more uptight and serious that makes him, and the more entrenched he becomes in his positions, which allows him fewer opportunities to laugh.

People certainly want to be informed when they turn on the radio. But they also want to be entertained. That's how the whole concept of "info-tainment" came about.

Right now, probably the closest thing we have to "liberal talk radio" would be some of the *proghhrams* you hear on National Public Radio (NPR). If you weigh in on the far left end of the scale and want your point of view validated every day, NPR is the place for you.

Granted, that's hardly a perfect parallel. There's a whole lot more to NPR than just talk radio. That said, if you listen to most of the talk shows you hear on NPR—and I say this with all due respect to my friends who host shows on NPR—you'll invariably find them urbane, thoughtful, and very informative. But they're not always particularly entertaining.

Naturally, liberals will take exception to that remark. "There is a different kind of entertainment," said Al Franken on my program last year. "I think that liberals are entertained by learning things . . . I think liberals tend to want information. Conservatives tend to want ammunition. I think that conservatives obsessively listen to things that confirm what they think they know. And I don't think liberals do that."

As much as I like Al, I'll tell you where he and I disagree. I think liberals and conservatives *both* want ammunition. The more extreme their position, the more they look for things that reinforce their point of view. Al can certainly point to plenty of examples of bombshells dropped by Limbaugh, O'Reilly, and other right-wing hosts. Then again, Al used a lot of that ammunition himself to satirize the right in his two best-selling books. And while Al is very funny, he's also very biting in the way liberals tend to be.

Say what you will about his politics, but Rush Limbaugh is fun to listen to. He took a hard and fast yet very colloquial conservative point of view and made it vastly entertaining.

People feel comfortable if they have someone they can identify with. Rush made it eminently acceptable for people in this country to have very conservative ideas. In a word, you could say he created a sense of community for the right-wing. Not only that, he made them feel as though they were no longer marginalized, but indeed mainstream. That in turn made his listeners feel good about themselves. It was as if they could now say, "Sure, I'm right. *You bet I'm right!*"

I have great respect for Rush. I may not agree with his view of the world, but I respect the fact that he has worked in this industry almost as long as I have, knows what's he doing, and happens to be very good at what he does.

That's why I've always appreciated the fact I have consistently topped him in the ratings, head to head. Whether it's sports, business, or politics, you're never truly satisfied in any competition unless you know you've beaten the best.

Content-wise, though, the kind of show that Rush does is obviously very different from mine. I encourage listeners to disagree with me. That's not the case with conservative talk radio. With right-wing hosts . . . Okay, maybe once in a while they'll put on someone with the opposite opinion just so they can put them down. But for the most part, you'll always hear the same continuous point of view day in and day out.

Now when it comes to style, there you'll find some similarity. I also strive to provide my listeners with an atmosphere of community. That has always been my approach to talk radio.

If there's one idea I try to convey, it's not so much "Here's my philosophy. This is what I believe in, and you'd better believe in it, too." It's more a matter of "Hey, folks, we're all going through life together. Let's be passionate as we talk about the issues, but let's also try to respect each other, listen to each other's point of view, and make the experience as enjoyable, or at least as pleasant, as we possibly can."

I may be the host, but I also consider myself a catalyst—a sounding board, if you will. My show is a sort of daily electronic town meeting where people can comment at any time on matters that concern them. I may not necessarily agree with your opinion, but I will always give you the opportunity to express it.

WHEN IN DOUBT, GO WITH THE PRICKLY GUY

Lack of a sense of humor is one reason why left-wing radio on the level of a Rush Limbaugh doesn't work as a concept. Reason Number Two is more a matter of common sense: In this medium, you can't just waltz in off the street and say, "Hey, I'm smart, people know who I am, my views are interesting, and I want a forum to get them across. I think I'll be a radio talk show host." It doesn't work that way. If it did, hosting a talk show would be as easy as running for governor in the California recall.

Name recognition is an obvious plus, but even that can only take you so far. Radio isn't about getting people to tune in and listen. It's about getting about people to tune in and listen *every day*. That's where you have to deliver. In that respect, it's also one area where conservatives will always have an advantage over liberals.

Generally speaking, conservatives come off as warm, outgoing, and positive. They always seem to have a sunny disposition when it comes to the future of this country.

Liberals, on the other hand, are often cold, aloof, and considerably more negative. They never seem to stop complaining about what's wrong with the United States. Their outlook on issues always seems to be bleak.

This isn't to say one view of the world is wrong and the other right. It's just that conservatives are usually "for" things, while liberals are usually "against" them.

Now you may say, "Wait a minute, Ronn. What about like Jim Hightower? He's bright, folksy, entertaining, funny. He could certainly compete with Rush on a national level." All of which is true.

I've known Jim for many years and he's an excellent broadcaster. In fact, at the time this book went to press, Jim was among the hosts in talks with the Gore group about their prospective left-wing radio network.

Problem is, Jim is a classic liberal cherry picker. He's always harping about what a corporate wet dream George W. Bush is ("Any CEO can make his fantasies come true by putting money in Bush's pockets."). Or how government in general is in the clutches of big business and private interest groups. Or how the evil conglomerates control the public airwaves, and how we've got to stop them before it all goes to hell in a hand basket. You rarely hear him mention Bush's track record for forging coalitions between Democrats and Republicans. Or how the evil conglomerates will finance just about anything—even a left-wing radio network—if they thought it could make them some money.

And that's the thing. Given the choice, who would *you* rather listen to every day: someone who looks on the bright side, or someone who bitches and moans?

When you think about it, that "glass-is-half-full" attitude toward the United States is not just what makes conservative talk radio entertaining. It also accounts for the overall appeal of conservatism in this country.

Disagree? Fair enough. Then how do you account for the fact that Americans have elected only one Democrat other than Bill Clinton in the last nine presidential elections? Going back a little further, only three Democrats besides Clinton have won the White House in the past 13 elections—a span of 52 years.

Still not convinced? Then let's go back to the 2000 election.

Forget Florida. Forget the Supreme Court ruling. Al Gore lost the 2000 election because he couldn't carry his own state.

Tennessee, you'll recall, went to George W. Bush. That means Al Gore ran so far to the left, even his own constituents rejected him.

I mentioned discussing the Florida vote on *Larry King Live* back on Thanksgiving Night 2000, when the outcome was still very much in doubt. At one point, I was asked to gauge how my listeners would react if the election were to go to Bush. I said, bottom line, they might grouse a little, but they would eventually accept the results. If it came down to choosing between a guy who's prickly and a guy who's patronizing, most people would go with the prickly guy. It's the lesser of two evils.

Sure, George W. Bush is still prone to verbal gaffes. As good as he is at delivering prepared remarks, he can often be downright awkward when it comes to speaking off the cuff, particularly at press conferences and impromptu interviews. Nor does he always appear graceful or polished in the way we've typically come to expect from our chief executive.

But give credit where it's due. George W. Bush is genuine. There's no pretense about him. That quality came out throughout the campaign, especially in the debates with Gore. Above all else, the man projects what people want to see in a president: a positive attitude about the United States. It's a quality that has shone forth consistently throughout his time in office.

I say this not as a Bush supporter, but as a political pragmatist who is proud of his country. I don't think we do everything right . . . but I've traveled a bit, and I can't think of a better place in which to live. I believe in our system of government, and I want to work within it. But it's tiresome to hear this constant left-wing whining about how lousy we are, that we're this aggressive super-power exploiting other nations and ultimately heading down a path of destruction.

I don't buy it. Nor does the vast majority of this country buy it either, no matter what the far left chooses to believe.

CLOSED-MINDEDNESS KNOWS NO BOUNDS

If we really care about the future, if we want to bring about change in important matters of policy, we not only have to put our heads together—we also have to keep an open mind. We can't tune ourselves out to aspects of reality that we may not happen to like. We need to listen to each other. We need to work through differences of opinion and find common ground.

That means allowing room to consider ideas you might not ordinarily tolerate for the greater good of this country. That, of course, isn't always easy to do.

For instance, I have very strong opinions on matters such as international terrorism and the conflict in the Middle East. Yet, I wonder to what degree some of my views on these issues are influenced by the fact that I'm Jewish.

I happen to be a huge supporter of Israel. Israel is one country that always been a complete ally of the United States. I also believe it's the one true bulwark of democracy in the Middle East. But I think because the Israeli government always responds aggressively to attacks, the world has it out for Israel, and that invariably the United Nations will condemn Israel for retaliation.

Consequently, I find it hard to listen to any arguments that equate Israel's attempts to effectively neutralize terrorist groups with indiscriminate suicide bombings at the hands of Palestinians. That sort of thinking is so far removed from that of basic human decency, I can't relate to it on any level.

That said, I'd like nothing more than to see the Road Map to Peace work. I think Ariel Sharon has shown more flexibility than I ever would have imagined possible from him.

I think the absence of Yassar Arafat has now given the Palestinians an opportunity to have their own state. I'd love nothing more than to see an Israeli and a Palestinian state, side by side, with enough protection so that they can finally live in peace without the need to attack each other.

Still, I'm hardly objective when it comes to Israel. It's one area where I tend to be very impassioned yet also very inflexible.

But then, I'm not making policy that could affect the lives of hundreds of billions of people. I'm just a radio talk show host. I can afford to be opinionated once in a while.

This isn't to say I'll never talk about the Middle East on the air. Obviously, if a story breaks in the middle of my program about an explosion in a Tel Aviv hotel in which innocent civilians are injured or killed, I'll definitely bring it up.

By and large, though, I would much rather consider issues where I can at least acknowledge the other side. I may not agree with the other side, but let's see what they think and how they came to that conclusion. Let's see if we can point out where we differ, why our side is right and their side is wrong. In other words, let's present an argument that weighs both sides of the issue on the basis of specifics.

Compromise on any major issue is hard enough. It becomes even more difficult to achieve when you're dealing with the extremes.

A true political zealot, regardless of his affiliation, will never admit he's wrong. You'll never hear him say, "Okay, you got me on that one," "I'm sorry, I'm afraid I'm a little weak on that particular point," or "You know something? I'd never thought of it that way." Instead, he will always have an answer for everything—a catch-all, simplistic excuse that never varies. When his policies fail, for instance, it never dawns on him that they may have been bad policies to begin with. Instead, they failed simply because he didn't take them far enough. "The tax cut wasn't big enough. The measure wasn't strong enough. The radio and TV ads didn't reach enough people," and so on.

With extreme liberals and extreme conservatives alike, you need to zero in on the same thing: a self-defeating tendency that stubbornly refuses to consider the other side's point of view, making communication of any kind impossible.

Extreme liberals tend to think in very broad strokes. Either everything fits into a neat little package, or it doesn't. With them, the closed-mindedness comes from an inability to believe that the United States is as good a country as it is. It stems from a perception that the United States has nothing but imperialism and conspiracies on its mind. It results from simply refusing to look at the failures of systems such as Communism around the world, from turning their back on the horrors that dictators have imposed on millions of people throughout the world.

Extreme conservatives are more apt to focus on specifics, but they're just as rigid in their positions. They share this myopic view of the United States that we've talked about before: "We're the greatest, we're the best, we can do no wrong." They don't question the actions of military governments that impose their will on other parts of the world. They see nothing wrong with the United States' ever-growing business interests abroad and the impact this expansion will inevitably have on local businesses in these countries.

The common complaint is that liberals want to spend while conservatives don't. In reality, though, it isn't quite that simple. Conservatives have no problem pulling out their checkbook if it's in their own best interest. Conversely, liberals can be fiscally responsible, too. They are perfectly capable of shutting off the spigot if they know the money is headed toward matters that they happen to oppose.

THE CHANGING FACE OF LIBERALS AND CONSERVATIVES

Still, it's interesting to note how on a national level fewer and fewer people today are identifying themselves as liberals.

Here in the Bay Area (and especially in the city of San Francisco), it's a completely different story. The political views expressed here are so far removed from what the rest of the country is thinking, it's really fascinating.

I think much of that independent thought stems from the transient nature of the region. That is not to suggest there's no such thing as a native San Franciscan. There are plenty of them. But there are also plenty of others who live here who originally came here from different parts of the country, either for college, grad school, a career move, the weather, or simply a chance to take in that laidback, freewheeling California lifestyle. Many come here because they're drawn to the eclectic nature of San Francisco, a city that's energetic, hip, and cutting-edge, especially in our arts and culture.

Granted, skyrocketing housing prices, not to mention the exorbitant high cost of living in general, has caused some people to leave San Francisco. In that respect, there really isn't the sort of permanence in the Bay Area that you might otherwise have in military towns, industrial hubs, or many other parts of the country. As a result, you'll often find that many people who live here tend to "remove" themselves from the action, and more or less flow with some of the more radical liberal politics espoused by, say, the People's Republic of Berkeley or certain members of the San Francisco Board of Supervisors.

Then again, San Francisco is also a city that attracts young people. When you're young, you tend to be more liberal in your thinking, no matter where you happen to live.

I can't help but think of that classic line often attributed to Winston Churchill (though among Churchill scholars that's a matter of debate): "He who is under 30 and is not a liberal has no heart. He who is over 30 and is not a conservative has no brains."

Regardless of who said it, there's obviously a lot of hyperbole in that statement. But there's also a lot of truth.

Young people will always be idealistic. There's nothing wrong with that. You might even say it's the natural order of things. Most of us have lofty notions in our youth, only to settle down and gradually become more conservative as we grow older. We start off headstrong yet naïve, hoping somehow to make a difference in the world before realizing it's hard enough just to make a living. As we grow older, wiser (and hopefully, wealthier), we often go one of two ways. We either become philanthropic and think about giving back to the community, or we grow increasingly conservative (in our pocketbooks, as well as in our views).

The problem comes with older liberals who won't remove the blinders of idealism. They become just as rigid as conservatives who are unwilling to look at some of the negative implications of the things that they believe in.

I, for one, was far more reflexively liberal as a kid. I'm much more open to conservative Republican philosophy now—but not because I buy it. As I've said before, when it comes to their positions on domestic issues that I happen to take to heart (such as abortion, gun control, and gay rights), there's a great deal about the GOP platform that totally turns me off. While I strongly believe in the notion of keeping government out of our lives as much as possible (which, again, is a traditional conservative position), I keep seeing that idea contradicted by the actions of Republicans today.

Then again, I should point out that the labels "liberals" and "conservatives" are really inappropriate. At least, they are when you consider the way in which both terms are commonly used today.

Once upon a time, a true conservative always stood for as little government as possible. Now conservatives want to tell a woman whether she can have an abortion. They want to tell gay people what they can do in the bedroom, or whether they have a legal right to be together in the first place. They want to tell you what you can smoke, what drugs you can take, or that you're going to have prayer in your school, like it or not. These are the people who ostensibly want to keep the government out of our lives, and yet they've clearly thrown their support to these and other areas that call for direct imposition on the part of the government.

All of a sudden it's the *liberals* who are saying, "No, no, no. We want freedom. We want the freedom to do our own thing. It's our choice if we have an abortion, do drugs, protest in the streets, marry someone of the same sex. It's our choice. It's our expression."

Strictly speaking, you would think liberals would *want* the government to intervene in these matters. After all, they're the ones who supposedly believe more government is better in the first place!

It's almost as if the two have become juxtaposed. The real liberals are now becoming conservative, while the classic conservatives are becoming much more liberal.

This brings us back to the difference between liberals and conservatives in general.

WHO WOULD YOU RATHER HAVE A BEER WITH?

I have a theory that as far as I know has never been articulated. It's an observation I've developed over the years, and it's based on interviewing hundreds, perhaps even a thousand or more, politicians.

By and large, I have found that arch-conservative Republicans have a great deal of concern for the individual, but don't seem to care about the group. One on one, they come across as caring, decent, even fun people, even as they support issues that either take away our rights or otherwise work to the disadvantage of large bodies of people.

A typical right-wing Republican sees a poor little Black kid panhandling in front of the Capitol. He's likely to stop, pull out his wallet, hand the kid a buck . . . then promptly vote against a bill that would fund a Head Start program or affordable housing for minorities.

Radical liberal Democrats, on the other hand, are very passionate when it comes to the group, but can't be bothered with the individual. They will fight to rid the world of terrible social ills, yet often have terrible social skills themselves on a personal level.

The typical left-wing Democrat is frequently so wrapped up in his particular cause of the moment (whatever that cause happens to be), he won't even *notice* the little Black kid asking for money.

Senator Orrin Hatch is about as right wing as you can possibly get. I've interviewed him many times. I watch this man whenever I talk to him, and I'm always impressed by how he deals with others and the genuine attention he pays to what you have to say. He is one of the nicest people you'd ever want to meet. And there are issues where the position he has taken is clearly right on. His support of stem cell research immediately comes to mind. But you look at his overall voting record or some of the other ideas he's tried to float past Congress, and the man seems either vindictive, oblivious to people's anguish, or just plain wrong.

Take, for example, the radical solution he proposed in 2003 to stop people from downloading copyrighted music illegally from Internet web sites. Hatch actually introduced a bill that would have allowed for the creation of technology that would somehow be capable of automatically destroying—yes, *destroying*—the computers of the offending parties. In other words, if the Senator had his way, you could download a song once, maybe twice, and only get a warning. Try it a third time, and all of sudden you're Jim Phelps on *Mission: Impossible*. Your computer self-destructs in five seconds.

Now, correct me if I'm wrong, but isn't that patently unconstitutional to begin with? Where's your trial? What if someone else is at your computer and downloads a file? You didn't do it. Should you still be held responsible? What if I did it at work? Do you therefore also wipe out every other computer connected to mine?

My station is owned by Disney. Does everyone at Disney have to suffer because of me?

Senator, that remedy is so Orwellian, it's frightening.

Fortunately, cooler heads prevailed. Hatch's idea never got past the talking stage. But it still makes you want to shake your head in amazement.

It would be like passing a bill that turned jaywalking into a capital offense. Sure, no one would ever cross against the light if they knew it meant the death penalty. But the law still wouldn't make any sense. The punishment really ought to fit the crime, don't you think?

On the far left side, Representative Barney Frank comes off like someone who really cares about the group as a whole. He's a champion not only for gays, but also for the poor and disenfranchised. Yet when you try to talk to him on a personal level, when you sit and watch him get ready to be interviewed, he comes across as really arrogant. He's pompous, he screams at people, he's just unpleasant to be around.

Now there's a combination for you. Barney Frank and Orrin Hatch. One doesn't treat people particularly well, yet votes for issues that will help groups. The other treats people with total respect, yet pushes for issues that will deny them opportunities. Or blow up their computers.

Pat Buchanan is another classic extreme in the Orrin Hatch mode. Now here's a guy whose take on major social and domestic issues couldn't be further apart from mine. Pro-life. Anti-gun control. Anti-gay. Seemingly anti-Semitic. I find his views on race and gender to be downright repulsive.

And yet on a personal level, he's terrific. You sit down for an interview and, sure, you get into it with him on the issues. But you also joke and schmooze, on and off the air. All in all, it makes for a great hour of radio.

One on one, I think Pat Buchanan is a pretty decent guy, despite the fact that deep down he probably hates Jews. That's why I've come to know him as "My Favorite Bigot."

You want another example, but on the liberal side? Try Ralph Nader.

This is a man who has been taking on big industries and fighting for the rights of consumers for over 40 years. No matter which industry—automotive, health care, banking, you name it—Ralph Nader has battled it on behalf of you and me. In many respects, he is the quintessential champion of the underdog. And yet when you first sit down with him one on one, it's as if he doesn't even know you exist.

Now in all fairness, I will say that Ralph has loosened up considerably over the years. We've developed enough of a friendship so that he and I can genuinely joke with each other on the air. But until we got to that point, Ralph was your classic liberal. Aloof. Distant. Uptight. Super serious. Self-absorbed to the point where he never seemed to care about, let alone notice, anyone else around him. Yet, look at all the issues he has cared about and taken on for all of our benefit.

Which brings us to that beer I mentioned at the beginning of this section. Given the choice, I'd much rather raise a glass with a guy like Pat Buchanan than I would with Ralph Nader.

By and large, extreme conservative Republicans are more pleasant to be around. That doesn't make their ideas any less far out than those of their liberal Democrat counterparts. But it does go a long way toward making those ideas seem if not more appealing, then certainly more tolerable.

What conclusions can we draw from this?

If you're a liberal Democrat, and are serious about winning the White House in 2004, it would behoove you to borrow a page from the Republican playbook.

Be positive. Be genuine. Don't just whine about what's wrong with the economy. Tell us what you're going to do turn it around.

That strategy worked for George W. Bush in 2000. It also worked for Arnold Schwarzenegger in 2003.

Common sense would say that's the only sensible way of winning an election.

Here's How to
Win an Election

How often have you heard a spiel like this from a radio or TV announcer? "Remember, today is Election Day. Polls are open till eight. This is your chance to participate in the process. This is democracy. People died so that you can have this right. It's important. So please go out and vote."

Now, I have strong feelings about voting. I believe it's important. It's a time honored tradition and a matter that I take seriously. To me, there's a certain inherent symbolism associated with going inside a voting booth and casting your ballot.

And while this may sound strange to you, I also like the little receipt I get once I finish casting my vote. I like the feel of it. Makes the act of voting seem that much more important. You fill out forms every day at home or at your job. You get a receipt every time you go to the store or fill up your car. But this is different. More than anything else, it proves you took part in the process. I like that.

That said, I've always had a different approach when it comes to reminding people to vote. Every Election Day throughout my career I say to listeners, "Hey, folks, if you want to vote, vote. If you don't want to vote, stay home!"

I have never understood why we push people to go to the polls. The way I see it, if you're not interested enough in what is being voted on, if you don't care enough about the future of your country or state or city, how intelligent a vote are you going to cast anyway?

People who follow the issues, who care enough to sift through all 300 pages of the voter information booklet and actually read every argument for and against each and every proposition and who have thought long and hard about which candidate on the ballot is the best person to lead their city, state, or federal government at this particular time *don't need* to be told to vote.

But that's never been good enough. Instead we insist on pushing *everyone* to vote. That makes no sense to me at all.

Now proponents for "getting out the vote" will almost always point to low voter turnout as their primary justification. They will argue the percentage of registered voters who actually go out to the polls is abysmal: *It's an embarrassment. We shouldn't tolerate it. We must do something about it now.*

I couldn't disagree more. A large turnout will not necessarily guarantee an intelligent vote. You're likely to have as many people vote for Arnold Schwarzenegger for governor of California because they like his movies as you will people who want him in office because they honestly believe he's the right man for the job.

As it stands, the people who go out to the polls year in and year out are the ones who genuinely give a damn. Consequently, the ones who genuinely give a damn are the ones making the decisions that affect the future of our city, state, or country.

From my standpoint, that's the way it should be.

That said, if you're really serious about improving voter turnout, make it easier for people. For one, don't hold the election on a Tuesday when most people can only vote before or after work. Hold the election on a weekend like they do in other countries. Either that, or come up with technology that would enable people to vote by computer. Devise some method of identification so that people can log in and cast their vote either from home or, if they don't own a computer, a public place such as a library. Make it foolproof, like a thumbprint, so that we know it's really you who's voting and not someone else. Not only would that make it easier, it would render a much more accurate count without any worry of chads, dangling or otherwise.

Politicians can also do their part to make voting more palatable. People get tired of election campaigns where the tone is always so negative. We're turned off by the endless parade of candidates who do nothing but complain about how lousy their opponent is, as if that alone were enough to convince us to vote for them instead. Just once we'd like to see an election that actually focuses on issues and solutions to problems instead of just harping about what's wrong.

It seems to me that a positive, proactive approach to elections is bound to get people excited. That in turn would inspire people to make their way to the polls. Not only will they be eager to vote in general, there's a good chance they'll also be keyed up about you, the candidate.

WHY WOULD ANYONE ENTER POLITICS TODAY?

In the world of radio, there are some issues a talk show host never has to worry about. For example, any time a public official asks the voters to consider a measure that would increase his salary (no matter what that increase might be), you can count on people picking up the phone to complain.

I'm of one mind on this. Being a politician is hard enough as it is. You need the kind of people skills, expertise, and dedication to issues that frankly not everyone has. It's also a fulltime job where 18-hour days and 80-to 100-hour weeks are not out of the norm. Therefore, we ought to treat politics like any other specialized field and compensate those who work in it fairly and competitively. Why shouldn't a good city administrator make as much as a good CEO? The more you pay elected officials, the more successful you'll be at attracting talented, highly qualified people from the private sector and convincing them to serve the public.

If you insist on being chintzy salarywise, one of two things will happen. You'll either get city council members who have to spend half their time at their "day job" in order to make ends meet, thereby precluding them from concentrating on the job for which they were elected. Or you elect people who are extremely wealthy and can afford to work for peanuts, but who otherwise have no real grasp of the issues that affect most people in the ordinary everyday world. (I can't help but think of George Herbert Walker Bush trying to figure out how much a loaf of bread costs.)

So Measure X would raise Joe Congressman's salary from $152,000 to $160,000. Why is that a problem? These people deal with trillions of dollars on a daily basis *and you're getting into a lather over 8,000 bucks?* Get real! Compared to the kind of economic decisions politicians have to make, that's like raising a stink over a grain of sand on the beach.

Then again, people tend to be two-faced when it comes to politicians in general. They'll call up talk shows and carp about what a lousy job Joe Congressman is doing. Then you invite the representative to come on the show, and all of a sudden it's "Oh, Congressman, I'm a longtime supporter. You are truly an inspiration. Keep up the good work!"

Which may account for the sizeable egos many politicians have, as well as why they put up with as much as they do on a daily basis.

I have strong ideas about what goes on in the Bay Area and in the state. For that reason, I've been asked on four occasions to consider running for political office. The most serious of which was a concerted effort by a group of Californians who wanted me in the House of Representatives. They had campaign money, they had a plan for raising more, and their views on the pressing issues facing the state at the time were very much in concert with my own.

I was flattered by their confidence in me, but I had to decline. I said I had no desire to run for public office. I still feel that way today.

Look, without question I'm about as big a political junkie as you'll ever meet.

I love talking politics. I can never read enough about it. I watch the Sunday morning shows. I've come to know a great many lawmakers and political insiders over the years. I know politics almost as well as I know radio.

That said, I am a talk show host. I provide an outlet for people to talk about the news. I'm more interested in exchanging ideas with listeners on issues than in exerting any influence of my own. If I did want to shape opinion, I figure I can do that far more effectively and reach far more people on a daily basis through my radio program.

And besides, you couldn't pay me enough to put up with the kind of headaches politicians have to contend with just to get elected.

So when you look at it that way, it's hard to imagine why *anyone* would want to enter politics today. Doesn't matter whether you want to be mayor of New York, governor of California, or president of the United States. Run for any office these days and you not only leave yourself open to public scrutiny, your entire life is dissected. The whole focus is on finding dirt in your past and leaking it to the media.

We saw this happen—well, we see this happen all the time. Here in California, we especially saw it come to the fore in 2003 in the effort to recall Governor Gray Davis.

That's right. We had a special election last year in California. You may have heard about it. Seems like everyone had an opinion on the matter . . . and we'll talk about that and more in the pages to come. For the moment, though, all you need to know is that under current California law the governor of our state can be recalled from office *for any reason whatsoever*. Yep, that's right. You want to oust the governor, you simply put together a petition, convince enough registered voters to sign it, and get the secretary of state to certify it. Then it goes on the ballot for the voters to decide.

Now in this case, you need to collect signatures from about 12 percent of the number of Californians who voted in the previous gubernatorial election for a recall election to qualify. That amounts to approximately 900,000 signatures. That's a lot of John Hancocks. And like any other political campaign, you need money to fund it.

As it happens, the major financial backer behind the signature drive was Republican Congressman Darrell Issa. As it also happens, Darrell Issa personally stood to gain the most if the recall made the ballot. Issa fancied himself as a replacement for Gray Davis—and in fact, he was among the 135 candidates to throw his hat in the ring once the petition was officially certified in July 2003.

Sure enough, in the days and weeks leading up to certification, opponents of the recall suddenly began leaking news items concerning Darrell Issa and his sordid past—just as Issa had been attacked in 1998 during his unsuccessful run for the U.S. Senate. Suddenly gun control advocates held news conferences attacking Issa as "an extremist friend of the NRA." There were reports that his Congressional campaign ran a booth at an L.A. gun show in 1998, where they supposedly sold Nazi memorabilia. Then there were allegations that Issa was arrested twice in the early 1970s on illegal weapons charges, including an incident in Michigan that led to a misdemeanor gun conviction.

This was one issue where it was difficult to choose sides. On the one hand, at the time I was adamantly opposed to the recall on general principle. I felt Davis did nothing to merit it specifically since his election in November 2002, plus I thought it set a bad precedent for state politics overall. I was also opposed to Darrell Issa on general principle because prior to entering politics he'd made his fortune selling car burglar alarms, which in my opinion are the single most annoying blight on urban living today.

I have long believed that before anyone is allowed to install a burglar alarm in a car, he or she ought to be required to sit inside a room and listen to it blare nonstop for an hour. I assure you if we did that, not only would no one ever buy a car alarm again, 95 percent of the car owners in this country would immediately remove them from their vehicles. That's how annoying, not to mention useless, car burglar alarms are.

Think about it. A car alarm goes off in the middle of the street. Immediately you race to the window. You're not thinking, "Oh my God, a car's being stolen!" You're thinking, "Oh my God, I hope mine didn't go off by mistake."

My feelings on car alarms aside, even I had to agree with Darrell Issa when he responded to the allegations. He said that "resurrecting 30-year-old misdemeanors [in the middle of an election campaign] was not fair play."

That's the way I look at an issue. I may not care for Issa's political views (he's way too far to the right for me). But that doesn't mean I won't give the man his due if he raises a valid point. And conversely, just because I support a political candidate doesn't mean I can't be critical if I believe the stance he or she takes on a particular issue is way off the mark.

HOW FAR IS TOO FAR?

Dredging up dirt on a 30-year-old matter that has nothing remotely to do with the campaign today is not only low, it smacks of desperation. More than that, it raises a fundamental question: In any political race, on any level, where do you draw the line?

For example, Joe Candidate blew a spitball at a girl in second grade. Clearly his character is suspect. Do we really want this man in the Senate?

To take it one step further, let's flip the question around. Do we really want candidates who would resort to such lame tactics just to get themselves elected?

Of course, the Democrats didn't stop at Darrell Issa. Once Arnold Schwarzenegger declared himself a candidate for governor, they couldn't wait to remind us of how many guns he fired or people he killed in the movies. Or how he smoked pot in the movie *Pumping Iron*. Or that he hasn't voted in every single election. Or that at his wedding to Maria Shriver he offered a toast to Kurt Valdheim after Valdheim's association with the Nazis had become public. Or for that matter, that his own father had been a Nazi.

All of which is true. None of which had anything to do with Schwarzenegger the gubernatorial contender. None of which had anything to do with Schwarzenegger's political views in support of gun control and gay rights, or the lengths he went to dig up the facts about his father's past and get them out in the open, or the lifetime of support he has shown the Jewish people.

If that weren't enough, some Schwarzenegger opponents managed to dig up a racy interview originally published in the now-defunct men's magazine *Oui*. In the article (which first appeared in

1977 to coincide with the release of *Pumping Iron*), Schwarzenegger spoke with typical Hollywood bravado about how much he liked to get stoned, party with other bodybuilders, and shtup lots of women. He also talked about how bodybuilders are often misunderstood and that they face many of the same stereotypes that gay people deal with: "People have certain misconceptions about them just as they do about us. Well, I have absolutely no hang-ups about the fag business."

Naturally the left wing jumped all over on these comments, claiming that a man of such gross moral turpitude was clearly unfit to lead the state of California. Meanwhile, gay rights advocates who happened to oppose the recall (and therefore wouldn't be expected to support Schwarzenegger anyway) chastised the actor for his use of the term "fag," equating that word with a certain racial epithet that begins with the letter N.

Let me get this straight. The Democrats kept telling us that Bill Clinton having oral sex in the Oval Office was no big deal. Now they have a problem with a reference about Arnold's sexual prowess from 26 years ago?

As for the other charge . . . while Schwarzenegger's use of the word "fag" may be unfortunate (or perhaps misinterpreted), the overall sentiment he expressed in the article is consistent with his views in support of gays today.

More to the point, Schwarzenegger was 29 at the time of the interview. His remarks may have said a lot about who he was then, but they revealed nothing about his current plans for reversing California's $38 billion deficit. They said nothing about where he stands *today* on the merits of legalizing marijuana for medicinal purposes, increasing vehicle registration fees, or granting drivers licenses to illegal aliens—all of which were pressing issues at the time of the recall election.

Of course, the Democrats aren't the only ones who hit below the belt. The GOP never misses an opportunity to blast Bill Clinton about Whitewater or his affair with Monica Lewinsky. Al Gore's penchant for exaggerating his record, including his legendary claim for inventing the Internet, was fodder for Republicans throughout the 2000 campaign. So it was no surprise to see conservatives retaliate on behalf of Schwarzenegger by digging up dirt on the leading Democratic candidate in the recall election, California Lieutenant Governor Cruz Bustamante. We'll talk about that in a second.

First, though, let's return to the question. How far back in a person's past are you reasonably entitled to go?

How many of us are the same people today as we were 25 or 30 years ago?

I strongly believe in taking responsibility for your actions. Everything we do is a reflection of who we are. That said, common sense would remind us there are limits.

I certainly wouldn't want to be held accountable for everything I did in the 1970s. The world was a much different place back then. The world has changed a lot since then. So have many of our values.

Sure, I had some good times when I was 29. But I also did some things I'd just as soon forget. Most of us have.

A politician's actions today mean a hell of a lot more to me than anything he may have said or done two or three decades ago. Especially if those comments or actions have nothing to do with the campaign at hand.

There comes a point where we should draw the line and simply say "Enough."

No wonder it's so hard to find good candidates for public office these days. Who could possibly have the stomach for it? Even if you did find a perfect person, one with no flaws at all, would you want him? How many of us can relate to that?

POLITICS TODAY CAN BE HAZARDOUS TO YOUR HEALTH

Problem is, everybody loves negative campaigning. I know we all *say* we hate it, but for most of us, deep down it's one of those guilty pleasures we just can't get enough of. And as topics go, it's ideal for talk radio. I mean, who doesn't love to dish?

My German ancestors had a great word for that: *schadenfreude,* or taking pleasure in the misery of others.

Like it or not, that's also a perversely human characteristic. As much as we like to build people up, we also like to see them fall.

Which again makes me wonder why anyone in politics would subject himself or herself to that. Especially since you need a small fortune these days just to get elected.

Now if you have money to burn, I say go to the Riviera and enjoy life a little. Instead, you're Michael Bloomberg. You say to yourself, "I have a ton of money. I'd like to take on one of the hardest jobs in the world. I want to be mayor of New York and have people verbally attack me, day in and day out. Not only that, I want to succeed Rudy Giuliani, arguably the most popular mayor in New York history—and who also happens to be leaving office *at the height of his popularity.*"

Why would you want to do that? So that you can see yourself on TV and in the newspaper?

To be a politician today, you'd have to be a complete glutton for punishment. Either that, or have an ego even bigger than that of a radio talk show host.

Think about it. The job in and of itself is not terribly exciting. The days are long. You spend half your time either flying back and forth across the country or sitting at a fund-raiser eating bad chicken and listening to even worse jokes. The rest of the time, when you're not cooped up in your office poring over budget figures or drafting legislation, you're either fielding complaints from your constituents, sucking up to special interest groups just to get their vote, or sitting in poorly ventilated chambers with the rest of your colleagues endlessly debating the merits of one bill or another.

Then again I shouldn't say, "It's all ego." There are certainly politicians who truly want to help people, who genuinely believe they have what it takes to turn this country around. And while the most cynical among us may suggest that everyone gets corrupted by the system, there are still enough politicians with strong principles and integrity who manage to keep themselves above the fray. Dianne Feinstein comes to mind. So does John McCain.

That said, even the most principled person in the world has to understand the meaning of compromise. That's the reality of politics. If you want to have any kind of impact, you've got to play ball with people. You have to make deals.

Lawmakers as diverse as Ted Kennedy and Orrin Hatch can work together on a health bill. So can Feinstein and McCain. That's why they're successful.

Look, if you enter politics because you genuinely give a damn about this country, that's terrific. I applaud you for it.

By and large, though, it seems to me that we have too many people who run for office sheerly out of ego. Once you're in, then it becomes like any other industry. You reach for the next highest rung on the ladder. You win a seat on the city council, then set your sights on the state assembly. After the assembly, you run for the senate. After the senate, you go for the treasurer's job. Never mind the fact you can't balance your own checkbook. You run for treasurer anyway because that's the next logical move for you, even if it's not necessarily the best move for the state.

IT'S NOT WHAT YOU DID BEFORE THAT MATTERS, IT'S HOW YOU RESPOND TO IT TODAY

People love to destroy politicians. With the possible exception of movie stars, there is no other group of people we love to tear down more.

Even with movie stars, we're not all that fazed about the things they did years ago. *Entertainment Tonight* airs an "exclusive, never-before-seen video" of Joe Boxoffice smoking pot in college. Like that's really supposed to shock us? It certainly doesn't faze him, so long as you spell his name right and mention the title of his latest movie. It's been said ad nauseam, but in show business there really is no such thing as bad publicity.

Now if it were a tape of a U.S. senator smoking pot, or a would-be U.S. president, or a would-be governor of California, then suddenly it's a whole other story. Remember all the hoopla over Bill Clinton *not* inhaling?

To me, the only positive outcome of negative campaigning is if it somehow exposes hypocrisy.

William J. Bennett, as most of us know, was one of Clinton's harshest, most unrelenting critics throughout the entire impeachment affair. He has given many speeches and written many books on the subject of virtue and morality. Turns out, he likes to go to Las Vegas from time to time for a little high stakes gambling himself.

Not that there's anything wrong with that. I myself have been known to go to Vegas now and then.

It's just that when you make a career out of putting other people down for gambling and other vices, don't expect the public to cut you any slack should word of your own habit ever become known.

Unless, of course, you stand up to the problem (no matter how embarrassing that may be) and address it head on.

If only more politicians could bring themselves to do that. Imagine how different it would have been for Bill Clinton had he not denied his affair with Monica Lewinsky. Or if he hadn't wagged his finger at reporters and insisted "I did not have sex with that woman." Or argued with lawyers at his deposition over what the meaning of the word *is* is. He could have avoided the entire impeachment proceedings and spared himself and his family a ton of embarrassment in the process had he just said, "Boy, did I bungle that one. What a really stupid thing to do."

Then again, all kinds of things happen in the course of a political campaign. More often than not, it's not so much what happens that can get you in trouble but how you react to it.

Take Arnold Schwarzenegger, for instance. Once the raunchy *Oui* interview from 1977 was leaked to the press, he addressed the matter head on. On the night the story broke, he told a Sacramento radio talk show host, "Look, I never lived my life to be a politician. I never lived my life to be governor of California. Obviously, I've made statements that were ludicrous and crazy and outrageous and all those things, because that's the way I always was."

Michael Bloomberg did the same thing when he ran for mayor of New York. When asked if he had ever smoked marijuana, Bloomberg said, "You bet I did, and I enjoyed it." The people of New York appreciated his honesty and directness. The issue went away. Bloomberg won the election.

Cruz Bustamante, Schwarzenegger's chief Democratic rival in the California recall, likewise had an opportunity to address an issue directly when faced with a scandal of his own. Instead, he whiffed.

While a student at California State University/Fresno during the 1970s, Bustamante was a member of MEChA, a national Chicano/Latino student association with chapters in hundreds of colleges, universities, and high schools throughout the country. Founded in the 1960s at the height of the Civil Rights Movement, MEChA tries to effect progressive changes in the Chicano/Latino community by advocating for educational equality through peaceful activity.

Conservative watchdogs, however, claimed that MEChA was a radical outfit with far more insidious goals ranging from spreading anti-White hate sentiment to returning California to the Mexican government. They went out of their way to point out the group's motto: *Por La Raza, todo. Fuera de la Raza, nada* ("For the Race, everything. For those outside the Race, nothing"). The implication was that MEChA was a thinly disguised Mexican equivalent of the Ku Klux Klan.

As it happens, the MEChA story turned up around the same time the 1977 Schwarzenegger *Oui* interview was posted on *thesmokinggun.com*. Maybe that was just a coincidence. Maybe it wasn't.

First of all, let me say that the MEChA flap had zero impact on my opinion of Cruz Bustamante. Number one, it happened three decades ago. And number two, I never would have voted for Bustamante anyway. I wanted to see a moderate win the recall, and Cruz was running way too far to the left.

That said, Bustamante could have easily put the matter to rest had he come right out and said, "Yes, I belonged to MEChA when I was a student. I'm proud of my affiliation. But I never had anything to do with the violent activities of which MEChA has been accused. That was certainly not part of the organization as I knew it, and they are certainly not views I would ever espouse."

That's what his supporters wanted him to say. That certainly would have been the sensible thing to say.

Only Cruz didn't do that. Instead he chose to issue a safe, bland "Hey, we were all just trying to get an education" statement that really didn't address the problem.

Then again, maybe Bustamante didn't have to. Compared to the uproar over the *Oui* interview, the MEChA story practically became an afterthought—especially after Schwarzenegger seemed to flip-flop on his 26-year-old comments during a press conference on the morning after the interview resurfaced. When asked specifically about the *Oui* article, Schwarzenegger told a reporter: "I have no idea what you're talking about. I'm here to talk about my economic agenda. I have no memory of any of the articles I did 20 or 30 years ago."

Huh? *I have no memory of what I said 26 years ago, even though I said I remembered it last night.* That's basically what he said. What kind of political strategy is that?

Now, as confusing as I found that answer, I will also say that part of me can understand where Schwarzenegger was coming from.

I've been in radio about as long as Schwarzenegger has been in show business. He has probably spoken to thousands of reporters. I've interviewed thousands of people over the years, and I talk to many different people on any given day. When I sign off the air at noon, I no longer think about the show I just finished doing. I'm already thinking about the next day's broadcast. So if you were to ask me about a certain guest or a specific topic on a particular broadcast (especially one that dates back several years), there's a decent chance I'd have no memory of it either. Not off the top of my head, anyway. But if my producer Susan Schustak were to say "Ronn, we did an hour on that last month" or "You talked to so-and-so last year," that's a prompt. Then I remember. (Okay . . . I *might* remember.)

Common sense would say that if someone were to show Schwarzenegger comments he'd once made in an interview—even an interview that was 26 years old—you'd think that would also provide enough of a prompt for him to say, "Yeah, I guess I said it." Especially since he'd just copped to the matter on radio a few hours before.

I'm sorry, but that doesn't bode well for the future. What, you think all of a sudden you're going to win over the religious right by simply denying that you gave the interview?

As much as I liked Schwarzenegger as a candidate, he really lost credibility on that one. But as the campaign continued, I wound up cutting him some slack.

If you want to win my vote, stay on point. Don't give me an answer about what you did 30 years ago and then come back the next day and say you don't remember. That's hardly any way to build confidence. That only serves to confuse. It only makes me wonder how well you'll handle the pressure of politics once you get in office.

"SPECIAL INTERESTS" IS A STUPID EUPHEMISM

Schwarzenegger also lost points when he tried to differentiate between business owners who contributed to his campaign and the so-called "special interest groups" that supported his opponents.

You might recall that when Schwarzenegger first jumped into the race, he made himself attractive to many Californians by saying that he would make the state more friendly to businesses and improve the economy overall without being beholden to special interest groups. "I will go to Sacramento and clean house," he said after he announced his candidacy on *The Tonight Show*. "I don't need to take any money from anybody. I have plenty of money myself. I will make the decisions for the people."

"I don't need to take any money," of course, was a direct jab at Gray Davis, whose relentless fund-raising efforts for his 2002 re-election campaign averaged a staggering $1 million per month throughout his first three years in office. Davis insisted that all of the money was obtained legally and that none of the donations have had any effect on public policy. Nevertheless, his endless drive for cash would lead many Californians to believe, rightly or wrongly, that he was a classic "pay for play" politician who governed simply on the basis of whoever lined his coffers.

About a month into the 75-day campaign, Schwarzenegger raised some eyebrows when he announced that he would return a $2,500 donation from a law enforcement union because he believed that ran counter to his earlier pledge not to accept money from special interests. Which is all well and fine—except that despite giving the impression that he wouldn't "take any money from anybody," Arnold in fact began accepting campaign donations from wealthy individuals, private companies, and small business owners shortly after entering the race. That appeared to be inconsistent with what he said before. Naturally, my listeners and I talked about it on the show.

Truthfully, I didn't have a problem with the campaign contributions in and of themselves. Schwarzenegger may have implied that he would never take any money, but if you look back at his original statement he never actually said that.

Now does that sound Clintonian? Yes. Did I like that about him? Not exactly. But it didn't exactly bother me, either. It was when Arnold began making distinctions between private businesses and other special interests that I began to have a problem.

Schwarzenegger's rationale was this: If at some point I have to sit down at a table to negotiate with you (as I would have to do if you represented a workers' union or an Indian tribe with a gambling casino), then I can't accept your contribution because I would be beholden to you. That makes you a "special interest group." But if you own a mom-and-pop store, or a large company, or simply want to make a donation as an individual, I wouldn't necessarily be sitting down and negotiating with you. That puts you outside the realm of "special interests." Therefore, I can take your money.

As much as I liked Schwarzenegger as a possible replacement for Davis, that explanation just didn't wash. Unions negotiate contracts with private businesses all the time. For that matter, so does the state when it comes to regulations, taxes, workers compensation, and other issues. So to differentiate private business on the basis of whether you sit down at a table with them seems as silly as the euphemism "special interests" itself.

The bottom line is, "special interests" is just a fancy way of saying "whoever gives you money." That's really what we're talking about. Whether you run a major corporation with offices throughout the country or operate a small business out of your garage, when people contribute to a political campaign they usually do so with their own interests in mind.

I'm not necessarily talking direct quid pro quo. But you do expect the candidate to support the causes you believe in and he espouses in a campaign in exchange for your financial support. So if you're pro-choice, and the candidate whose campaign you contribute to is running for governor on a pro-choice platform, and the Supreme Court decides to reverse *Roe v. Wade* and make legalized abortion a state issue shortly after your candidate wins the election, you would not expect him to suddenly flip-flop and ban abortions in the state once he takes office. Even if you had money to burn, why else would you contribute to his campaign?

Granted, I'm sure there are people who donate to political causes for purely philanthropic reasons. There are also probably a few corporations or individuals with legislation pending that relates directly to them, so they give money to everyone running for reelection and figure they've covered their bases.

By and large, though, if you give money to a political candidate, whether it's Gray Davis, Arnold Schwarzenegger, Howard Dean, or George W. Bush, you're usually doing it for a reason. And guess what? There's nothing wrong with that. That's how campaign finance works in this country. That's the way it will continue to work unless we find a way to make it public.

Now does that mean the candidate is always going to jump when you tell him to? Not necessarily. Ask a politician about this and the most he'll say, if indeed he concedes anything, is that it may buy you some access. This brings up the basic question of fairness, which is a topic unto itself.

But when you start looking at voting records, more often than not you'll find an interesting correlation between the amounts of money given to any candidate, left, right, Democrat, Republican, and the way they vote. I mean, why are we so naïve?

CAMPAIGN FINANCE REFORM: NICE IDEA, BUT NOBODY CARES ABOUT IT

As long as we're on the subject . . . I think campaign finance reform is a good idea in theory. In many ways, it's logical and addresses one of the biggest concerns people have with politics today: the feeling that politics is all for the rich.

Gray Davis raises $35 million to win a second term as governor. Michael Huffington sinks $27.5 million of his own money and comes close to beating Dianne Feinstein in the race for the U.S. Senate. The various candidates and committees in the California recall election raise and spend over $82.5 million in the course of the 75-day campaign.

On the face of it, those numbers are clearly obscene. Problem is, campaign finance reform is one of those ideas that has never really gone anywhere.

Up until John McCain and the 2000 election, you couldn't pay people to talk about campaign finance reform. And while McCain worked together with Democratic Senator Russ Feingold to pass the Bipartisan Campaign Reform Act of 2002, which was specifically designed to eliminate so-called "soft money" contributions to federal election campaigns (as well as tighten up loopholes that have allowed for virtually unlimited funding in elections on the state and local level), the constitutionality of that bill has been argued in court since practically the day it was passed. Even if the U.S. Supreme Court were to finally uphold the law (as the Court in fact did in a 5 to 4 ruling on the matter issued on December 10, 2003), the endless debate on the issue underscores the following point: People love to talk about campaign finance reform, but don't want to do anything about it.

And why is that? By and large people want nothing to do with campaign finance reform because deep down, they have their reasons for keeping the system the way it is.

Now you may say, "Ronn, look at big business. All they're doing is buying government. Don't you want to stop them from doing that?" And while that's certainly a valid point, don't forget that unions are also big political action committees. Most candidates would still like to bank on the support of labor, and vice versa.

There's an even more fundamental reason why campaign finance reform hasn't caught on, and it touches on something I feel strongly about. You do a talk show long enough, you get a pretty good sense of which issues resonate with listeners and which ones don't. And in my experience I have found that by and large, people care about and are opinionated on issues in direct proportion to how easy they are to understand.

When you think about it, it's the same as when we were in school. The harder the subject, the less we wanted to know about it. For some people, it was algebra. For me, it was science. The more complex the issue, the less passionate we tend to be.

Bill Clinton has oral sex with an intern in the Oval Office. Arnold Schwarzenegger is accused of repeatedly groping women on movie sets and behind closed doors. Kobe Bryant is accused of rape. Nicole Simpson and Laci Peterson are brutally murdered. While each of these issues had complexities in and of themselves, the basic issue in each of these cases was very straightforward. Obviously, our feelings ran deep in every instance, one way or the other.

The S&L scandals were horrible . . . but God, they were complicated.

Whitewater? To this day, I still don't think I understand everything about Whitewater.

Campaign finance reform fits into that same category. I would submit that if you asked the average person what soft money is, he probably wouldn't know. The only reason I know about soft money is because I talk about the news for a living. Otherwise, I probably wouldn't bother. That's how complex this issue is.

John McCain campaigns for president in 1999. McCain believes strongly in campaign finance reform. People get to thinking, "The man has a point. Let's do something about this."

Comes 2000, and John McCain gets trounced by George W. Bush in the South Carolina primary. McCain bows out of the race. Before you know it, campaign finance reform becomes as significant as the Washington Senators—the long defunct baseball team, that is, not the politicians.

Now we talked before about changing the rules so that elections are publicly funded. Once again, good idea in theory. But how do you make it work? What would you do if 135 people declared themselves candidates for president in the 2004 election? Would everyone be entitled to the same amount of money? What if one of the candidates was a porn actress, as we saw in the California recall? Are you honestly going to put her on the same par with Richard Gephardt or George W. Bush?

Get real. Most of these people are fringe candidates. They're people looking for attention. Sure, you may have a few who are lawyers with seriously passionate beliefs. But for the most part, these are people who have no business running for president. And yet they do it anyway. What, you're going to give them the same amount of money that you would a serious candidate?

Common sense would say you have to draw the line somewhere. So you decide that a candidate must maintain a certain minimum percentage in popularity polls to receive funding. That's more or less the standard right now. Question is, if you're a candidate how do you get that popularity? Without access to people, you're not going to register on the polls. Without campaign money, you're not going to have access. There's no easy way around this.

Once upon a time, we had a fairness doctrine in broadcasting that said if you're going to let one political candidate appear on your station in the course of an election, you have to allow equal time to each of his opponents. After many court battles, the FCC finally threw out that rule in 1987. And thank God for that.

Now why do I say that? Well, let's use the California recall again as an example. We had 135 candidates on the replacement ballot for governor. Three, maybe four of them had a realistic shot at replacing Gray Davis in the event he was recalled. Under the old fairness doctrine, if I wanted to do an hour with Arnold Schwarzenegger about his plans for California, I would have to spend an hour with each of the other 134 candidates even though 98 percent of them have zero chance of winning. That wastes my time. That wastes their time. That wastes my listeners' time.

Then again, I probably spent about 134 hours talking about the recall anyway. But that's beside the point.

If you're really going to be fair about it, you'd have to come up with a forum where they all appear at the same time and have an equal opportunity to speak. But you can't do it with 135 people. You can't do that with 15 people, which is about the number of participants you usually have in a typical San Francisco mayor's race once you count all the fringe candidates. What, you're going to let each of them talk for two or three minutes . . . and that's it? How informative is that?

Practically speaking, you can't do anything. You can't possibly have any meaningful discussion of who these candidates are and where they stand on important issues. And the public loses as a result.

Fortunately, reason prevailed. The FCC lets each station decide for itself which candidates it wants on. And as far as my own show is concerned, I think I go about it fairly and reasonably. I invite people who are serious candidates and who have a legitimate chance of winning. Or who are major party contenders. As long as we have the two major parties, I think that's the way to go.

BEWARE THE LAST WEEK OF ANY POLITICAL CAMPAIGN

We talked before about how perversely entertaining negative campaigning can be. But it can often be very predictable.

If you're a political candidate, you know you'll be attacked on your voting record. You know your opponent will dredge up even the minutest speck of dirt in your past. And you know your opponent will save the most vicious attack of all until the very last week of the campaign.

Call it what you will: a late hit, an October surprise, or simply politics as usual.

Conservatives will tell you this is an exclusive trademark of the Democrats. They'll bring up Bruce Herschensohn in 1992, Michael Huffington in 1994, Darrell Issa in 1998, George W. Bush in 2000. All were slammed by embarrassing revelations that were leaked to the media on the weekend before the election. All but Bush would lose to Democratic opponents.

Problem is, Republicans aren't exactly clean on this one. Or have they forgotten about George H. W. Bush, Willie Horton, and the election of 1988?

Granted, the famous ad that blasted Democratic presidential nominee Michael Dukakis for granting weekend prison passes to convicted murderer/rapist Horton while Dukakis was governor of

Massachusetts originally aired in September 1988. But that was the first of two "Willie Horton" ads produced by the Bush campaign. The second ad aired one week before the election. If that isn't a late hit, what is?

I bring this up to raise the following point. Politics are no different that any other game where strategy and momentum is involved. You want to save your best move or your strongest player for as long as possible for maximum impact. Sometimes that works. Sometimes it backfires. But that's the way you tend to play it.

That being the case, reason would say that when it comes to any damaging revelations against a candidate during the last week of a political campaign—regardless of how serious those allegations happen to be—you have to consider the timing of the story and look at the matter . . . if not completely askance, then at least with a healthy dose of skepticism.

This isn't to say you should disregard the story entirely. Nor do I think you ought to jump to conclusions by giving it total credence. What I am suggesting is that you look at the revelations intelligently and decide whether they are (1) a blatant attempt by a political party to manipulate you at the last minute into voting for their candidate instead of their opponent or (2) legitimate charges. If proof isn't easily forthcoming, go with the former.

Which brings us to the barrage of late hits unfurled on Arnold Schwarzenegger by the *Los Angeles Times* in the last five days of the California recall.

First, there was the report, published on the Thursday before the election, in which six women alleged that Schwarzenegger had groped, fondled, and somehow or other humiliated them sexually without their consent. The women were approached by the *Times* as part of a "seven-week examination of Schwarzenegger's behavior toward women." Four of the women spoke on condition of anonymity. All of them accused Schwarzenegger of mistreating them on movie sets, in studio offices, and in various other settings over the past 30 years, with the most recent incident allegedly taking place as recently as 2000. The report included lurid details about the allegations almost never seen in

any newspaper account of sexual harassment. It was tantamount to the kind of story you'd see in *Penthouse, Playboy,* or for that matter, *Oui* (were it still around).

Then there was the report, published in the *Times* the next day (Friday), in which a comment Schwarzenegger had once made about Adolf Hitler in a 1975 interview was used to create the impression that the actor was an anti-Semite and a closet Hitler admirer. In case you missed it, the quote the *Times* ran has Arnold saying that he admired Hitler "for being such a good public speaker and for what he did with it."

Now you see something like that in print and you can't help but think, "What do you mean, *what he did with it!?!*" That is, until you see the transcript of what Schwarzenegger actually said in 1975: "In many ways, I admire people. It depends on for what. I admire Hitler, for instance, because he came from being a little man with almost no formal education up to power. I admire him for being such a good public speaker, and his way of getting to the people and so on. But I didn't admire him for what he did with it."

Funny, how the *Times* forgot to include the word "didn't" when they ran the quote. That changes the whole meaning of the statement, wouldn't you say?

Finally, the *Times* ran not one, not two, but three different follow-ups to Thursday's story in the last four days of the campaign. By Election Day, a total of 16 women had come forward with allegations that Schwarzenegger had groped or made unwanted sexual advances toward them.

Now I'll make this as blunt as possible. In no way do I condone how Arnold acted toward these women. Nor do I want to minimize the serious nature of the allegations themselves. What he did was degrading, deplorable, and just plain wrong.

To his credit, Schwarzenegger understood that. Not only that, he once again addressed the matter head on and apologized for his actions. On the morning the story broke, he told the media, "I have behaved badly sometimes. Yes, it is true that I was on rowdy movie sets, and I have done things that were not right which at the time I thought were playful. But now I recognize that I have offended people. And to those people that I have offended, I want to say to them I am deeply sorry."

I said it before. I'll say it again. If only more politicians could bring themselves to do that.

Let's be clear about this. Number one, Schwarzenegger's treatment of women on movie sets had been widely known for years, especially in light of a story published in *Premiere Magazine* in 2001. One of the women interviewed for the *Times* story had also been featured in *Premiere*. No disrespect intended to any of his accusers, but this was not exactly news.

Number two, Schwarzenegger's strength has always been with men. His handlers knew that. That's why they made a concerted effort to try to sway women voters by planning appearances on *Oprah* as well as making Arnold's wife Maria Shriver a visible part of the campaign. Not only that, their efforts appeared to be paying off. Results of a Field Poll (California's equivalent of the Gallup Poll) released on the day before the *Los Angeles Times* broke its story indicated that Schwarzenegger's popularity with women voters had jumped eight percentage points to 31 percent heading into October, compared to 23 percent heading into September. That increase appeared to come mostly at the expense of Democratic rival Cruz Bustamante, whose support among women had dropped from 36 percent to 26 percent in the same period of time.

Number three, the *Los Angeles Times* has never been in Schwarzenegger's corner. They endorsed Gray Davis. They were against the recall. They have long displayed a Democratic bias. Unless you have the IQ of a squid (or have swung so far to the left, you're too blind to tell the difference), you have to wonder about the timing of a bombshell directly targeted at Schwarzenegger that comes out five days before the election. That's just too much of a coincidence.

We talked before about the double standard Democrats have when it comes to political leaders and sexual misconduct. Not surprisingly, that would surface again in the aftermath of the *Los Angeles Times* story. Every time I said, "Wait a minute— Schwarzenegger groping women is bad, Clinton having oral sex with Monica is okay," the Democrats would say, "That's apples and oranges, Ronn. Lewinsky and Clinton was consensual. That wasn't the case with Schwarzenegger. He's a sexual predator."

Granted, that was true about Clinton/Lewinsky. But what about Juanita Broderick, Kathleen Willie, or Paula Jones? Clinton allegedly made advances on each of those women. None of those instances were consensual. As a matter of fact, Juanita Broderick accused Clinton of raping her. Yet the Democrats never mentioned any of these cases. Instead they kept harping on how the *Los Angeles Times* story was written by a Pulitzer prize-winning journalist. Ergo, it must be taken seriously.

Talk about backward thinking. And I say this as someone who voted for Clinton twice . . . and who would probably do it again if given the chance.

I never questioned the veracity of the report. I only questioned the timing of it. When you release a highly charged story concerning a political candidate in the final days of a campaign, even an article written by a journalist with impeccable credentials, you leave yourself open to criticism by readers with a skeptical eye.

It's interesting to note how that the *Los Angeles Times* chose to run all of the sexual allegations against Schwarzenegger on the front page. Yet when Broderick came out with her allegations against Clinton, that story was buried in the middle of the paper. Not only that, George Will once wrote a column on the Broderick case that the *Los Angeles Times* refused to publish! Are both of those coincidences, too?

Finally, I lived in L.A. part-time in 1997 and 1998 when my show was simulcast in Southern California. During that time, I was interviewed by the *Los Angeles Times* on approximately 12 occasions.

Make of this what you will, but only twice did they quote me accurately.

HOW TO WIN AN ELECTION—ANY ELECTION

I mentioned before how politically speaking, the Bay Area is an island unto itself. The views here are blithely out of step with what the rest of the country is thinking. If you live here and didn't know any better, you'd think ours is a nation where everyone hates George W. Bush, thinks the war in Iraq was even more un-popular than Vietnam, and cares more about our inability to find weapons of mass destruction than the fact that we toppled Sad-dam in the first place.

Then again, we've been hearing complaints like these from left-wing extremists across the board since Bush took office.

Which goes to show that even a broken watch is right twice a day.

Liberals look for any sign of weakness they can find in the Bush administration. They latch onto the U.S. exit strategy for Iraq (or lack thereof) just so they can say, "See, I told you! People are waking up. The worm is about to turn. It's only a matter of time before the rest of the country realizes what a lousy president they have in George W. Bush." Never mind that opinion polls con-sistently show that by and large, people in the United States are quite happy with the job Bush has been doing. Never mind that polls also indicate that most Americans don't care about weapons of mass destruction. Most Americans look at Iraq in terms of "We did what we said we would do. We went in and we won." You can talk all you want about civilian casualties, but there were far more civilian casualties every day in Iraq when Saddam Hussein was in charge, and no one said a word about that.

Then there's the economy. The jobless rate in this country at the time this book went to press was roughly 6.1 percent, more than two points above the standard barometer of 4 percent or less. The national debt was roughly $6.9 trillion. Consumer confidence was still down. There was no guarantee that Bush's plan would pull us out of the fire. Conceivably the Democrats could use this to their advantage and take the White House in November just as Bill Clinton did when he ran against Bush's father back in 1992.

If the Democrats are serious about winning in 2004, there are three things they need to do:

1. *Stop living in denial.* Stop deluding yourself into believing the rest of the country is "finally waking up" to George W. Bush. Instead, wake up and face facts yourself.

Smart politicians realize that what wins elections in this country more than anything else is likeability. Sure, political philosophy counts. So does one's experience. By and large, though, what we really want is a candidate we like. We want to think, "Hey, he seems like a good guy. She's a woman I can relate to. They're people just like me." And as much as it pains liberals to admit this, this accounts in large part for the popularity of George W. Bush.

Bush's appeal is based on the feeling shared by many Americans that this is a man who understands people. Sure, he may have done his share of partying in his day, but he also has high moral standards—as well as unbridled optimism about the future of this country. And when you have somebody who's personable, you tend to cut him slack on points of view that you may not happen to like or behavior that you yourself would never condone.

Bill Clinton had the same thing going for him. He was eminently likeable. That's what helped get him elected twice. That's also what helped him survive the embarrassment of the Monica Lewinsky scandal. I know for myself that if Clinton had been anti-choice and a big second amendment guy, I'd have been far harsher on him about Monica than I actually was. When I look back and realize the man was actually impeached for fooling around with an intern—whoops, make that "lying under oath"—it makes me shake my head and wonder. I mean, the only thing Clinton should have been impeached for was his lack of judgment in morals and people.

So enough already. Stop dreaming that Bush is unpopular. Because he isn't. And so long as he isn't, that's the biggest obstacle you have to overcome.

2. *Come up with a candidate who is articulate, dynamic, and middle of the road.* Left of center is okay, so long as the candidate is closer to the center than he is to the left.

The closest Democrat who meets this criterion is Senator Joseph Lieberman. Now, I happen to think the world of Joe Lieberman. He's a fine human being, an excellent politician, and a man of great conviction. But he has two strikes against him. Number one, despite his convictions he has yet to sound as though his heart is really in this race. That makes him the Peter Ueberroth of presidential candidates: solid, dedicated, but not exactly passionate. There's no fire in the belly. If you want my vote, you have to show me how badly you want it. From what I've seen thus far, Joe hasn't been able to do that.

Then again, that kind of problem is relatively easy to overcome. Lieberman's second obstacle is considerably more difficult. He's an Orthodox Jew. A man like that, no matter how impassioned he is, will have a hard time getting votes in the Bible Belt. And I say that as a Jew myself.

Former Vermont Governor Howard Dean was the leading contender for the Democratic nomination when this book went to press in November 2003. Howard Dean is also Sanskrit for "Mondale." Nominate him in Boston and all you've done is guarantee another four years of George W. Bush.

The Democrats can't possibly be that stupid. Pin your hopes on someone who's as far to the left as Dean and you might as well run behind Dennis Kucinich. Either way you're committing political suicide.

You want to win the White House in 2004, you need a "New Democrat" like a Bill Clinton, the kind of candidate I had hoped Al Gore would be in the last presidential election, but ultimately was not.

3. *Don't settle for negative politics as usual. Be positive. Offer solutions.* Don't complain about how bad the economy is or how many millions of people remain unemployed under George W. Bush's watch. We already know that. Instead, tell us what you're going to do to fix the problem.

Don't whine about how about the GOP "stole" the 2000 election. There's no instant replay in presidential politics. The referees aren't suddenly going to reverse the results "upon further review." Get over it and look ahead to the race at hand. Make your case for why I should vote for you instead of Bush.

In fairness, it isn't just the Democrats. Republicans are just as guilty of campaigning by complaining. So is just about any candidate in any political party in any given election.

We've reached the point in politics today where it seems the only thing we hear at election time is "Vote for Me Because the Other Guy Is Worse." If you're on the outside looking in, as the Democratic party is in the case of the 2004 election (and as the GOP was in the case of the California gubernatorial recall), common sense would say it's self-defeating to devote the entire campaign to criticizing the incumbent without also offering some solutions.

When I step into the ballot booth, I'd like my vote to be a positive one, not negative. I'd like it to be a vote *for* a candidate, not a vote against his opponent. I'd like to believe most people feel the same way.

Here in California, Gray Davis took "Vote for Me Because the Other Guy Is Worse" and practically made it an art form. That's how he got elected governor twice. Faced with the prospect of being kicked out of office and replaced with Schwarzenegger, Davis resorted to the old slash-and-burn (that is, when he wasn't busy challenging the legality of the recall in court or blaming it all on a "right-wing conspiracy") instead of campaigning on his record. And while it's hard to draw conclusions from an election where the top contender is as larger than life as Arnold Schwarzenegger, the fact remains that Davis lost—or I should say, he was recalled—by a 55 to 45 margin. Politically speaking, that's a mandate.

Conversely, Arnold stayed above the fray and ran an upbeat campaign. Sure, he criticized the mostly Democratic Legislature for its "tax and spend" methods. So did every other candidate in the race—even Democrat Cruz Bustamante. Sure, he criticized Davis. But he also offered a plan that he believed could improve California. He promised to set a positive tone through the campaign and generally stayed on point.

Gray Davis, on the other hand, sunk to new depths, latching onto the barrage of sexual allegations that besieged Schwarzenegger in the final days, even calling for criminal investigations against Arnold when absolutely none were warranted.

I'll say this. I felt Davis did a lot of positive things for California while he was governor. But I got sick of all the negative politics as usual. So did a lot of other Californians, Democrats and Republicans alike.

Look, maybe your opponent *has* done a lousy job. But unless you offer me a viable alternative, unless you come right out and tell me what you're going to do to make a difference, how do I know if I put you in office that you're going to be any better? Which brings us to . . .

THINGS POLITICIANS SHOULD AVOID
IF THEY WANT TO GET ELECTED

If you're serious about getting yourself elected to any political office, you can't cherry pick on the issues. You have to be prepared to honestly tell people where you stand on the matters that concern them, especially when those issues also happen to be on the ballot!

This is one area where I found Peter Ueberroth particularly disappointing.

That wasn't always the case. There was a lot I liked about Peter Ueberroth early in the campaign. For one, I knew he was an intelligent man. Anyone who could work with the International Olympics Committee and run an Olympics that went as smoothly as the 1984 Games in Los Angeles (and turned a profit, to boot) pretty much has to be. Politically speaking, he also struck me as a pragmatist—I mean, the man was once commissioner of baseball! You deal with George Steinbrenner and some of the other fractious personalities who own Major League Baseball franchises, you'd better know the meaning of compromise.

Ueberroth originally opposed the recall. Once it qualified for the ballot, though, he supported the idea, accepting it as a statewide mandate for change. At first he urged Dianne Feinstein to run for governor. Like many Californians (myself included), Ueberroth believed Feinstein would have been elected hands down had she entered the race. But she stayed out, holding fast to the basic principle that the recall was unjustified and that to participate in the process would only serve to validate an idea that she did not believe in. So Ueberroth finally agreed to run, positioning himself as a moderate Republican as well as a fiscal problem solver.

He pledged that if elected he would only serve out the remaining three years of Gray Davis's term, during which time he would balance California's budget and then leave.

Ueberroth spent an hour on my program shortly after he announced his candidacy. On the one hand, he was refreshing in that he steered clear of negative politics as usual. He refused to take shots at any of his opponents—not even the man whose job he was gunning for. He insisted that California's budget problems were not the fault of Governor Gray Davis, but rather that of a flawed economic structure that dictates how large amounts of state revenues must be spent.

Like Schwarzenegger, Ueberroth felt it was important to bring more jobs into California to help build up the tax base. Not surprisingly, he spent most of his time talking about his economic platform. Fair enough. That was Ueberroth's expertise. That was the crux of his campaign. Even so, he proved to be as vague, evasive, and noncommittal in his answers as Schwarzenegger was early in the campaign. I felt like a dentist trying to extract even the tiniest bit of information out of him.

That was not a good sign. If you want to win an election, you've got to give the voters something to go on. You can't expect them to vote for you on good faith alone.

Where Ueberroth really disappointed me, though, was his lackadaisical approach to some of the other pressing issues facing California. He supported a controversial bill that would award drivers licenses to illegal immigrants. He totally whiffed on the subject of legalizing marijuana for medicinal purposes, saying repeatedly that he "had no opinion" and "knew nothing about it."

I was dumbfounded. The man was a candidate for governor of California. Using marijuana to help alleviate the suffering of people with AIDS, cancer, and other debilitating illnesses has been a long-debated, highly controversial issue in this state for many, many years. California voters passed a measure to legalize medical marijuana in 1996 by an overwhelming 70 to 30 margin. Yet the federal government has been relentless in its efforts to overrule the will of the people and throw out the law. I couldn't help but ask Ueberroth, "How could you not have an opinion on this, one way or the other?"

If you're running for political office and are serious about getting elected, you should be prepared to tell people where you stand on *every* issue—not just the ones you're good at.

Two weeks after appearing on our show, Ueberroth took part in a nationally televised debate with four of the other five major replacement candidates at the time: Lieutenant Governor Cruz Bustamante, Republican Senator Tom McClintock, Green party candidate Peter Camejo, and Independent Arianna Huffington. (Arnold Schwarzenegger was the only major contender who declined to participate.) Beyond hammering home his economic message ("We need to bring more jobs into this state. We need to get more people working"), Ueberroth abstained from commenting on every other issue raised in the debate with one notable exception. When asked specifically about medical marijuana, Ueberroth gave a passionate answer in support of the law.

I had to smile when I heard him say that. Just goes to show that every once in a while, even a voice of reason can make a difference in a political campaign.

Political Pragmatism and the California Recall

People like predictability. I know that doesn't sound particularly sexy, but that speaks to who we are. We like to know what's coming and who we're dealing with whenever possible.

Part of what's made me No. 1 in the Bay Area is that people know that every Monday to Friday, nine to noon, except for vacations or holidays, I'm going to be there. They may not know what I'm going to say, but they know I'm going to be there. People are comfortable with that.

Well, the same thing applies to politics, especially if you belong to the extremes. Political extremists would like to believe that everything is totally predictable, that people are divided into Democrats and Republicans and vote strictly along party lines. That's a nice, neat picture, very straightforward, eminently comfortable.

It doesn't work that way if your beliefs are in the middle, because the middle is much more fluid. People in the middle don't ascribe to any one party line. When it comes to choosing a political candidate, they weigh developments as they come and decide on a case-by-case basis. Some decisions come easily. Others are the result of a long, agonizing process.

In 35 years as a broadcaster, I have never experienced an election that was more baffling than the California recall. I've never seen an election where not only did developments change day by day, but in many ways my views on the matter also changed—maybe not literally every day, but certainly more times than I ever would have imagined.

Then again, that's what it means to be in the rational middle. That's what it means when you think for yourself. Sometimes you just have to vote your conscience, no matter how uncomfortable that proves to be. You live in a city where four out of five people vote one way on the recall, and you're the one-in-five who votes the other, you're going to alienate a lot of people.

But you can surprise a lot of people, too. Sometimes you even surprise yourself.

That's how it was for me and my vote on the California recall. It was a debate of principle over pragmatism that didn't completely crystallize until the day I cast my ballot.

THE LEMON LAW

The original concept of the recall came from Hiram Johnson, the progressive governor of California referred by some as "the patron saint of populism." When Johnson took office in 1911, he sought to clean up state politics, just as he had cracked down on local politics while serving as a special assistant to the San Francisco district attorney. Believing that the greatest source of corruption in California was the Southern Pacific Railroad, Johnson set about ending the railroad industry's influence on elected officials and returning power to the people. With that in mind, Johnson used his 1911 Inaugural Address to introduce three reforms that would usher in what President Theodore Roosevelt called "a new era in popular government": (1) *the initiative,* which allowed voters a direct say in the creation of laws or constitutional amendments; (2) *the referendum,* which enabled voters to veto acts of the legislature; and (3) *the recall,* "a precautionary measure by which a recalcitrant official can be removed" from office. Though Johnson knew his directives were hardly a panacea, he nonetheless believed the reforms bestowed on the electorate "the power of action when desired" and "the means by which they may protect themselves."

Without question, this changed the face of government. President Theodore Roosevelt, himself a progressive, went so far as to hail Johnson's reforms as "the greatest advance ever made by any state for the benefit of its people."

Problem is, while Johnson's rationale for the recall process was very explicit, the actual law he enacted is exceptionally broad.

Unlike the Constitution of the United States—which requires evidence of treason, bribery "or other high crimes and misdemeanors" for Congress to impeach the president—the California Constitution simply states that "recall of a state officer is initiated by delivering to the secretary of state a petition alleging reason for recall. Sufficiency of reason is not reviewable."

Talk about loopholes. Strictly speaking, this means the people of California can remove an elected official *for any reason whatsoever*. Even if they just plain don't like him. Not surprisingly, the recall rule has come to be known as the "lemon law."

That may be how the law appears on the books . . . but it still doesn't make any sense. That's why I believed from day one that the effort to recall Governor Davis was flat out wrong. No law that serious should ever be that capricious. There ought to be legitimate grounds.

Larry Sabato, the political analyst who is also director of the Center for Politics at the University of Virginia, agreed with my assessment. "The progressives of the early twentieth century established [the recall process] specifically to remove corrupt public officials from office *once the corruption was discovered*," he said on my program. "That was the point of recall. It wasn't simply to remove unpopular public officials. There's a real distinction there, and I think the people [behind the petition] have missed it."

Boy, did they ever.

Let's be blunt. Forget the energy crisis. Forget the budget crisis. The main reason for the recall election was Gray Davis himself.

Remember when we talked before about how we tend to elect politicians who are personable, and how we tend to cut them some slack if we like them? For all his experience in politics, Davis never seemed to get that. He failed to grasp the importance of reaching out to his constituents and connecting with them on a personal level.

I'm not saying you have to be a cheerleader all the time. What I am saying is that it never hurts to show a little warmth once in a while. That worked for Bill Clinton. That works for George W. Bush.

Being a leader isn't just telling the people you're the boss, or that your values resonate with those of the majority of people in your state or country. It's showing people that you're one of them. It's letting them know you care about your state or country just as much as they do, and that you seem as genuinely interested in their personal welfare as you are in your political welfare.

That's how you build trust. That's how you build confidence. And yet Gray never bothered to learn that. Not only did he not care whether people liked him, sometimes it seemed as if he went out of his way to make sure no one did.

This is a man who once said that the purpose of the state legislature—that is to say, *the people he has to work with every day in Sacramento if he hopes to get anything done*—is "to implement my vision."

Now we've talked before about the egos of politicians. But this takes hubris to a whole new level.

You may not agree with everything going on in the senate and the state assembly. Very few governors do. But at the end of the day, you still have to work with these people. You may not like taking your lumps right now, but common sense would say that you do it anyway. That's politics. That's also part of being a leader. You have to know when to compromise. There's always another bill or project where you can stand tough. Practically speaking, it doesn't do you any good to isolate the people whose help you'll need again sometime down the road.

And yet in July 1999, six months into his first term, after a prolonged dispute with lawmakers on matters such as health insurance (one of the issues that helped get him elected in the first place), Governor Davis had the audacity to tell the editorial board

of the *San Francisco Chronicle* that his victory the previous November entitled him to call the shots in Sacramento as he saw fit.
"People expect government to reflect the vision that I suggested,"
he said. "Nobody else in the Legislature ran statewide. Their job is
to implement my vision. That is their job."

Davis was roundly panned for making that remark, and de-
servedly so. Even his fellow Democrats were embarrassed by it.
And yet he never seemed to learn from that. He may have perceived himself as a competent administrator, but on the surface
he came across as a cold, aloof, arrogant tyrant. He had absolutely
zero connection with people, and the just-as-cold numbers bore
that out. Davis registered an abysmal 33 percent approval rating
in July 2003, when talk of the recall began heating up. By Election
Day (October 7), that figure was down to 21 percent.

Twenty-one percent. That means four out of every five Californians either didn't like what Davis was doing in office or simply didn't like *him*.

But that alone should not have been the criterion for the recall
of Gray Davis. If you're going to kick a man out of office, there
ought to be grounds for discharge beyond his sheer arrogance.
There ought to be a case for incompetence or gross malfeasance.

Now you can argue that the way Davis handled California's energy crisis was incompetent (and in fact, *it was*). But the energy
crisis took place in early 2001, midway through the governor's
first term of office. The time to take him to task for that was in
November 2002, when Davis ran for reelection.

Guess what? The people of California *reelected him anyway*.
That closed the book on anything that took place during Davis's
first term. Therefore, any basis for recall should be based on what
Davis did during his *second* term, not his first. And at the time the
recall first began to surface, the governor hadn't done anything to
justify his ouster!

You can also say Davis was less than honest about the size of
the deficit, choosing not to reveal how serious the problem was
until after he won a second term. But if that's your rationale,
then we'd have to recall every politician who winds up fudging
on the truth during an election campaign. That would leave the

entire country in the hands of one, maybe two people. And even *they* would get thrown out of office eventually. Not even the most honest person in the world can expect to get anything done in a way that pleases everybody. So that in and of itself is not reason enough to knock out Davis.

Then again, for the life of me I couldn't understand why the Republicans wanted the governorship so badly. It was like "Play to Win," except once you win *you're stuck with the prize.* And the prize in this case was a $38 billion deficit where you're going to have to make cuts. No matter where you cut, people are going to be upset. Why would you want to do that? That made about as much sense as the recall itself.

DOMINO THINKING

State law requires that once a recall petition is certified, a special election must be held within 60 to 80 days. Since the recall petition was certified in July, that means the recall election had to be held in October.

This brings us to the first of the two principal arguments against the recall. Opponents would say that holding a special election in October in addition to the one already scheduled for November would cost too much money—upwards of $67 million, according to the *San Francisco Chronicle.* With California already facing a $38 billion deficit, a recall election would be fiscally irresponsible.

I'm sorry, but I just don't buy that. Even if you strongly believed the recall was wrong in principle (which again was my position), the fact remains that the law is on the books. If the law provides for a recall, and you gather enough signatures and get the secretary of state to certify your petition and put it on the ballot, then we have to live with it and spend the money for the special election. That's just the way it is.

You can't the change the rules in the middle of the game just because you don't like them. If the state constitution needs to be amended, the time to do that is after the recall is over. Not before.

The other principal argument, espoused by prominent state Democrats such as former San Francisco Mayor Willie Brown, was that the recall would set a precedent that could possibly spell the end of democracy as practiced today. If the Republicans succeed in removing Gray Davis from office, then what's to stop the Democrats from instigating a petition to recall the new Republican governor once he's been inaugurated? They couldn't do it right away—according to the state constitution, they'd have to wait 180 days before filing such a petition. But once those six months are up, it's logical to assume the Democrats would want revenge. Assuming the Democrats succeed, the Republicans would then retaliate. And so forth and so on. Before you know it, we'd have in effect a political structure whereby elected officials are subject to expulsion every six months. "Not only would that totally destabilize the entire democratic system," said Brown on my show, "it would conceivably eliminate any possibility that an elected official can do his job."

This is a classic example of the domino theory—a form of argument first made popular by President Eisenhower to justify our involvement in South Vietnam. Eisenhower believed that if one nation succumbed to communism, all nations surrounding it would also succumb to communism. But if the United States were to somehow take out Vietnam, then all of Indochina would likewise fall as though they were dominoes falling in a line.

I've never been one for the domino theory. To me, that's just an easy way of getting out of an intellectual argument.

I have no way of knowing the future any more than you do—if I did, I'd spend every day at the race track! That's why I believe in approaching each particular issue purely on the basis of what we know now. If the story advances two weeks from now to the point where my views on the matter have changed, that's fine. I have no qualms about saying so on the air. For now, though, let's just focus on what's happening *today* because that's where our concerns are.

That said, I have to admit that for a while I shared Willie Brown's concern. There's something to be said for letting the electoral process remain the way it is. There's something to be said for nipping a potentially divisive problem in the bud before it polarizes us even further.

Problem is, you do a show for as long as I have, your views on certain matters become fairly well known. You take a position that runs counter to your views and sooner or later someone will nail you on it.

Sure enough, an astute listener called in one day and said, "Ronn, you can't argue the recall will destroy the democratic process. That's domino thinking. I thought you didn't believe in that."

I had to admit . . . the caller got me on that one. I *was* thinking like a domino theorist, and that's not something I ordinarily do. So while I still opposed the recall on principle—and would have voted no without hesitation at that particular time—I had to pull back on that aspect of my argument.

THE RECALL BECOMES REALITY

By early July, the people behind the recall petition had gathered well over 1.6 million signatures—nearly twice the amount required by law to require a special election. The effort to remove Governor Davis from office was moving further away from conjecture and ever closer to reality. While political insiders speculated on who might run in the replacement election, Davis and his supporters initiated a lawsuit on July 14 that challenged the legitimacy of the signatures gathered on the petition. This marked the first of several attempts to throttle the recall on legal grounds.

To anyone who even remotely follows California politics, this came as no surprise. Gray Davis the person is duller than watching paint dry, but Davis the politician is as tenacious as they come. This is a man whose career looked like road kill on more than one occasion, yet he always managed to bounce back.

I thought Davis was finished in 1998, when he faced airline magnate Al Checchi in the Democratic gubernatorial primary. Checchi was a charming, straightforward businessman with common-sense ideas and moderate political views. He looked like a shoe-in for the Democratic nomination, and yet Davis mopped the floor with him.

With the recall looming, Davis was now facing the battle of his political life. No way would he take this lying down.

The only question was whether Davis was smart enough to go about it the right way. Early indications said the answer was no. That also came as no surprise.

We talked before about how deep dissatisfaction with Davis ran with voters throughout the state, how he always seemed more concerned with lining his coffers and planning the next phase of his political career than in staying in touch with his constituents. And while Davis often acknowledged his dissenters ("I'm not asking you to marry me, I'm asking you to vote for me"), deep down he seemed to believe that nothing he could do could ever change that perception. So he never bothered trying. Instead he perfected a political strategy of presenting himself as the lesser of two evils: making his opponent look so bad that Gray Davis looks good by comparison. Or as we put it before, "Vote for me not because I'm the best candidate. Vote for me because the other guy is worse."

Look at how he ran his reelection campaign in 2002. Faced with the prospect of running against former Los Angeles Mayor Richard Riordan, Davis spent $10 million on ads designed to sabotage Riordan in the GOP primary so that right-wing conservative billionaire Bill Simon could win the nomination. Why did he do that? Because Davis knew he stood a better chance of beating Simon in November than he did Dick Riordan. Riordan was a moderate Republican with pro-choice and pro-gun control views identical to those of Gray Davis. Unlike Davis, Riordan was exceptionally popular with Democrats and Republicans alike. Most insiders believed that if Riordan won the nomination, Gray Davis would be history in the general election. To prevent that from happening, Davis ran a series of ads that blasted Riordan for abandoning the party line on abortion and gun control (which Riordan had once espoused on those issues) and adopting a more progressive stance. The ads were targeted at voters on the bubble about Riordan, as well as doctrinaire conservatives likely to support Bill Simon.

Long story short, the strategy worked. Riordan was out. Simon was in. Davis took advantage of Simon's political inexperience by presenting himself as the lesser of two evils. Davis beat Simon in

November. In effect, this means that the governor manipulated the GOP primary to achieve the match-up and result he wanted.

Illegal? Hardly. Dishonest? Not really. Bad taste in the mouths of voters who would have liked to have seen how Davis would have fared against a much more formidable challenger like Dick Riordan? Definitely yes.

Grounds for a recall? Definitely no. Voters had their chance to voice their disapproval over the governor's tactics in November 2002. And as we pointed out before, Davis not only won a second term, he did nothing to warrant removal from office since beginning his second term.

At the same time, though, I strongly believed that if the recall made it onto the ballot, and Davis chose to fight it by running the type of "slash and burn" negative campaign for which he was known, he would soon be out of a job.

As a matter of fact, I said that on the air on July 15—eight days before the recall was officially certified by California Secretary of State Kevin Shelley.

Common sense would say that if you're Gray Davis, and you're facing an election that calls for your ouster at a time when 80 percent of Californians don't even like you, going negative and attacking the process (instead of being positive and playing up your accomplishments) will only serve to alienate you further from the people who are already dissatisfied with you in the first place.

PRINCIPLE VERSUS PRAGMATISM: THE ARGUMENT OF THE TWO TOMS

On July 24, the date of the special election was set for October 7 (or 75 days later). Prospective replacements for Gray Davis had until August 9 to declare their candidacies. Republicans from across the board were rumored to be candidates, from right-wing conservatives Bill Simon, Darrell Issa, and Tom McClintock to moderates Dick Riordan and Arnold Schwarzenegger. Democrats regrouped to determine the best strategy: keep a united front behind Davis and fight the recall, or put up a replacement candidate of their own to cover their bets in the event the recall passed.

In the meantime, I invited two longtime prominent Bay Area political observers to come on the air and hash out the issue: Tom Campbell, the onetime U.S. Congressman who is now dean of the Haas School of Business at UC/Berkeley, and Tom McEnery, the former mayor of San Jose who has also taught at Stanford University and the University of Santa Clara. Campbell is a moderate Republican, McEnery a moderate Democrat.

On the one hand, the two Toms agreed with me that the recall was wrong in principle and should not be taking place. Like it or not, Gray Davis won reelection in 2002 and should be allowed to serve out his second term.

That said, the two Toms then asked me to consider two simple facts: (1) like it or not, the recall *is* reality and, (2) given the massive budget deficit, California is in a state of crisis. That being the case, you should therefore consider the other candidates on the ballot and ask the question, "Who among these people is the best person to lead the state of California out of this crisis?" If you think the answer is Gray Davis, then vote no on the recall. If you think it's someone else, then vote yes on the recall and vote for that person.

I had to admit, the argument of the two Toms was not only sound, it appealed to my sense of pragmatism. While their rationale didn't completely persuade me, it was compelling enough for me to keep an open mind on the matter.

Up to that point, I considered the recall a "slam dunk"—the kind of issue where one side was so obvious from a common sense standpoint, it wasn't even close. The recall was wrong in principle. There was no other way to go.

But after listening to the two Toms, I could see an argument for the other side that actually made sense. For the first time I was beginning to look at the recall not reflexively, but rationally, weighing each development on its merits as it comes up and considering the issue as a political pragmatist should.

GRAY MOVES TO THE LEFT

At that point, my family and I left for a two-week vacation. By the time I returned, two significant developments took place that dramatically changed the landscape of the recall (not to mention, my own feelings on my matter):

1. *Arnold Schwarzenegger and Peter Ueberroth, who both espoused political views that appealed to my own basic philosophy, entered the race as candidates on the replacement ballot*; and

2. *Gray Davis began doing some strange things.* After years of positioning himself as a moderate (a strategy which, by the way, got him elected governor twice in the first place), he suddenly started courting the left . . . not because he supported the left, but because he felt doing so was his best chance of staying in office. Not only that, he appeared to adopt this tactic without any consideration of how it might affect his established political base—especially after he flip-flopped on two controversial issues.

Let's look at the second development first.

I've known Gray Davis personally and professionally for over 25 years. I've followed his career very closely. I even voted for him twice for governor. He may be totally bereft of personality, but in his own way he was a man of principle. By that I mean he was consistent. His style of governing may have left much to be desired. But rightly or wrongly, he stayed on point and stayed within himself. You had to hand it to him for that.

Politically speaking, Davis was also consistent. For years he presented himself as a politician who was somewhere in the middle—perhaps left of center, but certainly not tilting all the way to the left. I didn't agree with everything he did in Sacramento, but at least I knew where he stood. I could respect him for that, too.

That's why I was so troubled by his blatant pandering to the left. To me, it was a move that smacked of desperation. Gray Davis went from being a man of principle to a man who would do just about anything to keep from losing his job.

I'll give you two examples of that. While I was away, Davis announced that he would sign into law California Senate Bill 60, a bill that would grant drivers licenses to illegal immigrants. (Davis in fact signed the bill in September, and the new law was scheduled to take effect in January 2004. However, immediately after taking office in November 2003, Governor Arnold Schwarzenegger called a special session of the state legislature for the purpose of repealing the law. One week later, the state Senate then voted to rescind the bill.)

SB 60 was an issue I felt strongly about. I thought it was a bad idea. I felt the law essentially said, "Sure, you may have circumvented the law when you entered this country, but now that you're here let's make you as legal as possible."

What disturbed me most about this development was the fact that Gray Davis originally felt the same way about SB 60 that I did.

Maybe it's me, but I don't understand how one morning you can say, "No way can I support a law that would reward people for coming to this state illegally" . . . and then change your mind the next day *for no apparent reason.*

I say that facetiously, of course. Davis knew exactly what he was doing. He flip-flopped purely for political reasons. But that still doesn't make it right.

Now you can say that in any given election any candidate for political office will use polls or focus groups as a way of measuring how best to position himself on issues that are important to the electorate. Whether you're an incumbent or someone challenging the incumbent, sometimes it might be smart to shift your views on certain issues if that's what it takes to stay in the race and attain a winning outcome.

That's the way Willie Brown saw it. "Every issue doesn't require your adherence," he said on my show. "In the case of Governor Davis, he clearly sees that the right has [exerted its influence in certain areas of the state] and occupies all of those votes. He knows that he is very comfortable, philosophically, with being on the left. Therefore, he is doing exactly what he should do to achieve his survivability."

Willie Brown, it should be noted, is a partisan liberal Democrat. Like Davis, Brown viewed the recall as a right-wing power grab, an attempt by the GOP to win a Governor's race they felt they should have won in November. Davis had no chance of swaying conservatives. Polls indicated his best bet for defeating the recall was by moving to the left. The left strongly opposed the recall. The left strongly supported the driver's license bill. Davis wanted to keep his job. So he supported the bill to appease the left. Nothing wrong with that. The way Brown saw it, the governor simply "changed his position after obtaining new information about the bill that convinced him that his earlier position was not the way to go."

I didn't agree with Willie's rationale for the flip-flop, but I could at least accept it if it were just an isolated incident. But it wasn't. Davis did a 180° on another controversial issue after the recall was certified: the increase of vehicle registration fees.

On May 14, 2003, at a time when the recall was still very much conjecture, Davis announced a plan to triple the fees that drivers in California pay each year to register their cars. The rate hike would (and in fact, did) go into effect on October 1 . . . only to be repealed six weeks later by Governor Schwarzenegger. He promised to make it his first priority. He kept his promise.

On the one hand, I didn't like this any more than my listeners. I didn't want to pay a 300 percent rate increase. Who would? For the average car owner, this amounts to an additional $136 per year per vehicle. Many households have more than one car. Depending on the number of cars you own, that's a big chunk out of your pocketbook. But Davis essentially said, "California is in trouble. We need to increase revenue so that we can bail the state out of this $38 billion hole. This is the right thing to do." That didn't make me any less unhappy about it. But at least I could understand the rationale.

Fast-forward to August. Now Gray Davis is in trouble. Gray Davis is facing a recall. He looks at the vehicle rate hike and realizes, "Wait a minute! Triple the car tax? Voters aren't going to like that. That can't be good for me. I'll just tell the people of California I've changed my mind."

Look, it's one thing if a politician changes his mind on an issue after carefully weighing it from all sides, or because over time one's views and convictions can and often do change. I've been known to do that myself. So have the rest of us.

But when a politician changes his mind simply to curry favor, as Gray Davis was clearly doing . . . that's altogether different. And don't try to convince me otherwise. I'm not stupid. I'd like to think most voters aren't stupid, either.

Which brings us back to the question raised by the two Toms. "The state of California is facing a crisis. Who is the best person who can lead us out of trouble?"

Before I went on vacation, I would have answered "Gray Davis." I voted for him before. All things considered, I was inclined to vote for him again. But once he started blatantly pandering, *I no longer believed that.* I had no idea which Davis I'd be getting: the one I voted for in November, who was slightly left of center but otherwise positioned in the middle—or the one who suddenly tilted all the way to the left!

It's hard to have allegiance to someone when you don't know where he stands. And that's the way I felt about Gray Davis. He went from being a man of principle to a man who would do *anything* just to stay in office. That would ultimately cost him.

THINKING OUTSIDE THE BOX

If you live in a state with a special election that essentially asks people to choose between keeping a governor who's eminently qualified but not exactly likeable, or supplanting him with one of 135 possible replacements (many of whom are likeable but not exactly qualified), you're going to catch a little flak. I mean, when you literally have candidates from all walks of life, you really have to expect that.

We had everything from politicians (Darrell Issa, Tom McClintock, Cruz Bustamante), political pundits (Arianna Huffington), and erstwhile political candidates (Bill Simon, Peter Camejo) to movie stars (Arnold Schwarzenegger), porn stars (Mary Carey), and erstwhile sitcom stars (Gary Coleman). Not to mention to Leo Gallagher, the comedian best known for smashing watermelons on stage with a sledge hammer.

Now how do you choose between Gary Coleman and Gallagher? When you think about it, there's really no contest. All

Gallagher has to do is take that sledge hammer and WHAM!, there goes the budget deficit.

All humor aside, I knew all eyes were on California. How could they not be? California has the fifth largest economy in the world. The recall dominated the news every day for two solid months. Sure, in many ways it was as farcical as it was fascinating. There was certainly a perception among some of my listeners that once again, "the rest of the country is laughing at us."

I think much of that was overblown.

For one, more people voted in the October recall election than did in the previous gubernatorial election held in November 2002—an increase of up to 30 percent, according to figures from the state registrar of voters. Certainly the star power of Arnold Schwarzenegger had a lot to do with that. You can argue the merits of that either way. The point is, for whatever reason, a large percentage of the electorate decided to get involved. Whether you believe the essence of democracy is participation, or if you simply care about politics, that kind of news is manna from heaven.

Number two, you can laugh all you want, but the fact remains that California sets more trends in this country than any other state, be they trends in the arts, business, or politics. As I saw it, the recall presented California with yet another opportunity to lead the way for the rest of the nation.

What do I mean by that? Well, as I mentioned earlier, at the time of the recall California was a state where only one political party was in power. The Democrats controlled the state assembly by a 48 to 32 margin. They controlled the state senate by a 25 to 15 margin. Both of California's U.S. senators are Democrats, as are the majority of the state's representatives in Congress (33 Democrats, 20 Republicans). Not only that, every major political office in California was likewise held by a Democrat: John Burton (senate president pro tempore), Phil Angelides (treasurer), Bill Lockyer (attorney general), Kevin Shelley (secretary of state), Cruz Bustamante (lieutenant governor), and of course, Gray Davis (governor).

You may disagree, but how is that possibly a good thing? This is the United States, not the old USSR. How can you be happy knowing that one party can decide by itself what it wants to foist off on you?

I didn't like seeing that on the state level any more than I like having one party controlling the House, the Senate, and the presidency on the national level.

I want both sides represented in government. I want both sides to engage in healthy debate and work together so that the interests of all Californians are served, not just those of whichever political party wields all the power.

Were the situation reversed, and every state office in California held by a Republican, I'd feel the same way. I'd want at least one Democrat in there. There has to be some viable opposition. There has to be a semblance of a two-party system.

That alone was reason enough for me to consider voting in favor of the recall. Because if Gray Davis were to be unseated, his replacement would likely be a Republican. As someone who hoped to restore balance to California politics, I didn't mind seeing that at all.

Then again, I wouldn't vote for just *any* Republican. Not if the GOP continued to shoot itself in the foot and put up candidates like Bill Simon, Dan Lungren, Matt Fong, Bruce Herschensohn, or some of the other ultra-conservatives they banded together behind in recent California elections. All ran for key state offices on platforms that were far to the right. All went down in defeat. Simon went down in defeat in the 2002 gubernatorial election. Yet, he ran as a candidate to replace Gray Davis—as did fellow right-winger Darrell Issa, the man who bankrolled the recall in the first place.

You had to wonder how many losses the GOP had to absorb in California before they finally realized that running far to the right is no way to win an election.

The Republican party faced the same challenge heading into the gubernatorial recall that the Democratic party faces in the upcoming presidential election. Their best bet at winning the governor's mansion in October, just as the Democrats' best chance of winning the White House in November 2004, is *by moving to the center.*

That's where the votes are. That's how the majority of people in this country think, politically.

It used to be that people voted strictly on a doctrinaire basis. It didn't matter who your party nominated: if you were a registered Democrat, that's who you voted for. The same goes if you were a registered Republican.

My father was that way. My father was a lifelong registered Democrat, and I just loved him. But Dad would have voted for Mister Ed if he were a Democrat running for political office.

(Then again, if Mister Ed ran for political office, maybe that wouldn't be so bad. After all, Mister Ed was smart enough never to speak unless he had something to say.)

The days of doctrinaire voting are over. Sure, you still have your 15 percent to 20 percent on the far left who will vote the party line, and another 15 percent to 20 percent on the far right. But the vast majority of people today—that remaining 60 percent to 80 percent that comprises the political middle—prefers to look at candidates on a case-by-case basis. They look at what a candidate says (and to some degree, how he runs his campaign) before they make up their minds.

That being the case, you have to think outside the box. In the case of the California GOP, that meant coming up with a candidate who espoused traditional conservative values while also appealing to the state's vast Democratic base. Call it what you will: a moderate Republican, or perhaps even a "new Republican" (in the same sense that Bill Clinton was a "new Democrat"). Someone who ideally is pro-choice, pro-gay rights, and pro-gun control while at the same time fiscally responsible. Someone who understands the meaning of compromise and who can administrate in a way that keeps the Democrats honest, if not completely in line. Someone who could offer Californians a real choice, instead of the choices the Democrats give us.

Arnold Schwarzenegger was such a Republican. So was Peter Ueberroth. Both announced their candidacies during that two week period I was on vacation. Both immediately piqued my interest.

Schwarzenegger particularly appealed to me for three reasons: (1) his views on social issues meshed with mine; (2) he seemed committed to running above the fray and not resorting to negative campaigning, which I found refreshing; and (3) he seemed determined to make it easier for businesses to come into California and employ people. Small companies have especially felt overly regulated in California in recent years. As a result, more and more of them are taking their businesses elsewhere in the country.

Schwarzenegger wanted to reverse that. He wanted to ease up on regulations as an incentive for businesses to come back to California and thus build up our tax base. The bigger the tax base, the more money coming into our state. The more revenue coming in, the more that helps the state get out of the red. It seemed like a sound, straightforward solution to a problem that I felt the state sorely needed to address.

The operative word was "seemed." Schwarzenegger, as we alluded to before, was especially vague on specifics early on. For that matter, so was Ueberroth. I may have liked them both, but I wanted more from both. I wanted details out of Schwarzenegger. And I wanted some fire out of Ueberroth. As appealing as I found him, he also struck me as a man whose heart wasn't really in the race. If you want my vote for governor, you have to show me you really want the job. Up to that point, Ueberroth hadn't done that, and I was hoping he might prove me wrong.

More importantly, I wanted to see if the GOP in California was smart enough to realize that the only way to win was by uniting behind a "new Republican" candidate.

If they were, and they somehow pulled it off, then perhaps the rest of the country might once again follow California's lead in realizing that "moderation" in the political sense is no longer considered a sin. Were that to happen, perhaps those of us who are in the middle might actually be heard.

That was something I really wanted to see.

WHY SOCIAL ISSUES MATTER

Within a few weeks, the field of 135 candidates on the bottom half of the ballot began to narrow considerably. Bill Simon quickly dropped out of the race, as did Darrell Issa. They were joined by

Peter Ueberroth shortly after Labor Day. All bowed out because of low poll numbers.

By mid-September, with Election Day a month away, the choices to replace Davis essentially came down to Cruz Busta-mante, Tom McClintock, or Arnold Schwarzenegger.

I must say, though, that I grew to like Gary Coleman. I couldn't vote for him . . . but I found him likeable as a person and refreshingly candid as a political candidate. How can you not like someone who comes right out and says, as Gary did on my show, that he's "probably the least qualified candidate for the job" and that his chances of actually getting elected were slim at best. When's the last time you heard a politician say that?

Along with that, some of the solutions Coleman proposed (such as a flat tax) weren't bad at all. He was genuinely passionate when he spoke about the need to move away from politics as usual in Sacramento. But when a candidate himself knows he hasn't got a prayer, then why should I throw my vote away?

You may disagree, but I'd rather cast my ballot for someone I honestly believe can win. I'd like my vote to matter. I like to think most voters tend to choose among the most viable candidates on the ballot so that their vote will matter, too.

That's why for all intents and purposes, it really came down to three candidates. If you count the question on the top of the ballot ("Should Gray Davis be removed from office?"), then you had a fourth choice: voting no on the recall and keeping Davis.

At this point, I was still on the fence as far as how to vote on the top of the ballot . . . and would in fact remain that way right up until the day of the election. As troubled as I was by the flip-flops and pandering to the left, I still felt in my gut that the recall was wrong in principle and that Davis should be allowed to serve out his term.

Then again, I am a pragmatist. Polls indicated that Davis stood a very good chance of being recalled. That being the case, I wanted a say on who his replacement might be regardless of how I voted on the top.

One thing was certain. I couldn't vote for Lieutenant Governor Cruz Bustamante, the lone Democrat on the ballot. Not when he proposed hiking the tax rate for anyone making over $100,000 a year. Not after the smarmy way in which he ran his campaign. He was supposed to be the fail-safe for the Democratic party, running under the banner "Vote No on the Recall, Yes on Bustamante." But the further along in the campaign, the more he emphasized the second part of the slogan at the expense of the first. That's when his true colors began to show.

A listener hit it on the head one morning. He sent me an e-mail that said that "Bustamante" is Spanish for "back-stabbing weasel."

Tom McClintock, on the other hand, was a man I had come to respect. He offered sound fiscal policies for helping California out of its economic bind. Plus I admired him for sticking to his principles and staying in the race to the very end, even when his own party leaders were urging him to quit.

But I could never vote for Tom McClintock—just as I could never vote for Bill Simon, despite how much I genuinely like Bill as a person. In both cases the deciding factor was their stance on social issues.

McClintock supporters would invariably call in and tell me that a candidate's take on social issues aren't that important. What really matters is getting California out of its financial woes. McClintock has a plan. McClintock has a track record for getting things done. Therefore, he's your guy.

I'm sorry, but I beg to differ. A candidate's views on social issues *do* count. Why? Two reasons. One, there are the various judicial appointments a governor makes throughout the state. And while people insist there's no litmus test for that, the fact of the matter is when it comes to making appointments, most administrators tend to choose people that think much like they do. Nothing earth shattering about that. That's just common sense.

Number two, there's a good chance that as many as three Supreme Court justices will retire from the bench in the next few years. If George W. Bush wins reelection in 2004, he will have to fill those three spots—most likely, with conservative judges. There would then be a chance *Roe v. Wade* would be overturned in the next presidential term and thrown back to the states. At which point, the governor's views on abortion will have tremendous significance. And if the governor of California were Tom McClintock, that would scare me.

Tom McClintock is so adamantly anti-choice, he went out of his way to bring this up even when it wasn't an issue.

It's one thing to say "I personally do not believe in abortion, but I could never support legislation that would deny a woman's right to choose. I believe that's a decision each woman should decide for herself, without any government imposition." I could support your candidacy even though you and I disagreed on the first part, because we would be in agreement on the second. It's another thing to fervently go out of your way, as Tom McClintock did throughout the campaign, and say "I believe this is wrong and no one should do it."

Why he did that, I don't understand. It was political suicide. But I'll give him credit for integrity. Abortion is obviously an issue he feels strongly about. And though McClintock supporters insisted he wouldn't let his bias show if abortion were to become a state issue again, I had a real problem believing that.

I go back to the point we discussed before about politics and principles. Even the most principled politician in the world has to know how to compromise. Nothing in McClintock's record indicated he could do that. Certainly nothing about his stance on abortion indicates that he would ever give any ground on that particular issue. For that reason alone, I couldn't possibly support him.

That narrowed the field even further. Either keep Gray Davis, or roll the dice with Arnold Schwarzenegger. If you are of a middle of the road philosophy, as I am, how could you not go for Arnold?

Now, was I completely comfortable with Schwarzenegger? Hardly. I still wasn't crazy about his flip-flop in response to the *Oui* controversy, owning up to his remarks from 1977 only to deny making them the next day. I didn't care for the way he ran his campaign in the early going, announcing his platform in dribs and drabs without ever really saying anything. And though he finally did publish position statements on his campaign web site six weeks before the election, I still wanted to hear from him directly. I wanted to be sure those were his views, not just those of his backers or advisors.

I was also troubled by a remark Arnold had once made when he was chairman of the President's Council on Physical Fitness under George H. W. Bush: "My relationship to power and authority is that I'm all for it. People need somebody to watch over them. . . . 95 percent of the people in the world need to be told what to do and how to behave." This statement, which originally appeared in a November 1990 profile of Schwarzenegger in *U.S. News & World Report,* resurfaced about a month before the recall election.

Now did find I that quote scary? Yes. Did I find it scary enough to not vote for Schwarzenegger as a replacement for Gray Davis? No. I still liked the idea of having a moderate Republican dealing with the Democratic majority in Sacramento. I liked the idea of an Arnold Schwarzenegger as governor because he understands compromise. And compromise is something I admire.

Say what you will about Schwarzenegger's acting career. But the fact remains that he comes from an industry where compromise is understood. Everyone involved in the motion picture business, from the executives sitting in the black tower to the crew members below the line, wants to see that movie made.

Arnold has an agent—as a matter of fact, he probably has more than one agent. And what do agents do? They find a way to compromise. You want x-number of dollars to make the picture. The studio wants to pay you less than that. You tell your agent to figure out how to make it work. It's a matter of making the right deal.

The same principle applies to politics. Schwarzenegger understands that from both sides of the desk. He's been a successful actor and has run successful businesses. He understands finances and treats employees fairly. He knows the importance of compromise.

WHERE GRAY WENT WRONG (OR, WHAT NOT TO DO IF YOU'RE FACING A RECALL)

Meanwhile, Gray Davis continued to implode. For a man facing a referendum on whether he should keep his job, he displayed a remarkable capacity for making the wrong moves, thereby isolating himself even further from an electorate in which 80 percent of the people who will decide his fate already hated his guts. Common sense would say there are certain steps an unpopular politician facing a recall should never take if he hopes to stay in office. Yet, Davis took them anyway. To wit:

1. *He goes the legal route.* First, as we mentioned before, he initiated a lawsuit that tried to block the recall by challenging the validity of the signatures on the petition that put the recall on the ballot. He lost on that count.

Then once the recall was certified, he tried to get the courts to rule that the process was discriminatory because his name was not included on the list of possible replacement candidates on the bottom half of the ballot. Davis argued that if the recall was passed, a replacement candidate could be elected governor with less than 30 percent of the vote—a percentage significantly less than the number of Californians who actually opposed the recall, according to polls. Davis reasoned that if his name were included on the replacement ballot, those who voted no on the top of the ballot would vote for him on the bottom. Therefore, he could still remain governor even if he was recalled.

That argument was rejected, and rightfully so. If you're subject to a recall election, by definition that means that people want to replace you with someone else. Therefore, your name has no business being on the bottom of the ballot. The governor can cry discrimination all he wants, but rules are rules. You can't have it both ways.

And you wonder why people don't like this man.

Then Davis tried to get the courts to delay the recall until March 2004 and make it part of the ballot for the California presidential primary. This would serve two purposes: It would keep Davis in office at least another five months, and it would likely ensure a much larger voter turnout than would be the case for a special election in October. There are more registered Democratic voters in California than there are registered Republicans. The way Davis saw it, a larger turnout in March means more Democrats. More Democrats means more votes for Gray Davis.

Though that effort was blocked initially, Davis would get a reprieve in mid-September when a three-judge panel on the Ninth

Circuit Court of Appeals ruled in favor of a case filed by the ACLU that also tried to delay the recall, albeit on different grounds. We'll discuss that case in just a bit.

2. *He acts defiantly.* When your administration is under fire for its handling of a statewide energy crisis (not to mention continuing to spend money despite massive drops in state revenue), and you find yourself rightly or wrongly on the verge of being thrown out of office as a result, common sense would say your best chance of stemming the tide is to be proactive about it. Come right out and say, "Look, here's where I stand. These are the accusations against me. This is what I'm going to do about it." Be strong when you make your case, but don't be defiant. Instead, be conciliatory and maybe even show some humility. After all, your political future is in the hands of the public.

That would certainly be the smart thing to do, especially when 80 percent of the public doesn't like you in the first place. You need to do everything you can to endear yourself to the people and convince them that they should keep you in office.

Gray Davis had such an opportunity on August 19, seven weeks before the election. Only he didn't do that. Speaking before a partisan crowd on the campus of UCLA, he was not only insolent, he blamed everyone for California's problems but himself. Not only that, he stole a page from the Hillary Clinton playbook by denouncing the recall as a "right-wing power grab" on the part of Republicans who felt they should have won the governor's seat in November 2002.

Now, let me get this straight. You had Arnold Schwarzenegger leading in the polls at the time Davis gave his speech. Schwarzenegger is a moderate Republican. Not only that, many prominent Democrats throughout the state were firmly in the Schwarzenegger camp, including investment mogul Warren Buffett, former San Jose mayor Tom McEnery, and (later on) California Attorney General Bill Lockyer. Where's the right-wing conspiracy in that?

True, it was a right-wing conservative, Congressman Darrell Issa, who financed the petition that put the recall on the ballot. But dissatisfaction with Davis ran deep across the state and knew no bounds. Democrats signed the petition, as well as Republicans. If

Issa hadn't put up the money, no doubt some other financier on one side or the other would have stepped forward and done it anyway.

Besides, the recall was originally the work of a disgruntled bipartisan group whose efforts began a few weeks after Davis won reelection in November 2002. The GOP did not throw itself into the mix until late in the game, when they were certain the recall would pass. So for Davis to cast the recall in a purely partisan light while continuing to blame everyone else for the state's problems didn't seem smart at all.

Then again, as we established before, there are more Democrats than Republicans in California. Obviously, Gray's strategy was to rally registered Democrats around him. But that strategy was clearly based on the assumption that all Democrats would vote doctrinaire. That would hardly be the case.

3. *He continues to pander and govern by polls, creating the impression in the minds of Democrats and Republicans alike that he would do just about anything in order to keep his job.* We talked before about the blatant political reasons behind Davis's flip-flops on the vehicle tax increase and granting drivers licenses for illegal aliens. In addition to that, the governor refused to parole a reformed female murder convict—whose request for parole was supported by the sentencing judge, state legislators, domestic violence experts, and *members of the victim's family*—for the second consecutive year. The woman, now 35, was convicted of second degree murder in 1987. The parole board, citing self-help programs, improvement in anger control, and newfound maturity (she was just 18 at the time she killed her boyfriend, a man who had abused her for years), said that she "posed no risk whatsoever to society." Yet, Davis denied her parole anyway. Why? Because he didn't want the GOP to accuse him of being soft on crime.

A little background here. In some circles, Gray Davis was considered a viable Democratic candidate for president, possibly as early as 2004. Davis himself had voiced such ambitions on more than one occasion. In that respect, every move in his political career can be seen as a calculated step toward an inevitable run for the White House.

Ever the shrewd tactician, Davis knew that he didn't want a "Willie Horton"-type of scenario coming back to haunt him like it did Michael Dukakis in 1988. And if you look at the record, you'll notice that of the nearly 300 convicted murderers whose release was recommended by the parole board during his five years in office, Davis vetoed the release of all but eight.

Coincidence? I don't think so. And I'm not alone in my opinion. As a matter of fact, on the morning after the recall, I received several calls from listeners who cited the governor's tyrannical stance against parolees as one of their reasons for supporting his ouster. One caller identified herself as a Democrat employed as a correctional counselor for a California state prison. She said she voted for Arnold Schwarzenegger because she was uncomfortable with Davis's close association with the prison guard union, which had contributed heavily to his campaign chest. She also told stories of inmates who worked hard to turn their lives around, who did everything the parole board recommended they do in order to win their release . . . only to find their hopes dashed by a governor too ambitious for his own good.

Sports teams speak of the difference between "playing to win" and "playing not to lose." Teams that play to win are loose, poised, and aggressive. They're focused solely on the task at hand and never worry about making mistakes—confident that if they do make a mistake they'll somehow overcome it. More often than not, they do just that and manage to win the game.

Teams that play "not to lose" are comparatively tentative. They worry so much about what might happen later on in the game, they become prone to making even more mistakes than ever. More often than not, they end up losing anyway.

That's what we had with Gray Davis. As a person, he seemed like a man uncomfortable in his own skin. As a politician, he governed like a man who played not to lose. You look at not only his stance against prison parolees but the preponderance of actions he took as governor and you'll find that philosophy bears out. And in the end it would cost him his job.

A WEEK IN LIMBO

Davis appeared to catch a reprieve, though, on September 15 when the Ninth Circuit Court of Appeals postponed the recall until

March 2004—a decision that would seem to benefit the governor. A three-judge panel upheld an ACLU lawsuit originally filed in the U.S. District Court claiming that punch-card ballots used in six California counties comprising 44 percent of the state's total electorate could disenfranchise voters because of inherent flaws in the punch-card system. This, of course, was a direct reference to the problem of "hanging chads" in Florida that became headline news as a result of the 2000 presidential election. The ACLU asked the Court to delay the recall until March to allow sufficient time to replace punch-card ballots in six counties with new voting methods allegedly less prone to error.

Here's the way I saw this. As much as I opposed the recall in principle, I just as firmly believe in the principle that the will of the people should be upheld. The recall petition was certified. The date of the election was set for October. The election should be held as scheduled. To have three judges suddenly delay it five months struck me as a blatant act of political manipulation.

If punch-card balloting machines were really the problem, why weren't those machines replaced in 2002 when Gray Davis was reelected? Furthermore, the three-judge panel said nothing about postponing the regularly scheduled local elections in November 2003. Shouldn't they have been delayed, too? Why focus simply on the special election in October?

Of course, we know the reason why. It's politics as usual.

The Ninth Circuit Court of Appeals is without question the most liberal court in the country. And I say that as someone who does not consider "liberal" to be a pejorative. The three judges who blocked the recall were all appointed by Democratic presidents: Harry Pregerson, appointed by Carter; Sidney Thomas, appointed by Clinton; and Richard Paez, also appointed by Clinton. How much you want to bet which way those three judges would have voted on the recall, in the privacy of their own voting booth?

Funny how many of the same people who thought the Supreme Court's ruling in *Bush v. Gore* was political suddenly looked at the Ninth Circuit decision and thought, "Oh, no, that seems pretty fair to me."

I repeat, if punch-card balloting was good enough to re-elect Gray Davis in November, it ought to be good enough to recall him in October.

Fortunately, reason would prevail and uphold the will of the people. One week later, on September 23, all 11 members of the Ninth Circuit Court of Appeals voted to overturn the decision of the three-judge panel. The recall was back on for October 7.

DARRELL ISSA GOES OUT ON A LIMB

Meanwhile, polls indicate that the GOP vote was split between Arnold Schwarzenegger and Tom McClintock, while Cruz Bustamante maintained a solid percentage among Democrats. There was growing concern among Republicans that unless the party coalesces behind one candidate, they may yet lose the replacement election to Bustamante even if Davis was successfully recalled.

With that in mind, Darrell Issa went out on a limb. At a speech before the Commonwealth Club of San Francisco, the Congressman from San Diego County urged California Republicans to vote against the recall and keep Gray Davis in office if neither Schwarzenegger nor McClintock dropped out of the race by the day of the election.

"In every poll, more than 50 percent of the people of California favor candidates who stand for fiscal restraint, for no new taxes, [and for eliminating] waste, fraud and abuse in government," said Issa on my program. "It's clear that's what the people want. If there are two Republicans, and one Cruz Bustamante, we don't get that. That would be a tragedy for the people of California."

Darrell Issa, of course, was the man who poured $1.6 million of his own money into financing the petitions that got the recall on the ballot in the first place.

I rarely agree with Issa politically, but I gave him his due on this one. It takes guts to say, "I spent $1.6 million to finance this thing, and I may vote against my own recall." And make no mistake: Issa funded the petition because he believed he stood a good chance of winning the replacement election in the event the recall went through.

At the same time, he proved himself to be a man of principle. Once Schwarzenegger declared his candidacy, Issa knew he had no chance of being governor. So he immediately dropped out of the race. More to the point, though the recall was always painted as a GOP power grab, Issa never said "I want a Republican in there." All he wanted was a leader who would restore fiscal responsibility to California. As fiscally irresponsible as he found Gary Davis as a leader, he strongly believed Cruz Bustamante would be even worse.

Frankly, I couldn't disagree with him on that point. Many leaders in the Democratic party felt the same way.

On the other hand, Issa was confident that either Schwarzenegger or McClintock would drop out of the race for the good of the party. That didn't happen. No way was Arnold going to bow out. McClintock not only vowed to stay to the end, he kept insisting that he was rising in the polls despite evidence to the contrary.

Then again, Issa's perception of a split GOP vote was before the big debate in Sacramento sponsored by the California Broadcasters Association. That debate would mark a turning point in Schwarzenegger's campaign . . . and the outcome of the election itself.

THE SUPER BOWL OF DEBATES

When a politician engages in live debate—whether standing behind a podium on stage or sitting behind a microphone on a radio talk show—the dynamics are obviously quite different from delivering a prepared speech. There is no teleprompter. There are no handlers sitting next to him to whom he can deflect questions he doesn't want to answer. For that matter, the politician doesn't even know what questions the host or moderator will ask, nor what questions the callers, e-mailers, or members of the audience will ask. So you have to be ready for anything. You have to think on your feet.

In that respect, live radio can provide us with a window into a politician's mind. We get to see who that person is, how he thinks, where he stands.

One curve ball I like to throw at politicians is asking them to do something we radio people call a "live spot"—a 60-second commercial that isn't prerecorded but instead read live on the air. I'll hand them the script for the spot, and as they read it I'll joke or schmooze or try to do something that will make them laugh or at least throw them off their rhythm.

Why do I do this? Two reasons. One, it's pure fun. There's something about the idea of an Al Gore or an Orrin Hatch doing an ad for a local bed company or patio furniture store that listeners (not to mention, the sponsors) really enjoy. More importantly, it's a small yet effective way of gleaning a little of the person behind the political façade. You can tell a lot about a politician if he's willing to laugh at himself, or at the very least risk losing his place as he looks up from reading a script he's never seen before.

Of all the politicians I've asked to do this over the years, only two have said no. One was former President Jimmy Carter, and he doesn't count because he's not really a politician anymore. He's more like a permanent ambassador or statesman, and besides I like the man. Before coming to San Francisco in 1975, I spent a year at WRNG in Atlanta. As part of my show, I did a monthly interview with then-Governor Jimmy Carter. He's had my respect for 30 years. So I cut him some slack.

The only other politician who refused was Gray Davis. No surprise there. Gray has no discernible sense of humor.

Arnold Schwarzenegger first appeared on my show in October 2002. At the time, he was stumping for Proposition 49, an after-school initiative that made state grants available to middle schools throughout California to create after-school programs for children. Arnold authored the measure. Voters approved it in November. To many political observers, Prop 49 served as a practice run for an eventual Schwarzenegger gubernatorial bid in 2006. That, of course, was before anyone knew that the recall effort would bring about that opportunity much sooner than imagined.

Schwarzenegger spent an hour in the studio that morning. He impressed me as being bright (far more so than I had anticipated), charming, dedicated, astute, witty, and well-informed—not just about his own initiative, but the state of California in general. He seemed to have substance. I respected him for that.

At some point in the hour, I asked Schwarzenegger to do a live spot for Sleep Train, a respected sponsor. He not only agreed, he ad-libbed the entire thing to often hilarious effect. It was one of the few moments in my 35 years in radio where I was practically left speechless. He was that good. He made me think, "Hey, this guy may actually have a future in politics."

That's why I was so disappointed in the way Arnold ran his campaign early on.

The biggest knock against Schwarzenegger once he entered the governor's race was that he was nothing but an actor, all style and no substance, a paid stiff who spat out lines written by somebody else. I knew he was more than that—at least, I was *confident* he was more than that. I was eager to see him show his stuff and prove everyone wrong.

But I didn't care for the fact that it took him an entire month before finally revealing his platform. I didn't like the selective approach he took to the media (focusing mostly on conservative talk radio programs), or that he spent the bulk of his time campaigning in Southern California at the expense of exposure in the Bay Area.

True, he did make several trips into Northern California, especially during the last three weeks of the campaign. True, it's doubtful whether he could have changed many minds here in the ultra-liberal Bay Area—and the numbers bear that out. Eight of the nine Bay Area regions voted against the recall. In San Francisco County, where I live, the divide was just as great. Four out of five people voted to retain Gray Davis. That said, you'd think people even in way-out San Francisco would want to know what Schwarzenegger might do for them in the event he were governor.

That's why I couldn't wait for September 24, when Arnold joined Cruz Bustamante, Tom McClintock, Peter Camejo, and Arianna Huffington in a nationally televised debate sponsored by the California Broadcasters Association. It was the one debate during the 75-day campaign that Schwarzenegger chose to participate in. For that reason, all eyes were on Sacramento that night. Arnold himself called it "the Super Bowl of Debates." This was the public's big opportunity to see him think on his feet, show his grasp of the issues, and make his case for why he should be governor.

By now you've heard the controversy—the debate behind the debate, if you will. The 10 questions that reportedly comprised the bulk of the debate were provided to the candidates in advance. Naturally, Arnold's opponents seized on this with glee. They again accused him of being a stooge for old guard Republicans like former California Governor Pete Wilson and onetime U.S. Secretary of State George Shultz (two of Schwarzenegger's chief political advisors), an empty suit incapable of thinking for himself.

Ironically, Arnold was opposed to having the questions supplied in advance. That was according to Stan Statham, the president of the CBA and the man who moderated this Super Bowl of Debates. Stan also told me that the flap over the debate was much ado about nothing. The advance questions would only comprise about 20 percent of the 90-minute debate. The remaining 80 percent would be a free-for-all among the five candidates. Schwarzenegger would have ample opportunity to show his mettle.

Stan was right about one thing. Not only was the debate a free-for-all, it was the equivalent of a cafeteria food fight. Tom McClintock came across the most dignified, Arianna Huffington the least. Arianna and I have been friends for over three decades, but she was completely over the top. She acted as though her entire purpose for being there was to take shots at Schwarzenegger. I didn't care for that at all.

Then again, I didn't care for Arnold's performance, either. I wanted to see him distinguish himself. I wanted him to show a grasp of the issues, and I didn't want clichés. Aside from one good line (when he said to Cruz Bustamante, "You've only signed the back of a check, not the front"), I came away disappointed. I wanted him to show me more than he actually did.

Ironically, I felt the real winner of that night's debate was Gray Davis. All along, Gray's strategy was more or less a variation of "Vote for me because they're worse." He believed that voters would be so disgusted by the farcical element of the recall process that they would gradually return to him. And to be honest, after watching the Super Bowl of Debates, I began feeling that magnet myself. As troubled as I was by Gray's flip-flops and pandering, I wasn't convinced that any of the five leading contenders were significantly better.

For that reason, I was tilting back to my original principle. If the election were held September 25, I would have voted no on the recall.

And yet, Arnold's numbers soared after the debate, while Bustamante's continued to drop. Already dogged by the flap over how he accepted campaign money from Indian gaming interests (not to mention, the sneaky way he tried to circumvent campaign finance restrictions by funneling the money into a "No on Recall" account), Cruz hurt himself even further that night by coming across as condescending. That helped moved Schwarzenegger into the lead. With two weeks to go in the campaign, polls indicated that Arnold had enough of a majority to win the replacement election even if McClintock stayed in the race.

As support for Schwarzenegger increased, so did the numbers in favor of the recall. With time running out, a desperate Gray Davis challenged Arnold to debate him. Arnold said no, again giving rise to the perception that he was just an empty suit.

Then again, it is true that in a campaign, you want a debate when you're behind. You don't when you're ahead.

One week before the election, Arnold Schwarzenegger appeared on my program. Among other things, I asked him directly why he refused to debate Davis. This is what he had to say: "The first item on the ballot is 'Should we recall Gray Davis or not?' That is a matter between him and the people of California. There is no other candidate involved in the first round. If he wants a debate, he has to debate the people of California. They're the ones—63 percent of the people of California are saying, 'We are mad as hell and we're not going to take it anymore.' That's why 1.6 million people signed the petition for the recall. That's why 63 percent of the people say they want him recalled. The numbers keep going up. Every time he's out there campaigning in a negative way, the numbers go up. It's between him and the people. There's no debate with me.

"My debate is every day. I'm talking to you, I'm talking to other radio hosts, I'm talking to television interviewers, I'm talking to the people, I'm traveling up and down the state, talking and reaching out to business leaders, vendors, farmers, everybody. That's my debate. I don't have to debate with him."

That was the first time I'd ever heard that answer . . . and to be honest, part of me had to wonder where it came from. That's the thing about having Arnold Schwarzenegger as a political candidate. So many answers are pat and crafted. Almost too good.

That said, it was a damn good answer. It was so good, and so commonsensical, nothing I could say could refute it.

WHEN PUKE POLITICS GOES TOO FAR

I mentioned the prediction I made in July before the recall was certified that if Gray Davis went negative, he would be out of a job. Three weeks later, while I was on vacation, that sentiment would be echoed by a prominent member of the Democratic party: California Attorney General Bill Lockyer.

Speaking at a meeting with the *Sacramento Bee,* at a time when most political observers believed Dick Riordan—not Arnold Schwarzenegger—would emerge as the leading Republican candidate on the replacement ballot, Lockyer admonished Davis for sabotaging Riordan's campaign in 2002 and implored him not to do the same if Riordan entered the race. "It was a puke campaign and I didn't like it," said Lockyer of Davis's tactics. "I think it's a disservice to voters and the profession. I'm just tired of that stuff. I want to talk about the things that we need to do that are positive and affirmative and consensus-building—not all this divisiveness. Gray says he's going to end the divisive time in politics, but he just sort of adds a new kind."

Lockyer also said that if Davis resorted to trashing his opponent, he wouldn't be surprised if Democratic voters decided to "pull the plug" on him. He elaborated on that comment when he appeared on my show a few weeks later. By that point, Schwarzenegger had entered the race and was drawing support from Democrats and Republicans alike. "I'm disappointed in the kinds of the campaigns that Gray has over-relied on in the past," he said. "It's disappointing to find in this recall environment that you can't get the mandate that you need to provide good leadership without some kind of consensus. I see other parties patching together an electoral coalition. I don't see that going on in ours."

It takes courage to speak out against your party, especially at a time of such political divisiveness. Not only that, it takes guts to admit on your own volition that you *voted* against your party—as Lockyer did in revealing at a political conference two weeks after the recall that he voted no on the recall, but supported Schwarzenegger instead of Democratic replacement candidate Cruz Bustamante on the bottom of the ballot. "I have learned to trust my intuition and to value authenticity," said Lockyer on my program. "People in public life ought to just say what they do and why. And that's what I did. I voted no on the recall because I thought that it was bad for the state. But as I looked at the options, I realized while there were reasons to be critical of Arnold—and I've known him for over 12 years, which perhaps gives me a little different sense of who he is than most people—I felt he represented hope and optimism and reform and independence.

"People don't like the partisan bickering on both sides of the same aisle that has characterized Sacramento politics for too long. This was my personal view of the right direction in which to take the state."

Predictably, Lockyer was criticized by fellow Democrats for going against the party line and abandoning his party's principles—which is an interesting charge, considering that the man Lockyer voted for supports gun control, supports the rights of domestic partners, is pro-choice, and pro-environmental protection. Last I checked, those were all considered key Democratic values.

I applauded the attorney general for two reasons. One, Lockyer has long been considered a leading Democratic contender for governor in 2006. Knowing the political risks involved, it would have been prudent for him not to reveal his vote. Yet, he did it anyway. That again takes courage. I admired him for being open and honest about it.

I also admired Lockyer for his independence. Just because you're a registered Democrat doesn't mean you must always be in lock-step with the party line. If you've weighed all the options intelligently and have come to decide that your party's candidate may not be the best person to lead the state at this time, that doesn't make you any less loyal to the party. Rather, it makes you a person who's not afraid to think for himself . . . a voice of reason, if you will.

If Gray Davis had respected the intelligence of the public, he might still be governor today. Instead of being positive and offering solutions, he again went to the well of puke politics. His conduct during the final days of campaign was as desperate as it was disgusting. At a time when his own political base was rapidly shrinking, Davis latched onto the various allegations against Schwarzenegger like a parasite.

First he jumped on the Hitler story. Then he started blatantly pandering to women, orchestrating photo ops in which he surrounded himself not just with major Democratic players such as Dianne Feinstein, Barbara Boxer, and Nancy Pelosi, but ordinary women of every shape and size.

Then, after initially claiming that he would have no comment on the sexual allegations against Schwarzenegger, Davis did an about face on the Saturday before the election when he called for a criminal investigation into the matter. "Some of those events are clearly a crime," he said at a rally attended mostly by women. "Electing a governor who might have committed a crime is obviously going to distract the state from the work it has to do."

That last one really bothered me. With all due respect to Schwarzenegger's accusers and the serious nature of their charges, the governor's call for criminal charges against Schwarzenegger was a cheap shot, pure and simple, with no basis in reality. What's worse is that Gray Davis should have known better.

Susan Estrich has been a professor of sex discrimination law for two decades at UCLA, a renowned expert on sexual harassment, and a former rape victim. She understands the issue of sexual harassment arguably better than anyone else in this country. She wrote an op-ed piece about the Schwarzenegger allegations that appeared in the *Los Angeles Times,* of all places, on October 3—the day *before* Davis made his spurious charges. Here's what she had to say:

> I certainly don't condone the unwanted touching of women that was apparently involved here. But these acts do not constitute any crime such as rape, sodomy, or even assault or battery. As for civil law, sexual harassment requires more than a single case of an unwelcome touching. There must either be a threat or a promise of sex in exchange for a job, benefit, or demotion, or the hostile environment must be severe and pervasive. But none of these women, as the *Times* emphasizes, ever came forward to complain. The newspaper went looking for them. And then waited until five days before the election to tell fragments of the story.
>
> What this story accomplishes is less an attack on Schwarzenegger than a smear on the press. It reaffirms everything that is wrong with the political process. Anonymous charges from years ago made in the closing days of a campaign undermine fair politics.

Susan Estrich is also a liberal Democrat. She ran the presidential campaign of Michael Dukakis in 1988. She was also a long-time political strategist for President Bill Clinton.

Gray Davis built his entire career on the puke politics of "Vote for Me Because the Other Guy Is Worse." But this time, he went too far. And it would cost him dearly.

WHY I VOTED FOR THE RECALL

As I said at the beginning of this chapter, I have never experienced a vote that I have agonized more over than I did with the California recall. I strongly believed the recall was wrong in principle. I felt that voting in favor of it was tantamount to saying, "Yes, it's okay to recall anyone from office if you don't like the results of an election." I said that consistently on the air.

That said, one thing I've always prided myself on is that I try to listen to what people have to say . . . and every once in a while, new facts and circumstances get to me and convince me to change my mind. And it got to the point where I felt I had to send a message to those who engage in the slash and burn politics of the extremes.

The way Gray Davis took advantage of the last week of the campaign was the last straw. I was sick and tired of it. So were a lot of other Californians.

And you know something? That's a principle, too. The principle of wanting someone who is decent, upbeat, and refreshing. Someone who represents the middle ground. Someone who could restore the two-party system to California and get Democrats and Republicans working together instead of sniping at each other.

I believe that's the best thing for California. That's why I voted yes on the recall and yes on Arnold Schwarzenegger.

What does this all mean? Has California sent a message to the rest of the country? It's too soon to tell.

The problem with "sending a message" is that unless you articulate it directly, you never know what that message is or whether people will react to it.

What would the message have been had Gray Davis survived the recall? That dirty campaigning works? That Californians really loved what he was doing, despite approval ratings that suggest otherwise?

Obviously, the governor did not survive the recall, and the margin wasn't even close—55 percent of Californians voted to oust Davis; 49 percent of the electorate also voted to elect Schwarzenegger. That means that Schwarzenegger received more votes on the bottom of the ballot than Davis received on the top. Not only that, more Californians voted for Schwarzenegger last year than for Davis in 2002, when Davis won reelection with 47 percent of the vote. Is that a measure of Arnold's star power, or a reflection of just how much people in this state hated their governor?

Chris Matthews of *Hardball* saw the recall as "a triumph of hope over fear"—a revolt at the hands of an electorate angry at the way in which Davis "gamed" the political system by virtually handpicking his opponent in the 2002 election. "One thing I've learned from covering politicians and working with them for so many years is that *they do not like elections,*" he said on my program:

You see a guy walking around Capitol Hill with his head down in February, it's because he knows he's facing a tough opponent when he runs for reelection in the fall. Well, dammit, you're supposed to have opposition. That's like playing in the Super Bowl and expecting to be coronated without actually playing the game. You have to expect the other team to give you a battle. And if you game the system by eliminating opponents who could actually give you a fight in the general election—if you take away the right of voters to make a decent decision between two acceptable candidates, don't expect the voters to like you.

If there's one thing voters have learned in this country, it's this: Don't tell them they can't vote for Reagan because he's a movie star. Don't tell them they can't keep Clinton in office because he screwed around. Don't tell them what they can't do, because the voters will always come back and do it anyway.

Not to disagree with Chris—because when it comes to understanding politics, I think he's the best. But I think if there's any lesson to be gleaned from the recall, it goes back to what we said before: the best way to win an election today is to *be positive.* I really believe that works.

Certainly in my case, that was the difference between voting for the positive attitude of Arnold Schwarzenegger and the smarmy, sleazy campaigning of . . . not so much Gray Davis per se, but the California Democratic party in general. Once the *Los Angeles Times* story came out, they milked it for all it was worth, generating a ton of faxes and e-mails that essentially said, "Hey, we finally hooked onto something we could use. This is why you should keep Gray Davis in office. Not because he's done a good job. Not because Arnold would do a lousy job. But because Arnold groped women."

And because I'm on their media list, I was constantly deluged with press releases on the matter from state Democratic party spokesman Bob Mulholland. I have never seen anyone more buzzard-like in terms of picking away at every single slight negative nuance against Schwarzenegger that he could find. And if there's a message in that, it's "Enough already!"

There was a time when negative campaigning worked. And it probably still can in some cases. But I think voters are growing increasingly weary of "Vote for me because the other guy is worse." Sometimes you have to draw the line.

Finally, you can say that the recall sent a second message to California Democrats: that the way to win an election is to come to the center. Otherwise, they'll go the same way the Republicans have gone in the last decade. Which is to say, practically extinct.

You can say that Republicans were told same the same thing. As a matter of fact, state GOP Chairman Duf Sundheim said as much when he appeared on my show on the morning after the election. "We got the message this time," he said. "But we need to show it on a regular basis. I think what we do in 2004 will be a clear indication of whether we really do get it.

"I think the fact that Arnold was able to get more women votes than Bustamante is important, that so many Hispanics voted for the recall is also a huge potential advantage. But what's really going to make the difference is what we do between now and the next election. Do we make sure that women are equal partners in the party? Do we go out into those communities that haven't historically identified with the Republican party, listen to their concerns, engage them in the issues that are important to them? If we do that, then this will be an important event. If we don't, then it will have just been a flash in the pan and we won't have learned our lesson."

For the good of the country, I hope he's right. And I hope that the Democrats also take heed.

Wedge Issues and the Middle Ground

In some respects the show I do is pretty straightforward. If there's an item in the news that affects us directly, chances are we'll talk about it.

I know that covers a broad spectrum, but I like to mix it up. I have a wide range of interests. More to the point, so do my listeners. In any given week, on any given day, we're liable to explore everything from politics and current events to popular culture, personal issues, and just plain gossip. We tackle the major issues, but we also hash out water cooler stuff. There aren't many topics we won't bring up.

That said, given the kind of show I do and the way I tend to look at issues in general, some topics—or at least, certain angles on topics—are better than others.

I like issues that clearly have two sides. I like issues where I not only have an opinion, but where I also know there's a very good chance someone, somewhere will express a point of view that's different from mine. I like issues that will lead to a lively, animated, thoughtful, and intelligent conversation that allows for consideration of both sides.

How does that work in terms of specifics? Well, there are certain hooks that will always interest me. If it's a one-sided

Supreme Court decision, chances are it won't come up (unless, of course, I happen to think they're wrong). Even so, if it's a 9 to 0 ruling, where's the opposition? There isn't any. So you look for something else.

If it's a 5 to 4 decision, or even a 6 to 3 . . . now we're getting somewhere because here, there are clearly two sides. If the Court's split, chances are you and I might also be split. That being the case, I want to hear what you have to say.

If it's a matter that the American Civil Liberties Union weighs in on, that's also ripe for discussion. There is not a thinking person alive who cannot find anything on which he both agrees and disagrees when it comes to the ACLU. There are some areas where the ACLU's position is clearly right on, such as their support of medical marijuana or their defense of the rights of neo-Nazis to march in Skokie, Illinois (as repugnant as that is). But there are also times, such as when they work to abolish the death penalty in all circumstances, or when they oppose anti-gang injunctions sought by residents of minority neighborhoods who want to retake control of their streets, their parks, even their homes, when the ACLU's stance just makes you want to scratch your head. They are so all over the board, it's frightening.

If it's a hot button issue that concerns privacy or homeland security, or where political correctness is involved, or where we're hit directly in the pocketbook, or one that directly impacts the quality of our everyday lives, those are exactly the kind of issues that are bound to stir up opinions from both sides in the course of an hour.

From there, my producer Susan Schustak and I look for callers who are intelligent, articulate, but who don't necessarily agree with me on every aspect of the issue. This is especially important when it comes to the first caller of the hour. If the phone lines are jammed, and all but one of the people on hold happen to agree with me, I'll ask Susan (who, among her many other responsibilities, screens the calls on our show) to patch through the dissenting caller first. That way, we're most likely to trigger additional response on both sides of the issue.

If you side with the person who disagrees with me, you'll pick up the phone and call because you know your opposition is not alone. On the other hand, if you're listening to the first caller and think he's completely off base, you'll want to jump in and tell me why. From there, we continue to develop both sides of the conversation in hopes of finding some middle ground at the end of the hour on which we can all agree.

Of course, that isn't always possible. Most topics have some degree of wiggle room in them, while a few have none whatsoever.

Take wedge issues, for example. Either you believe in a woman's right to choose, or you don't. You either support the death penalty, or you oppose it. You either uphold the right to bear firearms, or you want to see it abolished. In each case, the lines are clearly drawn. There's no wiggle room at all.

This isn't to say we shouldn't try, though. So with that in mind, let's look at the three issues where we are most clearly polarized in terms of the politics of the extreme left and right: abortion, capital punishment, and gun control. Then let's see if we can find some areas of compromise in each that we can all live with.

ABORTION IN A NUTSHELL: PRO-CHOICE OR ANTI-CHOICE

For me, the divide on abortion is not so much between pro-choice and pro-life. It's more like pro-choice and anti-choice.

Think about it. You have two sides. One side—espoused by people like me—will say, "You believe in abortion? Go ahead and have one. It's your body. It's your right. It's your decision to make. If you don't believe in abortion, then don't have one. Either way, the choice is yours."

Then there's the other side. Forget any talk about the sanctity of life. The basic argument of anti-choice advocates comes down to this: "We believe abortion is wrong. You cannot have an abortion. If you agree with us, you cannot have an abortion. If you don't agree with us, you still cannot have an abortion."

Side One respects the right of people to decide for themselves what is morally and ethically right. Side Two wants to impose their beliefs on everyone else.

Now, people on Side Two like to say: "How very liberal of you, Ronn. Always thinking you can do whatever you want." Never mind the fact, as we pointed out earlier, that expressing your views without intrusion of any kind is an inherently *conservative* idea. Anti-choice advocates will still dismiss it as yet another Left Coast liberal idea. Either that, or they'll get all holier-than-thou on me and talk about the sanctity of life: "You're missing the point, Ronn. We're pro-life. That fetus is a human life. Only God has the power to abort. None of us has the right to make that decision."

On that I disagree. Sure, we can. *Of course, we can.* And we can because, strictly speaking, a fetus is not yet a human life. The majority of the medical community has made that clear.

That said, if you strongly believe otherwise and wish to carry that fetus to term, fine. I respect your decision. It's yours to make. It should *always* be yours to make. Why should anyone have the right to take that decision away?

That's what I don't understand about the argument of Side Two. People who don't believe in abortion will never have to have one. Yet, they insist on saying, "This is how we feel on the matter. This is how everyone else needs to feel, too."

Of course it's a matter of degree, but how is that any different from the actions of a Saddam Hussein, Ayatollah Khomeini, or Josef Stalin? Either way, you're being told "Your thoughts don't count. This is what you have to believe." You're being told that you don't have the ability, much less the right, to make up your own mind about anything.

People adamantly opposed to a woman's right to choose only care about the fetus. They never seem to take into consideration any extenuating circumstances where an abortion may in fact be the only decent thing to do.

What if the parents have an ultrasound and discover that their baby will be born with Downs syndrome? Not only would that significantly impair the quality of that baby's life, a child like that will also require specialized medical attention. That's not the kind of expense people ordinarily count on when they plan to start a family.

What if they simply can't afford to care for that child? Who's going to pick up the costs—the anti-choice activists who insisted that the mother carry the fetus to term? *I don't think so.* Once the mother gives birth to the baby, these people are nowhere to be seen!

If you know your child-to-be has a birth defect and you decide to have it anyway out of love and responsibility, that again is your choice. But if you know you can't care for it . . . what, you should still be forced to bring that child into the world just because somebody says so? You're bringing misery onto yourself. You're doing an even bigger disservice to the child. What purpose does that serve?

Now, I realize that many abortion opponents will make the argument for adoption. I'm sorry, but in cases like these I just don't buy it.

I don't wish to sound cold about this, but how many people do you know who would go out and look to adopt a child with Downs syndrome?

Even if it were a completely healthy child, there's no guarantee he'd ever find a good home once his parents put him up for adoption. So there's a good chance that kid will go through life without ever having a family. Would you want to wish that on anyone?

There are other instances where common sense would say that a woman's right to choose should prevail. One that immediately comes to mind is a pregnancy brought on by rape.

It's one thing if a rape victim decides on her own volition to carry that fetus to term. That's her choice. That's her right. But if she should decide not to . . . why on earth would anyone insist that she do so anyway?

The woman has barely begun recovering from the most horrifying moment of her life. Wouldn't you say she's been traumatized enough already? Why should she have to be reminded of that every day for the next nine months?

I can't help but think of the story from March 2003 about the nine-year-old Nicaraguan girl who was raped by a worker on a coffee plantation near Costa Rica. This set off a huge debate in the Roman Catholic Church. The girl and her parents were devout Catholics who were taught that abortion went against Church doctrine. Compounding the matter, Nicaraguan law only allows for abortion under the direst circumstances, such as if the mother's life is in danger. Nevertheless, the Nicaraguan government issued an exemption. The girl's parents ordered their doctor to terminate the pregnancy—as well they should have. Though Church officials initially excommunicated the family and the doctor for their actions, reason would prevail on that count as well. After much heated debate, the Church rescinded their decision and reinstated the girl, her family, and their doctor.

No one should be forced to carry an unwanted pregnancy. Especially not a nine-year-old girl who can barely understand what happened to her in the first place. Even if her parents chose to put the baby up for adoption, they would still have been wrong to put her through the ordeal of a nine-month pregnancy. She's just a kid!

Naturally, the pro-life/anti-choice people would then say, "What about the other side of the coin? If you believe an underage girl should not be made to give birth, why should she be allowed to have an abortion? Isn't that also a matter for the parents to decide?"

To which I would say, "Yes, that girl still should be allowed to have the abortion. But if she's under the age of consent—whatever that age happens to be—then her parents should be informed before she undergoes the procedure." That's basically what the state of New Hampshire said when they passed a bill in 2003 requiring that at least one parent or legal guardian of a girl under 18 must be notified 48 hours before she has an abortion. Prior to passing the legislation, New Hampshire was the only state in the United States not to have any abortion regulations.

We had a lively discussion on the topic after the issue first came down. Several abortion advocates argued that the law would compromise a teenager's freedom of choice and deprive her of her right to privacy.

Being reflexively pro-choice, I naturally understood their concerns and could easily sympathize. But I still had to disagree. Parental consent is the one area of the abortion debate where I believe the pro-life side has it right.

For one, the New Hampshire law doesn't deprive the minor of any rights whatsoever. If anything, it upholds them. Parents may have the right to know about their daughter's planned abortion, but the law doesn't necessarily allow them to overrule her. The choice is still the girl's. In addition, the law takes into consideration extenuating circumstances that would allow the girl to bypass the parental notification requirement altogether by seeking a judge's permission or a medical determination that her life is in jeopardy. That's fair and equitable.

But let's set New Hampshire aside for a moment and look at the issue in general. Common sense would say that when you're under the age of consent—whether that's 16, 18, or 21—your rights to privacy aren't exactly the same as an adult's, anyway. Especially if you're still living under my roof and being supported by me.

Think about it. Most parents impose certain restrictions on teenagers in the course of raising them (or at least, we try to!). More to the point, most privileges extended to young people usually carry some sort of probationary caveat until they reach a certain age. Driving is an example. So is drinking. For that matter, so is sex and birth control.

As I see it, until such time when you are either legally an adult or completely on your own, you're my responsibility. As a parent, as a guardian, I think I have a reasonable right to know what you're doing. I won't necessarily stop you from doing it, but I'd still want to know about it before the fact.

IF YOU WANT MY ATTENTION, DON'T GO TO EXTREMES

Sometimes it's not what you say that matters. It's how you say it. You could champion the most worthy cause in the world, but your efforts won't do you a bit of good if you choose the wrong way to express them.

Look, I came of age in the 1960s. It was a time of great tension and upheaval. Seemed like every night on the news I saw images of people throughout the country protesting Vietnam, marching in support of civil rights, demonstrating on college campuses, rioting in the streets. So I understand the concept of civil disobedience. Not only that, I believe in it.

But I don't believe in anarchy. I don't uphold deliberately overstepping the bounds of a civilized society. I don't advocate the efforts of anyone who shuts down a major thoroughfare and effectively holds me or you hostage just to get their point across.

That's imposing your will on others. That's stooping down to the level of the extremes. When you do that, you not only lose me, you stand a good chance of losing a lot of people who might ordinarily support your cause.

For example, I strongly support funding for AIDS research. AIDS has been a serious problem in our society for far too long. Too many people have suffered and died from this debilitating condition. We must do everything we can *within reason* to increase awareness of this terrible epidemic and work together to find a cure.

This is where groups such as ACT UP simply go too far.

ACT UP (an acronym for AIDS Coalition to Unleash Power) is a group of AIDS activists with chapters throughout the United States. No doubt, you've probably heard of them. ACT UP describes itself as "a diverse, nonpartisan group of individuals united in anger and committed to direct action to end the AIDS crisis." Their credo: "We advise and inform. We demonstrate. We are not silent."

They're not subtle, either. In fact, ACT UP is unapologetically "in your face" when it comes to AIDS awareness. No stunt is too outrageous for them, no form of demonstration too shameless or severe. They'll block entrances to buildings. They'll clasp themselves together like a human chain and stand in the middle of a downtown intersection. They'll yell, scream, even drop their pants and moon you, all in the name of AIDS awareness. They'll even resort to literally throwing a pie in the face of any elected official or dignitary who doesn't support their views.

It doesn't matter what they do. In their minds, the end always justifies the means—even shutting down the Golden Gate Bridge at the height of morning rush hour. Members of the Bay Area chapter of ACT UP tied up traffic for hours and irritated thousands of commuters coming in and out of San Francisco. That happened back in 1989, and just thinking about it still makes me angry.

In fact, were it possible, I would have loved to have seen each and every one of those jerks arrested. And I say that as someone who ostensibly supports what ACT UP believes in!

In any argument, on any issue, you have every right to try to persuade me of the merits of your cause. Provided, of course, you do so in an appropriate forum. Also provided I want to listen to you. If I don't want to listen to you, you have to respect that.

You don't have the right to impose your opinion on me or anyone else. You don't have the right to say, "My point of view is so strong and so correct, I can force you to listen to it." That's exactly what ACT UP was doing.

That's not being rational. That's being a bully. It's resorting to guerrilla tactics in an attempt to get your way. It's predicating your actions on an absolute narcissism that your ideas are so worthy of attention, you can do whatever you want to inflict them on others.

Correct me if I'm wrong, but I thought the world rejected communism.

We are not an anarchistic country. We are a country of laws. And as much as I believe in the right to protest, I also believe there are limits.

I don't care what your cause is or how important you may think it is. Once you start interfering with the rights of other people to drive their cars, run their places of business, or simply live their lives without impediment, your right to protest ends. At that point, they ought to lock you up.

There's a time and a place for everything. If you want to protest, if you want to stage a rally, do it the right way. Hold it in a park, a downtown plaza, or some other public area. Get a permit if you have to. Announce it. Post flyers. Use chat rooms and Internet bulletin boards to spread the word online. If necessary, inform the media.

Just don't spring it on me on my way to work. Do that and I guarantee that no matter what your cause, you will gain more opponents than allies on general principle alone.

Here in San Francisco, we have a "group" of bicycle-riding clean air activists who call themselves Critical Mass. I use the term loosely because most groups or organizations have some sort of structure, while Critical Mass defiantly claims to have no leadership of any kind. More than anything else, they consider themselves a living, breathing "movement" whose power lies in their collective anonymity.

In any event, on the last Friday of every month, at precisely 6:00 P.M., bicycle riders from all over the Bay Area congregate at a given spot in the heart of the financial district and parade across the City, disrupting traffic completely and infuriating motorists and pedestrians alike for hours at a time. Their purpose (aside from being an irritant) is to encourage people to leave their cars at home and consider using bicycles and alternate means of transportation because that's better for the environment. Never mind the fact that as they impede access to Market Street, they may be preventing an ambulance from getting to an emergency on time. Never mind that as they make people wait inside their cars, those cars are burning fuel, wasting energy, and otherwise creating a toxic atmosphere for everyone, including the riders themselves.

More to the point, you would think that protestors would realize for any demonstration to be effective, it's counterproductive to alienate the very people you're trying to win over to your side. It makes no more sense to act like Critical Mass on the far left and make people hate you as they wait inside their cars than it would if you were a pro-life group on the far right and blocked the entrance to an abortion clinic. Either way, you're shooting yourself in the foot.

Why anyone would ever want to do that is simply baffling.

A REASONABLE APPROACH TO CAPITAL PUNISHMENT

Capital punishment is another debate where there's no middle ground. You're either for it or against it. There really is no compromise.

Here in the Bay Area, you have people on the far left who go out to San Quentin every time there's an execution. They bring out their banners, practice their sound bytes, and argue passionately to anyone who'll listen that the death penalty is murderous, barbaric, inhumane, and therefore wrong. The fact that the man on death row whose execution they're protesting is a serial murderer himself is beside the point to them. Not to mention the unspeakable way in which he made his victims suffer before he finally took their lives. Or the traumatic pain and loss the families of the victims have to live with every day of their lives because of what that man did. It's a classic example of being wedded to an ideology that doesn't allow for common sense. They're hung up on the notion that the state should not kill: "He's still a human being. We should let him live."

The far right's view on the matter is much simpler. Capital punishment is always justified. They not only believe all murderers should be executed, they'd pull the switch themselves if they could.

That doesn't make a lot of sense, either.

We talked before about how our views are often liberal when we're young, but become more and more conservative as we grow older. That was certainly the case with my views on capital punishment.

I opposed the death penalty throughout my 20s. I just didn't believe it deterred people from committing murder. I felt that people who kill are probably going to kill anyway. People like that are so far removed from basic human decency they're incapable of seeing their actions in terms of consequences. So the fear of death should they be caught, tried, and convicted never enters the picture. I felt there had to be a more civilized way of dealing with murderers without putting them to death.

I changed my mind in 1979. I was 34 when I realized, "Well, maybe the death penalty isn't a deterrent. But that doesn't mean we still shouldn't punish the people responsible for these heinous crimes to the fullest extent we can."

Capital punishment is one of those issues where unless you believe for religious reasons that you should never under any condition take another person's life, I don't see how anyone can oppose it. I just don't. Not if you're a parent. Not if you're been a victim of assault yourself, or if one of your loved ones has. Not when you know that there are career predators out there like Richard Allen Davis who wouldn't think twice about invading your home, kidnapping your daughter right out of her bedroom, raping her, and then dumping her body in a shallow grave.

That's what Davis did in October 1993. The victim was Polly Klaas, a 12-year-old girl from Petaluma, California, a quiet suburb about an hour north of San Francisco. The story captivated not only the Bay Area, it attracted national attention—much the same as the disappearance of JonBenet Ramsey in 1996 and the murder of Laci Peterson in 2003. The Polly Klaas case would also have a direct impact on the landmark "Three Strikes, You're Out" law that went into effect in 1994.

Davis had been in and out of jail for over 20 years on various charges of assault, burglary, kidnapping, and attempted rape. Four months before abducting Polly Klaas, he was released from prison after serving only eight years of a 16-year sentence for kidnapping and pistol-whipping a woman. He was convicted of Polly's murder in 1996 and presently sits on death row, pending appeal.

What Davis did to that girl and the scars he left on her family (and to some extent, the collective psyche of the nation) is unconscionable. Yet, the people of California are paying $40,000 a year to keep him fed and alive.

My question to death penalty opponents is this: *Why?* Why shouldn't the state of California put Richard Allen Davis to death? Why should he be entitled to three square meals a day? He's never going to set foot in society again. Not once has he ever shown the slightest remorse for his actions. Why should he be allowed to breathe the same air that you and I breathe?

Some people in this country are just plain bad. I realize it sounds simplistic to say this, but that's what I happen to believe.

I don't buy the inherently liberal notion that each and every one of us has this intrinsic capacity for good, that all we need to do is find it, nurture it, and bring it to the forefront. That's like resorting to the old argument that even Adolf Hitler had a mother. What, like that's supposed to make us forget everything and let him off the hook?

Sure, Hitler had a mother. So did each and every person whose lives he extinguished during the Holocaust. People such as my grandparents, who I would never get to meet because they were sent to a German concentration camp and exterminated on Hitler's orders.

That said, reason would remind us that there are no more absolutes on the death penalty than there are on any other issue. I don't necessarily believe all murderers should be executed. There are degrees of murder. There should also be degrees of punishment. We should therefore evaluate each case on its own merits.

If there's an element of brutality, an element of sadism, a complete and utter disregard for the sanctity of life that elevates it to a crime that has what California law calls "special circumstances" . . . then capital punishment makes absolute sense. If someone should fall under that aegis—like a Hitler, like a Saddam Hussein, like a Richard Allen Davis—then without question they should die.

THREE STRIKES, YOU'RE OUT: A BILL OF REASON

As you may have gathered, I'm a huge supporter of Three Strikes, You're Out. Not only that, I've been given credit by none other than Mike Reynolds, the man who co-authored the bill along with then-California Secretary of State Bill Jones, as being one of the key people who helped make the law possible by keeping it in the public eye. It's an important law and I'm proud to have played a role in it.

Mike first came to me with the idea for Three Strikes in late 1993, shortly after the kidnapping of Polly Klaas—and I was the first media person to recognize its importance. Mike appeared on the program several times over the ensuing months. Listener response was so passionate, I even did a remote broadcast from a shopping center in Petaluma. I set up a couple of bridge tables and spent the day gathering thousands of signatures for a petition to get Three Strikes on the ballot.

Now if you are looking for labels, consider it a classic example of someone opening his eyes and realizing it's one thing to feel sorry for certain people who commit crimes. It's another thing altogether when you're dealing with scumbags like Richard Allen Davis. Mike's daughter Kimber had been kidnapped and murdered by a career felon just like Davis in 1992. That's what motivated him to start the movement that would result in the passing of Three Strikes in 1994.

Three Strikes struck me as being a common sense bill—a "bill of reason," if you will. Here you have a situation where, in the case of the first two strikes, you're dealing with serious or violent felonies. And my basic feeling is, if you've committed a serious or violent felony and been imprisoned for it (as was the case with Richard Allen Davis), then go out and commit another serious or violent felony for which you're likewise arrested, convicted, jailed, and released (as was also the case with Davis) . . . if that doesn't motivate you to live your life as straight and honest as you can, then nothing ever will. So if you screw up again, you deserve everything that comes to you.

That said, I will concede that Three Strikes and You're Out is not without flaws. Unlike the first two strikes, Strike Three doesn't necessarily have to be serious or violent.

Then again, the law also allows for discretion on the part of both the judge and the prosecuting attorney. If they believe you should not face life imprisonment on the basis of the third strike (whatever that crime happens to be), they can elect to remove a strike from your record, which would no longer make yours a Three Strikes case.

The other "flaw" (if indeed, you can call it that) has more to do with the concept of "the law" in general than the Three Strikes law in particular. This has to do with the notion that if you're convicted of a felony, you should therefore automatically go to jail.

Some people belong in jail more than others. I think drug dealers ought to be behind bars without exception. But should everyone who uses drugs go to jail? Our jails are overflowing with drug offenders. Common sense says let's look at each case on an individual basis and then decide.

One of the major purposes of Three Strikes was to keep the worst perpetrators of crime off the streets. That's a notion I've long believed in—and a point we'll return to in just a bit.

NEWSOM'S RULE: PRISONS SHOULD ONLY HOUSE THE WORST POSSIBLE PEOPLE

Invariably a person on the left will pick up the phone and point out that the vast majority of countries today have abolished the death penalty. Therefore, we should do the same.

To which I would say, "Yes, but that's not an entirely valid argument." For one, it doesn't take into account that while other countries have indeed done away with capital punishment per se, many governments still torture prisoners, often to the point of death. You tell me: Is that more civilized than a lethal cocktail, or less?

Second, other countries don't necessarily have the same problems we have here in the United States. We're a very open, very heterogeneous country. There's no single culture that tends to govern us. In many ways, that's good. In many ways, that's bad because it leaves the door open for a vast range of criminal activity. We also have one of the highest levels of murders and violent incidents in the world. As a consequence, we have the right and the responsibility to look at our own country from our own lens.

It's none of France's business to tell us how to deal with our own prisoners, no more than it's any of our business to tell France what to do with theirs. That's why we have independent countries. You can be allies with countries on certain matters, but that doesn't mean you have to be aligned on everything they believe.

Plus there's hardball even in matters of diplomacy. A convicted murderer flees California and seeks refuge in Mexico. He's captured in Guadalajara, but Mexican authorities may not agree to extradite him unless the United States promises not to impose the death penalty. Sometimes that's part of the negotiation.

The answer to that one is simple: Let him stay in Mexico. Their prison system is worse than ours.

I have strong feelings about prisons in general. The average maximum security state penitentiary in this country is a hellhole. The conditions are awful. Too many jails are overcrowded. It's a problem we need to address.

One solution I've maintained stems from an idea originally broached to me by a man named William Newsom. Bill is a former California Appellate Court Justice; his son, Gavin Newsom, was elected mayor of San Francisco in December 2003. Back in 1976 (long before Three Strikes), Bill introduced an idea that is so basic and commonsensical, it's hard to believe our state legislature has never bothered to adopt it.

Bill's notion is that prisons should only be a place for the worst, most violent, most degenerate people in the world—people who cannot live among other people in a civilized society. That's the way it ought to be. Prisons should only house people who, if you unleashed them among the general populace, would likely rape, pillage, murder, cause havoc, or otherwise clearly pose a threat to the safety of everyday ordinary people.

In other words, the main concern for all of us should be protecting our families and ourselves from any kind of physical harm. That's what we're talking about here.

I have many friends who work in law enforcement: police chiefs, sheriffs, beat cops, you name it. There's a term that cops will often use when it comes to neighborhood safety issues: "peaceful enjoyment of your home." You and I have a right to the peaceful enjoyment of our homes. We are all entitled to live our lives and enjoy our homes as we see fit, so long as it doesn't infringe on the rights of our neighbors to the peaceful enjoyment of *their* homes.

Carry it a step further, and Newsom's Rule basically says the same. We all want to be able to live our lives without fear, without worrying about the welfare of our children, without wondering about the safety of our streets, city, and country. We ought to do everything we can to guarantee that right to the extent it's possible. The best way to do that is to ensure that the worst element of society remains behind bars.

You want an either/or? Fine. I'll make it real simple.

If I had choose between locking away a CEO who swindled the life savings out of his own employees to the tune of millions of dollars and a 16-year-old kid who pulls a gun on an old lady in a parking lot and grabs her pocketbook so he can buy an ounce of crack—then ends up shooting her because she doesn't surrender her purse quickly enough—I'd pick the violent offender in a heartbeat.

Now, I realize bleeding-heart liberals will say, "Ronn, how can you say that? He's just a kid. Maybe he's had a rough childhood. Maybe he can turn it around if we just gave him the chance." I understand where they're coming from—it's the classic argument perhaps best exemplified by Officer Krupke in *West Side Story*. And at one point in my life I probably would've agreed.

But let's be real. If you're walking down the street with your wife and kids, and some guy sticks a gun in your back and asks for your wallet, you couldn't care less about his childhood. All you want to do is get out of there alive and make sure your family is safe. So that line of reasoning really doesn't wash.

You pull a gun on someone, you do them bodily harm, that makes you a menace to society. You ought to be put away.

Come up with another punishment for the likes of Ken Lay, Charles Keating, or Michael Milken. Their crimes are no less wrong, but in no way do they pose the kind of threat that violent offenders do.

Now, I realize there are folks on the far right who want to lock everybody up. The problem with that argument is that it's a Catch-22. Put all criminals in jail, and you'll accomplish what you want in the short term: that is, you've gotten rid of these people. But unless you're willing to keep them locked up for the rest of their lives, in most cases, they're going to make parole and eventually be released. And as we said before, jail is not a particularly nice place to be. The longer you incarcerate them, the more hardened they become. By the time you put them back on the street, they've completely lost touch with the normal feelings that human beings have and as a consequence are even more brutal and menacing than before. So what exactly have you accomplished?

That said, I'm not averse to putting the fear of God in white collar-types.

You want to crack down on corporate crooks? Treat them as you would any other convict. Don't put them in a nice, cushy minimum security country club environment. Put them in the state pen with the rest of the general prison population. Use that as a kind of proverbial sword of Damocles.

If some fat cat executive making $15 to $20 million a year, living in luxury, knew he'd be suddenly sharing a maximum security cell with "Bubba" instead of golfing every day or playing gin rummy, he might think twice about cooking the books or stealing from the company pension fund.

Of course, that's hardly a panacea. But hey . . . it's a start!

GUILTY, BUT INSANE

Then again, if we go back to the idea of "Give the kid a break, he's had a rough childhood," I do think the law ought to consider extenuating circumstances (or if you'd rather, "explanations") when it comes to judging crimes. I'm not just talking about felonies, either. This would apply to speeding tickets, jaywalking, panhandling, parking violations, and any other misdemeanor you can think of.

For lack of a better word, let's call this "Guilty, with an Explanation." In other words, the explanation would only apply toward your sentence—it would have zero bearing on your guilt or innocence. You broke the law, so you should still be held accountable. Were I a judge or juror in the case of the 16-year-old armed robber, and the kid's lawyer somehow managed to convince me that he really did have this lousy childhood that led him down the wrong path, I'd say, "Fine. Your client is still guilty, but I'll take that into consideration and factor it into his sentence."

Another example of how this would work is an idea I have espoused on more than one occasion. I have a great deal of difficulty with the ruling "Not Guilty by Reason of Insanity." I think we ought to change it to "Guilty, but Insane."

What's the difference? At the risk of sounding cold, "Not Guilty by Reason of Insanity" ascribes no guilt whatsoever to the perpetrator of the crime. Not only that, it implies the crime was never committed—or that the law somehow failed to apprehend the person responsible for the crime.

From the standpoint of the victim or the victim's family, that's a crock! They know a crime was committed. They even know who did it. And to sit helplessly by while a lawyer sways a judge or jury into accepting a "not guilty by reason of insanity" verdict is about as big a moral outrage as you can imagine. In essence, that's like handing the defendant a free pass.

"Guilty, but Insane," on the other hand, makes no bones about it: "You are guilty of this crime." Maybe you were insane when you molested those boys and left them in the woods to die. Maybe you didn't know what you were doing because you suffer from a chemical imbalance that prevents you from having complete control of your actions. Maybe you should spend the next 20 to 30 years in a mental facility and finally get the help you need. None of that changes the fact that you're guilty. You still committed those heinous crimes, and you still should be held responsible.

As a ruling, this serves two important purposes: (1) It provides closure for the victim and/or the family of the victim, and (2) it puts the onus back on the perpetrator by reminding him that a crime was committed in the first place, and that he is on record for committing it.

Now, should there still be compassion and understanding in these circumstances? Absolutely. Reason would agree that a defendant who was not in his right mind at the time he went postal is clearly not the same as someone who murders with malice aforethought. He doesn't belong in prison. He belongs in an insane asylum. I have no problem with that at all provided we understand and agree that the person still committed the crime.

WITNESS TO AN EXECUTION: COULD I WATCH SOMEBODY DIE?

One final aspect of capital punishment I'd like to touch on is the classic notion—traditionally espoused by the far left—that if you were to actually watch an execution and see what happens when the state puts another human being to death, your views on the matter would change forever.

Problem is, that argument holds no water. At least it didn't for me when I witnessed the execution of convicted serial killer William Bonin.

Bonin was the third death row inmate in San Quentin to be executed since California reinstated capital punishment in 1977. He was found guilty for the brutal murders of 14 people in Southern California between 1979 and 1980. Ten of his victims were teenage boys. Because of his propensity for abandoning the nude bodies of his victims near freeways close to gas stations, alley ways, and deserted roads, Bonin was dubbed the "Freeway Killer." Though originally sentenced to die in 1982, the appeals process would keep Bonin alive in prison for nearly 14 years before U.S. District Court Judge Marilyn Patel finally upheld his conviction in February 1996. Bonin was scheduled to die at 12:01 A.M. on February 23, 1996. As is the procedure in California, the execution had been to be witnessed by two members of the local media.

This was three years after the murder of Polly Klaas and the start of the Three Strikes movement. Anyone who listened to my show knew where I stood on the matter of William Bonin. I thought people like him were despicable and clearly deserved to die. I would say this on more than one occasion in the weeks leading up to his death.

One morning, we were discussing the case on the air when a listener called and issued a challenge. He was a death penalty opponent, but he also knew from listening to the program over the years that my views on capital punishment had changed. If I could shift before, perhaps I could shift again. At that point he posed the question: "Could you watch somebody die?"

My gut feeling said it wouldn't make any difference. Given the opportunity, I'd probably go in there thinking I was going to watch a savage killer be put to death, and that would be the end of that.

Then again, it was a legitimate challenge. I knew if it did change my mind, I'd have no problem saying so on the air. I told the caller I'd do it. KGO made the arrangements, and before long it was official. I would be a media witness to the execution of the Freeway Killer. I was going to watch a man die.

Fast forward to the night of the execution. There were about 50 of us seated behind the glass of a small L-shaped room. Members of the victims' families stood on a platform on the opposite side from where I sat. A few minutes before midnight, the guards wheeled Bonin into the chamber. He was already strapped down on a gurney, hypodermic needles taped to his arms.

I'm sorry, but when I looked him in the eye I felt nothing. All I could see was a man who had brutally snuffed the life out of 10 young boys. I couldn't imagine the world being any worse off with him gone.

Not only was I dispassionate, I felt the method that they used to execute him was about as gentle and antiseptic as any in the history of mankind. A lethal dose of poisons was slowly pumped into his veins as he lay there with his eyes closed. He heaved his chest, twitched his stomach, and expired four minutes later. It was certainly a hell of a lot more tranquil than the way in which any of his victims died.

The official time of death was 12:13 A.M. At that point, I looked over at the family members and I could see the sense of closure in their eyes. That, I felt good about. That was exactly as it should be. I walked away, and I felt fine. Justice had been served.

The one fascinating thing about it was the tension we all felt in the minutes leading up to midnight. I mean, it really was like you see in the movies: you can't help but look at the phone and wonder whether the guy just might get a reprieve at the last minute. Beyond that . . . I guess I was supposed to feel emotional about it, but I didn't. I won't say I was thrilled by the fact that the guy was gone—but I didn't feel bad about it, either. It may not have made me more vehement in my support of capital punishment, but it certainly didn't lessen my views. The way I saw it, William Bonin paid the price for what he did. If anything, it was way too cheap.

In fact, the best argument against capital punishment from a voice of reason standpoint is that compared to life imprisonment, it's much too good. I'd much rather have someone slowly drive a steam roller over Bonin (or better yet, unleash him among the prison population and let matters take their course, as they did with Jeffrey Dahmer) than to see him go so easily.

A PRAGMATIC SOLUTION TO GUN CONTROL

Like abortion and capital punishment, the right to bear arms is another issue that tends to polarize people. Either you're for it or you're not.

How often do you hear someone say, "Gosh, I don't know about gun control. Maybe we should regulate it. Maybe we shouldn't. I can go either way." You don't, because there is no middle ground to speak of. Most people are firmly in one camp or the other, and have no trouble finding company.

Having said that, I think there are areas in the debate over gun control where we can find common ground if we're willing to try.

On one side of the spectrum, you have extremists who categorically believe that any attempt on government's part to regulate ownership of their guns will ultimately lead to the confiscation of those weapons. They take the Second Amendment at its word, maintaining that the phrase "the right of the people to keep and bear arms shall not be infringed" ought to mean just that, despite numerous court decisions to the contrary. Nevertheless, that's their story and they're sticking to it.

Weighing in on the other side are those who reflexively say, "Guns are horrible. Guns are bad. There is no place for guns in a civilized society. There are too many criminals and nut cases out there. Too many innocent people have died because some loose cannon shot up an office building or a post office or a fast food restaurant or a high school campus with assault weapons that were far too easy for him to obtain. We must crack down on this. We must ban handguns altogether before it's too late."

Frankly, of the two positions, I prefer the latter. But I also know it's not realistic. There are already far too many firearms out there in this country today—nearly 276 million, in fact, according to the 2003 Small Arms Survey commissioned by the United Nations. "By any measure, the United States is the most armed country in the world," the report indicated. "With roughly 83 to 96 guns per 100 people, the United States is approaching a statistical level of one gun per person."

That being the case, a voice of reason would say there's no way you'll ever remove all guns from all those people. The bullet's out of the chamber, so to speak. Once it's fired, you can't put it back in.

This is where pragmatism comes into play. You can't take away guns from people who already have them, but you *can* control the number of guns that will be issued in the future.

How do you do that? By licensing and registering firearms the same way we license and register cars. Driving a car is a privilege, not a right. Owning a gun for private use should be considered the same. So come up with a test that all potential gun owners would have to pass before they can purchase a gun. Not only that, make it a real test: a true and vigorous evaluation that clearly proves they have the capacity to know right from wrong, and that they would own and use the gun responsibly.

Naturally, the Second Amendment people will say, "Are you nuts? That's a horrible idea. You regulate gun control and that'll bring us one step closer to totalitarianism." They'll automatically dismiss the idea simply because they think it's yet another ultra-liberal approach. And that's all well and good, except for the fact that argument breaks down once you hold it under the microscope.

Common sense says that if I'm a responsible gun owner, I would want other gun owners to be just as responsible about it as I am. I'd want assurance that my new neighbor across the street who has an impressive display of firearms mounted on the wall of his garage is really a gun aficionado with his head screwed on right, and not someone deranged or disturbed such as the individual behind the horrible McDonald's massacre in San Ysidro in 1984, or the man who shot up an office building in downtown San Francisco in 1993, or the two teenage boys responsible for the Columbine tragedy in 1999. That stands to reason, wouldn't you think?

Political Correctness and Other Slam Dunks

On wedge issues, we are clearly polarized. Both sides are so firmly entrenched in their positions, any rational consideration of the matter is nearly impossible.

Other issues are difficult to discuss for completely different reasons. One side of the argument makes so much more sense from a voice of reason vantage point, any serious consideration of the opposing view would seem ridiculous.

For example, I have yet to be convinced that the Arab world is more democratic than Israel or that women in Afghanistan were treated with any respect under Taliban rule. Nor has anyone ever swayed me into thinking that it is wrong to legalize marijuana for medicinal purposes when we know it can alleviate the pain of people suffering with AIDS, cancer, and other debilitating illnesses. The challenge with these issues and others like them is not so much finding common ground but getting the other side to recognize what they clearly appear to be missing: common sense.

I mean, you can always argue the other side. But to me, that's like trying to defend a slam dunk in basketball.

Think about it. Shaquille O'Neal has the ball. He's clearly in position to jam it into the hoop. You can certainly try to stop him but odds are Shaq is going to score anyway. It might be wise to step out of the way before you end up in the hospital.

This isn't to say I'm Shaquille O'Neal, or that I will never hear you out if you strongly oppose medical marijuana. I will always listen to your views. I will always try to keep an open mind.

It's just that some issues seem so clear to me as a matter of principle and common sense, it's hard to consider the other side because I've already done so and find my position to be solid and inflexible.

For example, I have a big problem with anything related to political correctness. I have a problem with this inherently liberal notion that we must always watch exactly what we say and how we say it (and exactly what we do and how we do it) for fear of offending anyone. I find that whole idea insulting, condescending, and just plain nuts.

Political correctness says you can no longer refer to a dark-skinned man or woman as a "Black" man or a "Black" woman. That's presumed to be offensive. Instead you must say "African Americans."

Now, I realize race is a touchy, highly charged issue. But let's try to look at this sensibly. I grew up with the term "Black." I've never thought of it as a pejorative, let alone ever used it that way. To me, it's always been a descriptive term, just as I've always described myself as "White" or a Jew—*whoops*. Almost forgot. We can't use either of those words, either. We have to say "Caucasian." We have to say "Jewish-American."

Nancy Pelosi represents my district in San Francisco, but I can't call her my "Congresswoman." That's considered sexist. Never mind the fact that she *is* a woman and she *does* represent me and everyone else in my district in Congress. The acceptable term these days is "Congressperson."

I'm sorry, but some things just are what they are. You're not an "undocumented worker." You're an *illegal alien*. You're not "vertically challenged." You're *short*. You're not a "substance abuser." You're a *drug addict*. You're not a "sanitation engineer." You're a *garbage collector* (or, in the case of Tony Soprano, a *mob boss*). It's as simple as that.

I also bristle at the notion espoused by political correctness advocates that whenever we see a male or female of any minority, or a woman regardless of her race, we must somehow feel sorry for them because of the extra struggles they had to endure in life because of their race or gender.

Get real. We all know people of every race, age, gender, and economic status. Some of them struggle. Some of them don't.

When I look at people like Colin Powell, Barry Bonds, Tiger Woods, or Jackie Chan, I don't consider them disadvantaged. I look at them in terms of their accomplishments, just as I would view Dianne Feinstein, Madeleine Albright, Condoleezza Rice, or any other successful woman in terms of her accomplishments.

And when I see a guy out on the street holding a cup and a sign asking for money, I don't necessarily consider him particularly disadvantaged, either. I see a man who appears to either be down on his luck . . . or just a bum.

Whoops. I forgot. *Homeless.* Can't say "bum."

Part of my problem with political correctness is that it automatically implies malice behind everything we say or umbrage in our every response. As a thinking person, I find that condescending.

Certainly the intent behind our thoughts and deeds is always important. But so is common sense.

I like to think I'm bright enough to know when I've insulted someone and when I've been insulted myself. I like to think we all are.

What troubles me most about political correctness is how reflexive it can make us. In that respect, it's not that much different than the thinking of the extremes. If you're that far to the left, it almost becomes engrained that you must always have this attitude or behave in a certain way. It's as if you're an elected official who governs according to the polls, making decisions strictly based on what's best for you politically instead of doing what you know to be right. You're more concerned with how others might react instead of thinking for yourself.

Fortunately, we seem to be reaching the point where more and more of us are rebelling against that. Common sense would remind us that no matter how hard we try, we're always going to be wrong about something. That's just reality.

It's impossible to hold yourself to a strict standard of political correctness and think you're never going to slip.

You're in a conversation and instead of saying "African American," you inadvertently say "Black" instead. Does that mean you've suddenly become a bad or bigoted person? Give me a break!

It is completely ridiculous to worry about every word we say. Otherwise, we become so afraid of offending anyone—or excluding anyone—that we can barely do anything at all. Exactly how productive is that?

Case in point: In January 2003, the Santa Clara County Human Relations Commission agreed to draft a resolution to denounce a certain six-letter word that begins with N and combat its use as slang and slur through education and awareness.

Now on the face of it, that's a sound, well-intentioned, commendable idea. The N-word is without question one of the most vulgar, offensive, emotionally charged and problematic words in our language. It connotes anger, hatred, oppression, and divisiveness. It provokes images of a period in our history that none of us are particularly proud of. Many young Blacks use it freely and often casually among their friends, and one can certainly question whether that's appropriate. (Then again, they obviously choose to do so and appear comfortable with their decision.)

The problem with the resolution is the same as the problem with political correctness in general. If the whole purpose is to combat the use of racial slurs in our society, why stop at the N-word? Why not include epithets that are equally offensive to Jews, Arabs, Italians, Spaniards, Mexicans, Chinese, Japanese, Afghanis, and other nationalities instead of just the one that offends the Black community? Are you saying that Blacks need more protection from hateful language than anyone else?

I'm not alone in my opinion on this. Both the Bay Area chapter of the NAACP as well as the San Jose-based Coalition of Concerned Citizens and Organizations (CCCO) raised concerns over early drafts of the resolution that singled out the Black community above all others. The CCCO's opposition is noteworthy because they were the group who approached the Commission to draft the resolution in the first place.

The more drafts this resolution went through, the more problems continued to crop up. The Commission went from calling for a blanket opposition to all derogatory words, to singling out some individual slurs as being more destructive than others, to debating over whether to include the euphemism "the N-word" as opposed to the actual word itself, to running into opposition from free-speech activists.

A year after the resolution was first proposed, the Commission still was trying to come up with wording that was acceptable to everyone.

That's the problem with political correctness. It sounds good in theory, but on a practical basis it can be more trouble than it's worth.

RESPONSIBILITY WITHIN REASON

I'm very liberal when it comes to social concerns, but on some things I simply draw the line. For example, I find it patently offensive that when a man robs a bank, rapes a woman, pulls out a gun and starts shooting people, or hijacks a 747 carrying innocent passengers and crashes it into the World Trade Center, someone on the left will say it's not politically correct to simply look at him as a dirty, rotten criminal. No, no, we must also understand his motivation. We must accept our share of the "blame." We must ask ourselves what kind of society we have that drove this person to inflict such violence upon his fellow man.

Excuse me, but aren't we forgetting something here—such as the fact that in both of the above scenarios *a terrible crime was committed and innocent people were victimized?* That's a ridiculous notion born out of liberal White guilt.

I'm sorry, but I don't feel guilty. I had nothing do with those horrible crimes, and don't waste your breath trying to convince me otherwise.

Understand, I believe strongly in individual responsibility. I think it's important that we hold ourselves accountable for our actions. But common sense would say there's a time and a place where individual responsibility goes beyond reason. I think it's wrong to assume we are equally responsible for matters or conditions we did not do, would never condone, or which took place long before our time.

The issue of reparations to the Black community for the injustices done to them as a result of slavery immediately comes to mind.

Now, I have no problem with reparations in and of itself. My parents received reparations after they came to this country in 1940. At the end of World War II, they, along with many other German Jewish emigrants, received restitution from the German government because their property had been confiscated by the Nazis during the Holocaust. While certainly not full restitution, it was a reasonable level of reparations, if you will, for what had been taken from them.

That made sense. The German government immediately acknowledged that a terrible wrong had been committed and reached out to the people who were directly victimized by it.

Slavery in this country is a low point in our history that was no less wrong than what occurred during the Holocaust. But I didn't bring anybody over in chains. I had *nothing to do* with slavery. It was 145 years before my time, and unfortunately those victims are no longer with us.

I go back to the question we raised before. How far is too far?

I think it's unreasonable to ask my generation to accept responsibility for slavery, just as I believe it would be unreasonable to ask future generations to accept responsibility for what happened to my Jewish ancestors 70 years ago.

Look, we've made great strides in race relations, but clearly we still have quite a ways to go. While we should never forget our history (and especially the progress and lessons we've learned), reason would say let's work together in making the present and future better rather than trying to remake the past.

We cannot rewrite history, although there are certainly those who would try.

WHEN POLITICAL CORRECTNESS IS APROPOS

Then again, if you reflexively oppose everything attached to political correctness without any consideration whatsoever, you're not exactly thinking either. A voice of reason is a thinking person. And even a voice of reason would concede there are times when political correctness has it right.

Let's look at an example: The battle over the use of Indian names by certain sports teams has been an ongoing debate in this country for years. The Cleveland Indians. The Atlanta Braves. The Kansas City Chiefs. The Washington Redskins. Political correctness would say the use of such names is offensive to Native American Indians. Therefore, we should drop them.

A voice of reason would say, "Let's look at the issue on a case-by-case basis and see where the trouble lies."

Kansas City Chiefs. Now to me, a chief is a title of respect. A chief is someone who has established himself as fit to rule over a group of people. A chief is someone the rest of the tribe turns to for advice, counsel, leadership, and strength, especially in the field of battle. All of these are good qualities. No one is being dishonored when the term *chief* is used by the team. So I don't see the problem here. Why would you want to change it?

The same goes for the Cleveland Indians and the Atlanta Braves. The Indians were here before we were. A *brave* is an Indian warrior. There's nothing inherently wrong with either one of those terms in and of themselves.

The problem with the Cleveland Indians is their logo: a buck-toothed mascot that really plays into racial stereotypes. That image is clearly offensive and should be dropped, as should the Tomahawk Chop in Atlanta. That chant is an insult to Native Americans, not to mention an assault on everyone's ears.

Now, the Washington Redskins . . . that's where you draw the line. Sure, the franchise has been around for over 70 years, but that doesn't make it right. You can argue all you want, but you can't get around the fact that "Redskin" is a pejorative term. There's no more need for that than there would be if the team chose "Wops,"

"Wetbacks," or any other racial slur as its nickname. Reason would say get rid of it.

That said, just as I abhor people on the left who feel we must say everything so cautiously, I have equal disdain for those on the right that wrap themselves in the political correctness flag just to get your vote.

When you think about it, people on the right couldn't care less about political correctness. Sure, there are exceptions, but by and large they don't. So when a right-wing Republican suddenly starts speaking of "undocumented workers," or supports a measure that amends anti-discrimination laws in this country to include the rights of "weight-challenged" individuals, there's a good chance he's pandering more than anything else.

LET'S GONG DIVERSITY TRAINING

Diversity training (a.k.a. sensitivity training) is another absurdly liberal concept. Not to keep dumping on the left, but if you were to break things down into what's liberal and what's conservative, I doubt you'd ever hear of a diversity training session held at the Coors Brewing Company. Certainly not in the old days, anyway. (Coors, of course, has always been a traditionally right-wing corporation.)

That said, most employment lawyers will tell you that companies mandate diversity training more for their own benefit than anyone else's. It's a fail-safe move to protect them from liability in case an employee sues them for sex harassment or discrimination. Often it's even a requirement of their insurer: that is, the insurer tells the employer, "We will only provide coverage, and defend you if necessary, if you sign up for our sensitivity training." That way, the employer can say in the lawsuit, "You can't blame us. We held the sessions and did everything we could to prevent this kind of behavior."

Don't get me wrong. I think businesses should always foster good working environments. If the employees are happy, they're liable to be more productive. The more productive your employees are, the better it is for the company. It's a win-win situation. It's common sense.

I just happen to believe that if there should be a problem among your employees, there are more effective ways of solving it than through diversity training. And if there *isn't* a problem, you're better off leaving well enough alone.

I have been with KGO nearly half my life. You couldn't find a better place to work. Up and down the line people like each other, respect each other, get along with each other, and work well with each other. And with the exception of one six-month period, it has always been that way.

KGO is an ABC owned station. Our general manager Mickey Luckoff is a legend in the business. But even the great ones make a wrong move once in a while, and boy did he miss on this decision. Mickey thought a mandatory diversity training session for the entire staff would be beneficial. One morning we all had to meet in this huge conference room. A fill-in host did my show that day . . . it was more important for me to be trained.

We all spent our time listening to some new-age guy with a gong. Yes, when he wasn't asking us to stare into each other's eyes as he spouted some new-age, touchy-feely mumbo jumbo, this clown actually *banged a gong* to call everybody to order.

You want to hear the irony of this? This guy made us all so annoyed and uptight, by the end of the session many of us could barely stand each other!

The problem with sensitivity training is that it's based on a flawed concept. If people don't respect each other to begin with, sitting them in a room for three hours is hardly going to make a difference.

People tend to get along on an individual basis, and some better than others. True, there are times when we have to work with folks we don't necessarily know very well or have much in common with. For the most part, though, we forge our best relationships with people on our own volition. So when you force people into a room and feed them a line about how we all must get along, you're not really bringing anyone together. If anything, you're driving them further apart. Why? Because nobody wants to be there. The only reason they're there in the first place is because management told them they had to be.

I've done several shows on this topic since we had diversity training at KGO. I've had trainers call up and tell me how wrong I am, how I'm missing the point, how it really is a good thing if I could just see it that way. They say sensitivity training affords us an opportunity to see how our own biases influence our relationships with our colleagues and clients. They say that, if done right, diversity training can be a powerful, productive, and positive experience that leads to greater understanding for all people involved.

I'm sorry, but I just don't buy it. I don't believe that people's minds are changed that easily. That's what makes this a slam dunk issue—at least for me.

Most people don't go home that evening and say, "You know, honey, my boss had this expert on sensitivity training talk to us, and boy, am I glad he did."

No. Most people say, "You will not believe what they made us do at work today!" Either that, or "You won't believe how much work piled up on my desk because of this session I had to go to on diversity training."

Common sense would suggest that people aren't likely to learn anything if they're forced to attend a three-hour meeting on diversity training. No more than they're likely to learn anything if they have to go through eight hours of driving school.

Think about it. You go to driving school for three reasons: You got a ticket, you don't want it to go on your record, and you don't want your insurance rates to go up. So you put in your time.

I went to driving school once. I can tell you where we broke for lunch. Beyond that, I don't remember a thing I "learned." What I *do* remember is a bunch of people speeding out of the parking lot when it was over.

If you have participated in diversity training and can honestly say you gained something from it, I commend you. But I would also submit that you were probably inclined to consider it worthwhile to begin with.

Look, I'll concede that our opinions of people are often shaped by our own experiences. But so are our opinions on issues. And I can't get away from the fact that the one time I participated in diversity training was an unmitigated disaster. We went from being a wonderful place to work to having six months of genuine acrimony between a lot of people at the station. That's how long it took to undo the damage. Naturally, that has had a huge impact on my opinion about this particular issue.

Then again, I will say I've done more hours on this topic than I ever would have imagined. So maybe I *did* get something out of diversity training after all.

I THOUGHT TOLERANCE WAS A GOOD THING

Personally, I'm about as heterosexual as you can get. I can't imagine walking down a beach, past a row of beautiful women, and saying, "Hey, check out the guy with the hairy legs and the buffed chest. What a hunk."

That said, you'd be hard pressed to find anyone on the radio that's a bigger advocate of gay rights than me. I believe you're born gay, and that your rights are just as important as anyone else's, and that any attempt to convince you otherwise is rude, absurd, uninformed, and just plain wrong.

It's your life. It's your business. And if you should find a partner that you want to spend the rest of your life with, God bless you. It's tough enough for anybody in life to find someone they're happy with. Why would anyone want to deny you that?

For me, gay rights is an issue that has always come down to logic. I have no idea what George and Laura do in the bedroom . . . and I don't care, anymore than I care about what you, my neighbors, or anyone else might do in the bedroom. So long as you're an adult, what you do in the privacy of your home is no one's concern but yours.

That's a very Libertarian point of view. Strictly speaking, it's also traditionally conservative, in the sense that conservative Republicans are supposed to believe in keeping government out of our lives.

That's why I've never understood how the GOP could consistently oppose gay rights. This is the party that says they want the government to interfere as little as possible in our private affairs, yet they keep pushing for laws that would discriminate against people because of what they do in the bedroom.

Case in point: the GOP's reaction to the historic Supreme Court decision in June 2003 that struck down a ban on gay sex in Texas, ruling that the arrest of two men in Harris County, Texas for participating in sodomy was an unconstitutional violation of privacy. The 6 to 3 decision reversed the Court's previous ruling on the matter of *Bowers v. Hardwick,* a 1986 case in which the Court said that states could in fact punish homosexuals for what such laws historically called "deviant" sex. "This Court's obligation is to define the liberty of all, not mandate its own moral code," said Justice Anthony Kennedy. "[The two male defendants] are entitled to respect for their private lives. The state cannot demean their existence or control their destiny by making their private sexual conduct a crime."

I thought it was a superb ruling. The decision opened the door for legal challenges to a host of laws that discriminate against gays and lesbians, including marriage laws, the "don't ask, don't tell" rule on gays in the military, custody and employment disputes, and other rulings based on the 13 remaining state sodomy laws, as well as the *Bowers* decision. The Court made the right call. It was about time it came down.

Naturally, conservative Republicans reacted as though Armageddon was coming. "Clearly, this law, having been overturned, is setting a dangerous precedent," said the Reverend Louis Sheldon, head of the Traditional Values Coalition, when he appeared on my program on the day of the ruling. "Public schools, state boards of education, and local school districts will now have to teach children that homosexuality is a viable life alternative. And when you say that homosexuality is a viable life alternative, you are delivering a devastating blow to our society. We'll go the way Rome went with its decadence."

I couldn't agree less with Lou's politics, but I always like having him on the show because he's lively, passionate, and presents the other side. What was particularly fascinating that morning is that once you dug through his rhetoric, *he actually agreed* with the principle on which the decision was based: that it is morally wrong for the police to barge into the bedroom of two people (whether it's two men, two women, or a man and a woman) when the only thing they're doing is having sex. That was the issue in the case involving the two men from Harris County. The Supreme Court said that was wrong. I told Lou that if he agreed with the principle, it followed that he should also agree with the decision.

To his credit, Lou conceded the first part of the statement, but he couldn't quite bring himself to yield on the second. Instead he kept harping about how bad it would be for schools to teach that homosexuality is acceptable.

"My God, Lou," I said. "You mean we might end up teaching tolerance?"

"Listen, Ronn," Lou replied, "this is not a matter of discrimination. This is a matter of discernment. Discerning what is morally right, and what is morally wrong. We have to make that very clear."

Except that the Supreme Court has already made it clear. For that matter, so has the state of California, where the law says consensual sex between adults 21 and older regardless of gender is none of the government's business. And any law that discriminates against people because of their sexual preferences is therefore wrong. End of discussion.

GAY DAYS, AGE APPROPRIATENESS, AND AN ASININE DECISION

Then again, there are some issues involving gays where even a voice of reason will find himself agreeing with the far right.

You might recall the instance from the summer of 2003 in which a nominee for a federal judgeship was attacked by liberal Democrats in the Senate because he had rescheduled his vacation so that it wouldn't coincide with the Gay Day celebration at Disney World.

The parties involved were Alabama Attorney General William Pryor, whom President Bush nominated to the Eleventh Circuit of the U.S. Court of Appeals, and Wisconsin Senator Russ Feingold. Pryor is a right-wing Republican, Feingold a liberal Democrat. In the course of the hearings reviewing Pryor's nomination, it somehow came to Feingold's attention that Pryor had once rescheduled a family vacation to Disney World in Orlando, Florida, when he realized his family would be there the same week as Disney's annual Gay Days. Pryor explained that at the time of his vacation, his daughters were six and four. He and his wife felt it was not appropriate for young children to be at a place where they would see men holding hands and kissing. "We made a value judgment," he told Feingold. "That was our personal decision."

Personally, I don't care for Pryor's political views. He has defended the Texas law that prohibited participation in sodomy by individuals who weren't legally married—the same law that the Supreme Court would later strike down. You look at his overall record, and he's about as far to the right as you can get.

That said, common sense would say you should be able to take your kids to Disney World whenever the hell you want. Disney World is crowded enough as it is. It's even more so during peak periods such as early summer, when Gay Days are traditionally held. If you're planning a vacation and suddenly discover you're going to be there during one of the busiest weeks of the year, you have every right to reschedule the trip. Especially if you have the flexibility to do it.

As I said, I'm as big a champion of gay rights as you'll find. But that doesn't mean I have to inconvenience my family by planning our vacation around Gay Days just to show my political support.

More to the point, when Feingold asked him about it, Pryor didn't duck the question. He said very plainly he felt the atmosphere at Disney World that week was not suitable for his young children. You may not agree with Pryor, but you can at least respect his decision as a parent. No one should hold that against him.

Guess what? Feingold did. He actually put Pryor through the wringer *over that*.

It would be one thing if Feingold were attacking him on his record. Because if Pryor believed in the Texas sodomy law, you have to wonder if you're a gay defendant whether you have a fair shot with a man like him on the bench. But that's separate and apart from the idea that he just didn't feel like taking his family to Orlando during the week of Disney Gay Days.

Are you telling me that in order to be a judge, you have make sure you don't go out of your way to avoid Gay Days because that might be politically incorrect? *Come on.*

I said it before. I'll say it again. No wonder we don't see more people entering public service today.

For me, the most uncomfortable aspect of this issue was not that I was defending Pryor. Were it up to me, I'd have blocked his nomination on the Texas sodomy issue alone. What bugged me most about this was that it put me on the same page as people like Tim Wildmon, the president of the American Family Association.

Ordinarily, I can't stand Wildmon, but in this case he was right. He thought Feingold's stance was "asinine," adding that the Senator ought to "be ashamed of himself for trying to take Mr. Pryor to task for avoiding a homosexual day at Disney World because he had two young daughters."

Just goes to show once again how problematic backwards thinking is. In his zeal to excoriate Pryor, Senator Feingold ignored the issue of age appropriateness. That was the bottom line my listeners kept returning to when we talked about this on the show. If Pryor's daughters are young, and he felt it was too soon for them to understand the atmosphere to which they would have been exposed on Gay Day, that's his decision to make. Several callers who identified themselves as either gay, lesbian, or bisexual all opposed Pryor's nomination on principle, yet supported his decision as a parent.

Interestingly enough, an emailer pointed out that at Paramount's Great America, the popular amusement park located one hour south of San Francisco, many of the toddler rides are closed whenever Gay Day is celebrated. Which suggests that even here in the way-out liberal, free-wheeling Bay Area, common sense can still prevail. Some events are not necessarily appropriate for young children.

WHY DO WE PROSECUTE PEOPLE WHO WANT TO END THEIR LIVES?

I cannot for the life of me understand anyone who believes they have a right to force you to stay alive. I just don't get that at all.

I'm not talking about suicide help lines or hot lines. That's different. If you're thinking of ending your life, but aren't necessarily sure, it's good to know there are people to whom you can reach out and talk. There are professionals out there who are trained to hear you out and help you if you need it. I think that's wonderful.

But if someone believes that his life just isn't worth living anymore, and he as an adult makes a conscious decision to terminate his life, how the government can impose its will on others by making that a prosecutable offense is beyond me.

"Quality of life" is a notion I feel strongly about. I believe we all have the right to lead our lives as we want to, within reason, and without impediments that would prevent us from doing so. Serious illness is one such impediment. If you should find yourself diagnosed with a terminal disease, or are hospitalized with critical injuries and face a future attached to a life support system, or have simply come to the point where you no longer wish to live because you believe the quality of your life in the future would be severely diminished, I believe you have the right to end your life on your own terms.

I come at this from a personal experience.

My mother was a unique individual. She was a wonderful mom and had a perspective on life that was refreshingly and unceasingly ultramodern. She was the type of person who, when I changed my name professionally at the start of my radio career, decided she was at a point in her life when it was time to change her name, too. So she did. I went from Ronald Lowenstein to Ronn Owens. She went from Maud Lowenstein to Monica Owens.

You might call her eccentric. I just called her Mom. Without question she was, and is, one of the major influences in my life.

Medically speaking, my mom was a mess. Even when I was a kid, she used to talk about how she was like an old car, falling apart piece by piece. She had health problems from day one and was often in pain, especially during her last years. So it should come as no surprise when I tell you my mom committed suicide in December 1988.

There was certainly no surprise on my end. She had talked openly about this for a long, long time. She was always her own person and she always enjoyed life. She simply believed that if she ever reached the point where her body was failing her to the extent that the quality of her life was significantly lessened, then it would be time for her to go. She was never sad or brooding about it. I suppose you could say she was pragmatic about it.

After she died, I remember going down to Orange County, where she had been living for several years. I was putting her affairs in order when at one point, while by myself, I just said out loud, "Mom, I'm so damn proud of you!!!"

How could I not be? She knew what she was doing. She was 77 years old. She had a good life. She just wanted to end it on her own terms. And when the time finally came, she did.

To think that attempted suicide and euthanasia are actually prosecutable in this country just strikes me as ridiculous.

I mean, think about it. Our legal system was designed to prosecute people who break the law. If someone successfully commits suicide, he escapes scot free! What are you going to do, throw the book at his family and loved ones? What purpose would that serve? Don't you think they're going through enough pain already?

What do you do with the ones who bungle it—put them in jail? For how long? The minute you let them out, they're only going to try to take their life again anyway. How are you going to stop them from doing that?

And as far as assisted suicide is concerned, that's also a slam dunk.

Now ostensibly, doctors are pledged to try to prolong our lives. Understood. That said, do you really think there aren't doctors that help people die every single day?

If you're an adult and you express to your physician a desire to end your life, or that the plug be pulled from the life support machine, or that you no longer want him to give you medication, what's he going to do, say no? If he does, find another doctor.

Doctors are people, too. They may not always seem human . . . but they still are. They deal with hundreds of different people every year, and they will always advise you based on that experience. But when they're sitting down talking to you, one on one, they never lose sight of the fact that the final decision on any aspect of your health care always lies with you.

HOW HEARTLESS CAN YOU GET?

Since we're on the subject of quality of life, let's take another look at the medicinal use of marijuana. From a voice of reason perspective, that's also a no-brainer.

You have people struggling every day from the debilitating symptoms of AIDS, epilepsy, glaucoma, multiple sclerosis, and the side effects of chemotherapy treatment for cancer. You have leading doctors recommending the use of marijuana for such patients to help alleviate their pain. You have statistics that indicate smoking pot can help make people with serious illnesses more comfortable and can even have a positive impact on their recovery. You have states such as California which vote overwhelmingly in favor of legalizing marijuana for medical purposes. (In most elections, 55 percent is considered a landslide. California voters approved of medicinal marijuana in 1996 by a whopping 70 percent.) You look at the issue through the lens of common sense, and it's hard to fathom how anyone could possibly oppose it.

And yet the federal government keeps saying no.

You have the U.S. Supreme Court ruling in May 2001 that a federal anti-drug law does not allow for the use of marijuana for health reasons. The federal government immediately shut down nearly two dozen marijuana dispensaries in the state of California while continuing to raid others. You have federal prosecutors asking an Appeals Court to override the decision of a District Court judge who had overturned the prison sentence of a marijuana advocate who was arrested and prosecuted *despite the fact he was hired by the city of Oakland to cultivate marijuana for medical patients.* And if that weren't enough, you have the Bush administration asking the U.S. Supreme Court in July 2003 for the right to punish doctors in California who recommend marijuana to their patients by revoking their licenses to write prescriptions.

You tell me. Does that sound like a government that's working for you?

George W. Bush professes to be a man of compassion. Then he tries to take away the ability of physicians to prescribe marijuana, even if they should happen to believe that's the best thing for their patients.

How good a doctor can you be if you can't do what you know to be helpful to your patients?

Talk about imposing your will on others. Because what this basically says is, "Politicians know more about your health than your own doctor."

That notion is not only absurd, it's frightening, crazy, and a classic case of overkill. It's like pummeling ants to death with a sledge hammer.

On some issues, the government seems determined to make our lives more difficult, not less.

In all fairness, President Bush is not alone in his stance against the medical use of marijuana. The Clinton administration was equally strident in its opposition—and I couldn't understand that, either.

Even so, the Bush administration is taking it a step too far. Their attempts to rewrite the ending to the Ed Rosenthal case made that very clear.

A little background. Rosenthal was a medical marijuana advocate who was deputized by the city of Oakland to supply marijuana to a local cooperative. Federal officials then turned around and arrested him on three felony charges in connection with marijuana plants he was cultivating for patients served by a San Francisco dispensary. But when the case went to trial in February 2003, the judge refused to let the jury be told that Oakland specifically hired Rosenthal to grow marijuana for medical purposes. Rosenthal was convicted and sentenced to five years in jail. Four days after his conviction, the jury was outraged to learn that key evidence had been suppressed. The jury foreman then told reporters that Rosenthal would never have been convicted had the jury known he had been hired to grow marijuana for medical purposes. This set off a huge controversy, the upshot of which was that U.S. District Judge Charles Breyer overturned the prison sentence, setting Rosenthal free after one day in prison.

Fast forward to July 2003. Federal prosecutors asked an Appeals Court to send Rosenthal to prison after all.

What do they want to do, squeeze blood out of the guy? How heartless can the government get?

The case is over. He won. You lost. Get over it.

Now, the rational part of me would to like think maybe it's simply a case of the White House catering to Middle America, the millions of people who simply may not understand the issue.

I could accept that as an explanation. I still wouldn't *like* it, but I could accept it in the sense that it would be an example of governing to the center, which is how I think government ought to lead.

But if that isn't the explanation, how do you justify the government's opposition? How can anybody be so cold-hearted? How can anybody just sit by dispassionately and say, "Let 'em suffer!"

I have never understood that way of thinking. Frankly, I can't imagine I ever will.

Fortunately, there continues to be hope that reason will ultimately prevail. In October 2003, the U.S. Supreme Court upheld a decision by the Ninth Circuit Court of Appeals that said that doctors and patients have the right to discuss the possible use of medicinal marijuana without fear of repercussions by the federal government. This ruling thwarts any effort by the Bush administration to rescind the licenses of physicians who prescribe marijuana to their patients.

TERM LIMITS ARE JUST PLAIN STUPID

Term limits is another issue that I feel strongly about, but on which I often find myself in the minority. Most people love term limits. Here in California, the voters in fact approved an initiative enacting term limits back in 1990. But I've been against them from the start, and my reason why is simple: Why would anyone want to limit their choices?

You go to a restaurant. You're about to order when the waiter tells you the best items on the menu are no longer available. Your heart is set on prime rib but you can't have it because they suddenly ran out. You have to choose from what's left.

Or better yet, you look at the wine list and say, "I know you have over 20 wines to choose from, but it's hard to make up my mind. Why don't you just offer me the house red or the house white, and I'll choose from those instead."

Either way, your options are limited. That's exactly what happens when it comes to term limits.

If you think the person already in office is doing a lousy job, by all means don't vote for him. Vote for his opponent instead. But if the incumbent is doing a good job, common sense says you'd want to keep him in power, right?

Except you can't do it here in California. Once a politician is "termed out," he can no longer run for that office even if he happens to be the best person for the job.

To me, the biggest problem with term limits is that it opens the door to electing people who have never been in office before. You wind up with candidates who may have a lot of upside—like, say, the longtime chief aide to a city councilman who's about to be termed out. The aide runs for the councilman's seat. He gets the councilman's endorsement. He wins a four-year term. Problem is, once he's in office, it soon becomes evident that the protégé has nowhere near the expertise of the man who served before him. It ends up taking him two years before he finally knows what he's doing. That's one huge learning curve. And by the time he learns how to do his job, he has to start campaigning for reelection or else he's out the door. So what exactly has been accomplished?

Either that, or you end up electing people who simply haven't got a clue. Like most members of the San Francisco Board of Supervisors.

Proponents would say that term limits is the only viable method of keeping certain politicians from being so entrenched in office and wielding so much power that you can't possibly defeat them—people such as Willie Brown, who held the same seat in the California State Assembly for over 30 years. During the last 15 years of his tenure, Brown held the pivotal position as speaker of the assembly and became a virtually unstoppable force in California politics. For that reason, Brown, an avid Democrat, became the target for the largely Republican movement that would successfully bring term limits to California in 1990. Though Brown was re-elected speaker in 1994, he would have been required to leave office at the end of that term under the new law. When the opportunity presented itself, he ran for mayor of San Francisco in 1995 and was reelected in 1999.

I understand the argument. But it seems to me that if you could tear down the Berlin Wall and put an end to communism, you could also come up with a way to unseat a politician who's been around forever—even someone as crafty as my friend Willie Brown—without resorting to term limits.

The entire concept of term limits is inherently flawed. Trying to keep powerful politicians out of office by invoking terms limits is like trying to outsmart a computer hacker. You come up with a firewall that you think will thwart hackers, and I guarantee you that within a week someone will find a way around it. And guess what? When it comes to their own futures and their own careers, politicians are just as savvy. They followed Willie Brown's example and figured out term limits in no time. So what we have is a game of musical chairs. The state senator who is termed out runs for the assembly. The termed-out assemblyman runs for the senate. Some other senator becomes lieutenant governor. The speaker becomes the mayor. Their addresses may have changed, but the power players are still in office.

Term limits are a stupid idea across the board. Even term limits for the presidency.

Now, I wasn't around for FDR, but I understand the rationale behind the Twenty-Second Amendment. That still doesn't make it right.

Bill Clinton had a sound proposal for a constitutional amendment for which he claims to have no ulterior motive. The idea he floated to amend the Twenty-Second Amendment is actually a reasonable compromise, and since we're always looking for compromise . . .

The Twenty-Second Amendment currently states that no person shall be elected president more than twice, and no president who has served more than two years of a term to which some other person was elected president shall be elected president himself more than once.

Under Clinton's proposal, you have a president in office. You limit that president to two terms in less than 10 years. He leaves office at the end of the second term. Four years later, after sitting out one full term, he becomes eligible to run again. I don't have a problem with that at all.

What, you think there aren't any Democrats today who would have liked to have seen Clinton run in 2004?

Now I suppose an argument against that would be, "Well, what's to prevent a Democrat like Clinton from serving two terms, then using his influence to get his vice president elected, then running again himself four years later, thus making it conceivable for one party to monopolize the White House for 20 years or more?"

Sure, if this rule were in effect we could conceivably have one party in power for 20 years. Only it wouldn't be a monopoly. The people would still have the right to vote. If they don't like the Democratic vice president, they can always vote for someone else. And just because you're eligible to run again four years later doesn't mean you're going to win. Who's to say the Republicans couldn't come up with a candidate the electorate likes more than you?

That said, as much as I like Clinton's idea—as much as I wouldn't mind seeing him in the White House again—it's hard to imagine he came up with the idea without himself in mind. If so, that poses a problem for me. I just hate it whenever a new law passes that allows for an exception that is designed to benefit one particular individual. But would I vote for this one? Yes.

I have the same dilemma when it comes to Orrin Hatch's proposal to amend Article II of the Constitution. Article II says that only natural born citizens of the United States shall be eligible to run for president. Senator Hatch would like to change it so that foreign immigrants who have since become naturalized Americans can also run for president.

Purists will argue that when the Founding Fathers first drafted the Constitution in 1789, they specifically wanted to prevent anyone coming over from England or France—that is, someone who may well have had the interests of their king at heart—and putting themselves in a position to lead this country. That would have defeated the purpose of why we seceded from England in the first place. If you're going to lead this country, you have to know what it's about. You ought to be steeped in its history. Therefore, you should be born here.

Liberals oppose the idea purely out of politics, seeing it as a thinly veiled attempt to open the door for a possible White House run down the road by someone like Arnold Schwarzenegger. As it happens, Arnold Schwarzenegger and Orrin Hatch are political allies.

Now I would agree with the argument as to what the Founding Fathers intended. But that was over 200 years ago. Reason would attest that if you come to this country, take the tests, and swear your allegiance (as you must when you become naturalized), and have established yourself as a citizen for 20 or 25 years, your roots as an American are pretty solid. If you have a vision for this country and have demonstrated the various leadership and political skills needed to implement it, you should have as much right to run for president as any natural-born American.

That's why I can support Hatch's idea, just as I can support Clinton's idea, even if they do turn out to be politically motivated. We shouldn't have term limits. We shouldn't have any restrictions. Why should we deny ourselves the option of voting for the best possible candidate, regardless of age, sex, nationality, or how many terms he's served before?

Common Sense Solutions
to Everyday Issues

I've never been one for sitting behind a microphone and telling my audience, "This is how you have to vote. This is how you have to think." I'd much rather talk things over with my listeners instead. That's why I particularly enjoy discussing issues where we can present both sides intelligently and come up with solutions together. Especially when they concern areas of life that affect us all on an everyday basis.

There are certain *voice of reason* issues. There are certain matters we can tackle and resolve with pragmatism and common sense.

For example, gay marriage in and of itself is a wedge issue. Either you're for it or you're not. Generally speaking, liberals back it. Conservatives don't. The debate has gone on for years. As recently as 2003, the Vatican once again condemned it while the ACLU reiterated its support. Then President George W. Bush further stirred the pot when he said "I believe a marriage is between a man and a woman. I think we ought to codify that one way or another."

Now you know where I stand on gay rights overall. I'm straight. They're gay. So what? People who love each other should have the right to have their relationship accepted and recognized, *period*. Who cares what they do in the bedroom? Their rights are no different than mine. That issue is a slam dunk. For that matter, so are my views on gay marriage.

That aside, I think the biggest problem in the debate over gay marriage is not so much with the *concept* as it is with the terminology.

No matter what you think of George W. Bush, the man is not alone in his belief as to what comprises a marriage. I say this not as a Bush devotee, but as a political pragmatist who's trying to look at this particular issue calmly and objectively.

I think most would agree that anyone who believes there haven't been homosexuals all throughout history is simply naïve. That said, there's a reason why many gays in this country have stayed in the closet until only the past 30 years. The very idea of homosexuality is something many people in our society are still adjusting to, particularly older generations. So while I clearly support the idea of gay marriage, I can understand the resistance to it from the other side.

But it seems to me we could all come closer to bridging the gap by agreeing on one thing. Don't call it a *marriage*. The word *marriage* is what ruffles the feathers of people who just can't bring themselves to think of matrimony as anything other than an act "between a man and a woman."

So let's compromise and call it something else instead: a union, a bond, an alliance, a lifelong commitment. All of these terms are equally strong. None of them make the act or ceremony any less significant. Two people are still professing their dedication and love for each other before an audience of family and loved ones.

Obviously, there's a lot more to the issue than that. My point is that if we can somehow agree on the language, that's a step in the right direction.

THE PROBLEM WITH "HOMELESS"

There are other matters we can likewise solve with the help of common sense. As libertarian as I am on social issues, I also believe there are times when government has every right to intervene.

Take welfare, for example. I find it odd that we live in a world where 4 percent unemployment is considered "no unemployment." Or where a poverty level of 11 percent is considered a good year.

The number of poor people in the United States rose for the second consecutive year in 2002. Nearly 34.6 million people are barely getting by, according to figures released by the U.S. Census Bureau in September 2003.

That's way too many. No one in this country should be left wanting. We should do what we can to help.

I'm no socialist, but I do think there ought to be a minimum level of subsistence for every American. If a family truly is in desperate need of money, and they're literally out on the streets without any means of fending for themselves, then I think it's only right and decent for the government to step in.

It used to be that the debate over welfare boiled down to this: "Why should we? Poor people have no desire to work. They're not doing a damn thing. We have enough problems of our own. Why should we take on theirs?" And while some people may well fit that description, I'd like to believe the vast majority of people living at the poverty level do not.

No one really likes a handout. Most people are inherently proud regardless of their economic status. If they're struggling or out of work, they want to do everything they can to get back on their feet and take care of their family without the help of anyone else. That's not only admirable, in many ways it's also human nature.

Trouble is, you look around and there's a lot of reality working against them. When the economy's down, they compete with more and more people over fewer and fewer jobs. Even with the economy up, it can still be a struggle for low income families to get by. Especially if they have no health insurance. Or find themselves priced out of the housing market. (Which reminds me: There's a certain hypocrisy when it comes to developing affordable housing. On the one hand, everyone's for it in principle. On the other hand, no one wants it in their neighborhood. And the poor get stuck as a result.)

It's a tough road and you truly hope those down on their luck can pull through. But there are times when everyone needs a little help to get through the rough patch. That's when government should step up to the plate.

Then again, whenever you talk about poverty or unemployment you will inevitably find yourself embroiled in a debate over the homeless. At the risk of sounding coldhearted, my feelings on that matter are entirely different. And they stem from the word *homeless* itself.

The problem with *homeless* is that it's a blanket term that covers a lot of territory. As such, it's very misleading.

There are people on the streets who are legitimately out of work, down on their luck, living hand to mouth with no roof over their head, no prospects, and no relief in sight. You see them sitting on the sidewalk, perhaps with a little child holding a cup and asking for help, and you can't help but feel sorry for them. These people truly are homeless. These are the people who genuinely need our help.

Statistically, many people on the street are drug addicts, alcoholics, or mentally ill. These people are so far gone, they need help more than they need a handout. Give them money when they ask you and what do they do? They buy drugs. They buy booze. On nights when they can't find a bed at any of the city-run shelters, you'll find them sleeping in the park, in an alleyway, in a dumpster.

These people are also considered homeless. We need more programs that would take them off the streets and give them the help they need to fight their addiction.

Then there are the scam artists, the aggressive panhandlers who "work" the same block, day in and day out. You know who they are. There's a certain number of them in every city in the country. They linger behind you at the ATM when you're trying to make a withdrawal. They crowd your space as you try to cross the street. They're all pleasant with the "God bless yous" as they hit you up for money. But when you politely decline, they suddenly turn mean and hostile and try to intimidate you into giving them money anyway.

These people aren't homeless at all. These people are bums. I realize it's not politically correct to say that, but that's what they are.

These people are bums who shamelessly manipulate you into feeling sorry for them because, after all, they're "homeless."

They're the ones who do the most damage to a city's quality of life.

WE COULD USE SOME MORE RUDY GIULIANIS

I want to return to *quality of life* because it's an issue I'm passionate about. Whether it's the guy in New York with the squeegee who cleans and washes your window when you don't want it washed (and who, adding insult to injury, only makes it worse), or the bum who blocks you from going into the pharmacy because he's in your face asking for money, these are all quality-of-life issues. These are the issues that made Rudy Giuliani such an excellent mayor. By the time Giuliani left office in 2002, the people in New York didn't see him as Democrat or Republican, liberal or conservative. They viewed him as a man who dramatically improved their quality of life by cleaning up the streets, getting tough on crime, and cracking down on aggressive panhandling. And when you look around the country, you'll see that more and more cities where panhandling is pervasive are beginning to follow his lead.

Take Winston-Salem, North Carolina. Under a new law that was passed in the summer of 2003, the city council made it illegal to solicit money at outdoor restaurants, bus stops, or ATM machines. Panhandlers under the influence of alcohol or drugs are also subject to immediate arrest. Residents said, "Panhandling to the point of disturbing people is a problem we don't need. Let's do something about it."

If only we can do the same in the Bay Area. Why we allow this blight on our quality of life to go on in cities such as San Francisco and San Jose, as well as surrounding suburbs like Walnut Creek, is simply beyond me.

Then again, I live in a city where the Board of Supervisors overwhelmingly voted *against* a law that would have prohibited people from urinating on public sidewalks.

It's one thing to always support the underdog. But there are times when the underdog is clearly in the wrong. And if someone is panhandling aggressively to the point where he's blocking your path and being obnoxious, I'm sorry, but that's wrong. Even if that someone hasn't a dime to his name.

Tourism is the No. 1 industry in San Francisco. Tourism these days is suffering in the City. Talk to people who visit this city from all over the world, and invariably within the first couple of minutes they will remark about all the homeless—excuse me, make that *street people*—who panhandle them or impede their paths by sleeping in the middle of the sidewalk. Take a walk around Market Street or Union Square and you'll see exactly what I mean.

Now, bleeding-heart liberals will call in and tell me these people have every right to do what they're doing. And to a certain extent, I'd have to agree. They have a right to panhandle *within reason*. But they don't have the right to block the entrance to a building, store, library, church, or business. They don't have the right to lie on the sidewalk in the middle of the day and prevent pedestrians from getting by.

How can we change this? Well, we could start by electing more people like Rudy Giuliani. When Giuliani was mayor of New York, you could walk down Fifth Avenue and not have anyone blocking your way or hitting you up for money. You no longer saw anyone with squeegees because those people were arrested—and when they were arrested, New York didn't kid around. It wasn't "We'll arrest you then let you out on your own recognizance," as you see in other jurisdictions. You get busted for panhandling in New York, you'd find yourself arrested, put on trial, and sentenced to a short term in prison. And if you went out and did it again, you'd end up back in jail.

Common sense reminds us that once a law goes into effect, you don't always need the police around to enforce it. Often the public acts as its own police. Under Giuliani's leadership, people with squeegees suddenly stood out . . . and the people of New York noticed them and helped squeeze them out.

WHEN THE WILL OF THE PEOPLE IS OVERTURNED

Then again, maybe there's hope for San Francisco yet. After all, the City did elect Supervisor Gavin Newsom as its mayor in December 2003.

A leader in the Giuliani mold, Newsom has shown a commitment to doing some of the same things Giuliani did to improve the quality of life in New York: cleaning up the streets, restoring the City's parks, and tackling the matter of the homeless. One idea he tried to implement during his tenure as a supervisor was a measure called "Care Not Cash," a controversial plan that would have dramatically revamped the City's general assistance program.

Welfare recipients in San Francisco receive monthly payments of up to $410—clearly the highest such figure in the Bay Area. San Francisco is also the last major county in California to provide such substantial monetary assistance to people who live on the streets. Consequently, this provides incentive for street people from outlying regions to come to San Francisco for refuge. Studies have shown, however, that the majority of recipients spend most of their stipend on drugs and alcohol instead of on rent and food. Over 1,000 street people died in San Francisco over the past decade. Nearly half of these deaths were the result of an overdose of drugs or alcohol. Local health professionals as well as the *New England Journal of Medicine* concur there is a direct correlation between cash payments to homeless individuals and the high number of overdose-related deaths. Problem was, budget restraints limited the City's ability to provide shelter and treatment to people living and dying on the streets.

Newsom proposed a plan to increase funding for additional services by reallocating how general assistance money was distributed. The measure would have transferred the money presently used for direct cash payments to fund additional homeless shelters as well as additional services for mental health care and drug and alcohol treatment. Welfare recipients would still receive cash in hand each month under the plan, only the amount would be significantly less. In exchange, they would have access to nearly 1,000 more single-occupancy rooms and vitally needed care.

Granted, it was hardly a perfect solution. Then again, few compromises are. What mattered was that the plan was a concerted effort at resolving a homeless problem that has baffled City administrators for over 20 years.

Newsom's measure went to the voters in November 2002 and was approved by a 60 to 40 margin. It was set to be enacted in

2003 until a superior court justice threw out the initiative on the grounds that it was unconstitutional. In ruling against the measure, Judge Ronald Quidachay declared that state law made it clear that implementation of any standards of aid for the downtrodden "is beyond the reach of initiative and referendum." In other words, the court said welfare is a matter for county officials to decide, not the general public.

Just like that, the will of over 125,000 San Franciscans who voted for the proposition suddenly went down the drain. Though Newsom's effort to revive the initiative ultimately failed, he remains dedicated to finding solutions to this important quality of life issue. Toward that end, he authored a measure similar to the Winston-Salem law: Proposition M, which not only outlaws aggressive panhandling in San Francisco, but also prohibits begging in parking lots, near ATMs, on median strips, outside check-cashing businesses and on City buses. Voters in San Francisco resoundingly approved Proposition M in November 2003.

Of course, we see this happen all the time. Someone comes up with a great idea such as "Care Not Cash." The general public supports the idea and puts it into effect, only to see the matter taken to the court and inevitably tossed out the window at the whim of a judge. The will of the people is overturned.

Now, we can argue all we want over whether this is wrong (and in fact, it is). From a voice of reason standpoint, it's far more productive to try to come up with ways of preventing other initiatives that we vote for from being thrown out in the future. Two ideas immediately come to mind:

1. *Once an initiative qualifies for the ballot, submit it to an impartial panel of judges. Have them rule on its constitutionality before the measure goes to the voters.* The panel could be comprised of sitting judges, retired judges, or "rent a judges" from different states or jurisdictions. If they say it's constitutional, the measure goes on the ballot. If it isn't, everyone saves time, money, and aggravation.

2. *Change the rules about the petition-gathering process.* Before you gather signatures, submit your petition to the secretary

of state. Let the secretary of state determine whether the new initiative you're proposing is constitutional. If it is, then go ahead and gather signatures. If you gather enough signatures, it goes on the ballot. Either way, at least people will know that when they step inside the ballot booth, their vote will actually mean something.

As it stands, my vote for "Care Not Cash" meant nothing. And you wonder why so many people have so little confidence in the electoral process. If you don't believe your vote will matter, what's the point in voting at all?

SMOKING IN PUBLIC IS IMPOSING YOUR WILL ON OTHERS

Smoking in public is another quality-of-life issue. Time was you could smoke in any office building, restaurant, supermarket, stadium, or just about any other public place in this country. Try that today in most states and at the very least, you'll be glared at by everyone else around you. And rightfully so.

Smoking is one of the first areas in politics where I decided to get directly involved. The year was 1980. A small group formed and called themselves "Californians for Smoking and Non-Smoking Sections." They sponsored an initiative that would have required every restaurant in the state to have, you guessed it, both "Smoking" and "Non-Smoking" sections.

Shows you just how much times have changed, doesn't it?

In any event, I liked the group and so strongly supported their efforts that I signed on to the campaign. I canvassed the state and held press conferences in San Diego, Los Angeles, San Francisco, and Sacramento, all in support of the measure.

When the issue was first presented to the voters, a Field Poll showed 66 percent of Californians favored Smoking and Non-Smoking sections. Now remember, this was back in 1980. That year, the tobacco companies poured $10 million to fight the measure. We had about $250,000. And as a consequence, the measure lost, 53 percent to 47 percent.

It would be another eight years before reason ultimately prevailed. Californians passed a second, even tougher law in 1988 that prohibited smoking in all public places—this, despite a $15 million campaign against it by Big Tobacco. Which goes to show that even money can be toppled at times by common sense.

As we said before, the public word is the most important word of all. You want to smoke in your house, or in your car, go right ahead. That's your choice. What you do on your own time and in your own space is your own business. So long as you have the door closed or the windows rolled up, that's all right by me. But your right to smoke goes out the door once *you* go out the door. I can't put it any simpler than that.

Most anti-smoking advocates will justify their opposition by zeroing in on second-hand smoke and its effect on our health. While that argument is certainly true, that's not why I'm against smoking in public.

Plain and simple, I don't want to breathe your smoke. I believe that's imposing your will on others.

Smokers and civil libertarians alike get upset when I say things like that. They accuse me of eroding "yet another basic human right" in difficult times such as these, when the fact is they're really more concerned about the rights of other smokers.

I believe there are times where common sense should prevail on certain matters. Smoking in public is one of them.

You don't have the right to smoke in public, any more than you have the right to be drunk in public or have sex in public. You have every right to express yourself and enjoy your life, but you don't have the right to disturb the rights of other people to enjoy *their* lives. That's imposing your will on others. That's not what this country is about.

A PRAGMATIC APPROACH TO
TRAFFIC AND PARKING

If you were to poll the citizens in any city in the United States and ask them to list their most pressing concerns, I'm willing to bet that driving, traffic, and parking will rank near the top. That's also part of quality of life. We'd all like to be able to drive to work, go to the supermarket, visit our friends, find a parking space, use the freeways, use the bridges, and come back home again with as little hassle as possible. The harder that is for us, the more frustrated and angry we become, which in turn diminishes our quality of life.

Driving is a privilege. For many people in this country, it's also a necessity of life. Most of us have to drive in order to get to work. All attempts to encourage us to use mass transit are just that—attempts. Like it or not, we are wedded to our cars. That isn't likely to change. And yet traffic remains one of our biggest irritants. Nothing bugs us more than sitting in gridlock. At its worst, traffic can lead to road rage and other incidents of violence.

A voice of reason would say, "Driving and gridlock are realities we cannot change, but we can definitely try to control them. And the way to do that is by being tougher on enforcement."

Problem is, I happen to live in San Francisco—the second-most congested region in the United States, according to a national survey of traffic congestion conducted by the Urban Mobility Study in 2003. Law enforcement in San Francisco is pressed enough as it is. They simply do not have the time and manpower to sit around and stop everybody who's making bad moves in a car. As a result, San Francisco can be a pretty dangerous place to drive, not to mention a hazardous place for pedestrians.

On the other side of the spectrum is Los Angeles—*the* most congested urban area in the country, according to the Urban Mobility Study. The average driver in Los Angeles spends an additional 90 hours per year stuck in gridlock beyond the number of hours they're actually commuting. By comparison, drivers in the San Francisco area spend an extra 68 hours stuck in traffic beyond the time they're in commute.

Now I've spent a fair amount of time in L.A. I even lived there part-time for a year when my show was simulcast in both the Bay Area and the Southland. And with all the other problems the police have in L.A., they *still* write you up for just about everything.

Look, I'm as a big supporter of law enforcement you'll ever find. That said, I don't know if I want to live in a community where the police have so much time on their hands, they're liable to cite you for even the slightest traffic violation.

I say let's put our heads together and come up with solutions where everyone wins. For instance, I'm intrigued by a practice recently started in London where they actually charge people a fee (beyond what they would ordinarily pay for bridge tolls) in order to enter the city. Elitist? Perhaps. But that's what they do. You pay an extra five pounds, or about eight bucks USD, for a sticker that will allow you into the city that day. You don't pay, you don't get in. That's one way to control traffic and congestion.

I'm also fascinated by so called "Lexus lanes," which is something Orange County has been trying on an experimental basis. These are specially designated lanes in the roadway that enable you to get from Point A to Point B quicker than everybody else. Lexus lanes are like car pool lanes with a catch: If you want to drive in them, you have to pay extra. Otherwise, you're restricted to the regular access lanes every other driver uses. In a way, it's like the difference between opening a regular account at a bank and paying extra for a premium account. Or between flying coach and first class.

While Lexus lanes may also be considered elitist, I can accept that because the concept is so eminently fair. For one, the city earns revenue from the people who are paying the extra fee for the right to use those specially marked lanes. More revenue means more money for addressing other transportation issues from which all drivers in the city will benefit. Number two, every driver who uses a Lexus lane is one less driver in the regular lanes. That means less traffic for people in those lanes. So if you're on a budget and can't afford to pay for the Lexus lane, or simply refuse to pay the premium as a matter of principle, you're still contending with fewer cars in your lane.

That's the kind of innovation I think we need to solve some of our driving problems. Instead of trying to pry people out of their cars (or give them tickets at the drop of a hat), let's be pragmatic about it. Let's focus on decreasing traffic and making the experience more palatable for people, rather than wasting our time and your advertising money on mass transit campaigns that when all is said and done are not likely to have an impact anyway.

Shifting gears, so to speak. . . . Parking poses other challenges, especially in a city as densely packed as San Francisco. Here we have over 790,000 residents in an area of only 47 square miles. That's close to 17,000 people per square mile. God knows how many cars we have. What we do know, however, is that there is nowhere near enough parking spaces. As a result, people started en masse to park illegally, double park, or stop in bus zones.

Well, you do that long enough and it's just a matter of time before the bus company gets upset. Sure enough, the San Francisco Municipal Railway (or MUNI, as we call our public transportation system) started lobbying the Department of Parking and Traffic (DPT). Guess how they solved the problem? They convinced the DPT to raise the fine for parking in a bus zone from $50 (which is how much it cost five years ago) to a whopping $275. And if you look around the City, you'll notice that nobody parks in bus zones anymore.

From a voice of reason standpoint, that's a surefire solution to many traffic-related problems. Whether you have an excess in parking violations, speeding tickets, cars going through red lights, or drivers who hit pedestrians, if you want to deter people from doing those things in the future, you have to hit them where it counts: in the pocketbook.

Then again, there's also an inherent unfairness to it. I mean if the fine was only 50 bucks and you felt you could afford to pay it, you might be inclined to say, "What the heck, I'll take a chance and park in the bus zone anyway." But $275 is a pretty steep ticket no matter how much you happen to make. As a result, people no longer do it.

Then again, we're right back where we started. There is still nowhere near enough places to park our cars.

Street parking is an issue that hits close to home. We have two cars in our family, but only have room for one car in the garage. My wife Jan uses the garage. And since you can't park in your own driveway here in San Francisco (the California Vehicle Code prohibits parking on any portion of the sidewalk, and says explicitly that the majority of driveways in the City are "part of the public right-of-way that is considered the sidewalk"), that means I have to park on the street in front of our house. So I know what a hassle it is to circle the block for a parking spot whenever I come home.

WHY ARE WE SO EASY ON DRUNK DRIVERS?

We are much too lenient on drunk drivers in the United States. Why can't we take this more seriously?

Driving a car under the influence of alcohol is much the same as waving a loaded pistol in the air. Cars are weapons. Cars can kill people. There are Scandinavian countries where if you get *one* driving under the influence (DUI) offense you not only lose your license for 12 months, you might also spend a year in jail.

I'm not necessarily advocating zero tolerance on drunk driving no matter what your alcohol level is. But I do think we can be a lot tougher. If you're brazen enough to disregard the law, you ought to be punished much more harshly than the law allows right now. As it stands right now, you look at some of the laws we have on the books and it almost seems as if we go out of our way to make it as convenient for drunk drivers as possible.

Here the California Highway Patrol (CHP) does periodic sobriety checkpoints at certain locations to crack down on drunk drivers. Now on the face of it, that's a good, sound practice. No doubt most other jurisdictions throughout the country do the same thing, especially during New Year's Eve, Memorial Day, Fourth of July, Labor Day, and other times of the year when our roads are busiest and people are more likely to drink and drive. Problem is, whenever there's a major holiday crackdown the CHP not only tells the media they're going to establish checkpoints, they also say *where* they're going to set them up two or three days ahead of time.

From a common sense standpoint that makes zero sense. You're basically telling drunk drivers, "Okay, here's where we'll be stationed Friday night. Whatever you do, stay away from there." Which means, of course, that you can drink, drive, and conceivably get away with it by simply avoiding those areas.

Dwight "Spike" Helmick is the commissioner of the California Highway Patrol. He's one of the most forthright, refreshingly honest public officials I have ever met, and for that he has my ut-most respect. So when I asked him to explain the rationale be-hind the CHP's checkpoint policy, he didn't duck the question. He agreed that it makes no sense to announce the locations for the checkpoints in advance—but added that state law nonetheless re-quires the CHP to do so.

That being the case, reason would urge that we change the law on that real fast.

Along the same lines, we should also tighten up on insurance laws and make it mandatory for all drivers to carry insurance. Yes, that *is* the law in California . . . but apparently three out of every 10 drivers in this state blatantly disregard it anyway. Why not make people think twice before being so reckless?

Now is that too much government intervention? Hardly. Some-one drives a car without insurance. They hit a four-year-old girl and paralyze her for life. Without mandatory insurance, technically speaking they would be off the hook because they don't have the money to take care of her.

Does that seem right to you?

AB 45: A COMMON SENSE BILL DONE IN BY ITS OWN HAND

California State Assembly Bill 45 would have made it mandatory for all drivers to use a hands-free phone device when driving. Sim-ply put, the bill said that if you have to make a call while you're on the road, go right ahead . . . so as long as you do so with the use of a head set, ear piece, speaker phone, or any other hands-free technology presently available. In other words, for obvious reasons of safety (not to mention common sense) the measure un-derscored the importance of keeping your hands on the wheel and your eyes on the road at all times.

AB 45 struck me as another straightforward and levelheaded "bill of reason." Speaker phones are standard features available in most new cars these days. Many people use head sets or ear buds with their cell phones anyway. All the measure would have done is require drivers to use these devices in the interest of safety if they're talking on the phone while driving. Why would anyone want to fight that?

But many cell phone companies did. AT&T Wireless, Sprint PCS, Cingular Wireless, Nextel, and T-Mobile all fought hard for amendments that not only severely watered down the bill, but also called for provisions that would have pushed the law in an entirely different direction. Among other things, they lobbied for an amendment that would have banned anyone under the age of 18 from using a cell phone while driving—an idea that Assemblyman Joe Simitian, the man who originally authored AB 45, didn't support at all. As a result, Simitian found himself in the awkward position of rounding up votes to *shoot down his own bill*. And that's exactly what he did.

As if you and I needed yet another reason to stay out of politics.

This one makes you scratch your head, folks. You would think that the cell phone companies would want a bill like this if only because they've already developed all the hands-free mechanisms that drivers would have to buy in the first place. In other words, from a moneymaking standpoint they would seem to have everything to gain. Not only that, their products all have disclaimers that plainly say, "For reasons of safety do not use a hand-held cell phone while driving. Use a hands-free device instead." And yet they band together to scuttle a bill that says exactly the same thing.

Reminds you of the cigarette companies, doesn't it? They include the warning from the Surgeon General on every pack of cigarettes, or put out campaigns that say young people shouldn't smoke, yet they fight tooth and nail any time someone speaks out about the hazards of smoking.

"It's a hard dynamic," said Assemblyman Simitian when he appeared on my show after the bill was defeated in July 2003. "New York has had a law similar to this one on the books now for about a year and a half. It certainly hasn't brought conversation or commerce or traffic to a halt in New York. Plus we have 30 countries around the world that have laws of one sort or another regulating cell phone behavior. It's a well-established phenomenon at this point, yet we still get this resistance from the very people who acknowledge that it's a problem."

In the meantime, it's back to square one. Here's hoping common sense will eventually prevail on this issue.

AN AGE-OLD DILEMMA IF EVER THERE WAS ONE

When a horrible accident takes place, it forces us to look closely at what happened and ask what can be done to prevent similar tragedies in the future. And while laws are invariably changed as a result, it isn't always easy. Because these issues are often so emotionally charged, we have to work just as hard to prevent reflexive reactions from impeding common sense.

Elderly driving, for example, set off a huge debate in California in 2003 following the report of a deadly crash at a farmers market in Santa Monica that killed 10 people and injured as many as 50 others. The driver was an 86-year-old man. Blood tests found no traces of alcohol or drugs in his system. The incident was clearly an accident. And while it was not the driver's first accident (apparently he had run into his own garage some months before), his overall driving record was solid. In fact, by all accounts he had led an exemplary life. Yet, he was charged with manslaughter.

From a voice-of-reason perspective, there are two key questions: (1) Should an 86-year-old man be driving in the first place, and (2) do you charge this man with manslaughter?

Let's tackle the second part first. As much as my heart went out to the families of the victims who were killed that day, I couldn't help but feel just a little compassion for the driver as well. Yes, without question he was clearly at fault. Without question he should face some sort of punishment. But at no point did he ever say, "I intend to use my car to kill or injure people." As a matter of fact, by the time his car finally stopped, the driver was so dazed he had no recollection whatsoever of what he had done. It was a freak accident. Now he has to live with the fact that he killed 10 people.

Short of revoking his driving privileges and making him spend the rest of his life in court settling civil lawsuits, how else do you possibly punish him?

Charging the man with manslaughter just struck me as a bit excessive. Wouldn't you say his life is already ruined enough as it is? What . . . you want to put him in prison, too?

I go back to the point we discussed before. As much as I believe we're always responsible for our actions, our intent has a lot to do with it.

It's one thing if you're speeding or driving under the influence. You deliberately chose to exceed the speed limit. You deliberately chose to drink and drive while drunk. You make a reckless decision like that and of course you should be held accountable for the consequences of your actions.

Now you can argue that if you're 86 and have already demonstrated impaired judgment such as driving into the wall of your own garage, then you really have no business being behind the wheel and are likewise responsible for what happened. I'll admit, that's hard to quarrel with. Even so, beyond taking away his license what more can you possibly do? He didn't mean to cause the accident. It was a terrible tragedy. And I just don't see what can be accomplished by throwing the book at an otherwise good and decent man. That doesn't seem right at all.

Elderly driving is such a touchy issue. On the one hand, common sense would remind us that our skills and reactions as a driver naturally diminish as we get older. Therefore, we should pay particular attention to drivers once they reach a certain age. Years ago California Senator Tom Hayden tried to pass a bill that would have required an additional test for drivers 75 and older beyond the regular written and visual test. In addition, Hayden's bill not only would have reduced the interim between renewing licenses from five years to four, it also would have required drivers to renew their licenses every year after age 90. But the American Association of Retired Persons shot down that measure on the grounds of age discrimination. The AARP pressured the state legislature to water down the bill to the point where it became meaningless.

On the other hand, when I advocate punishing the man who caused the tragic accident in Santa Monica by revoking his driving privileges, I don't say that lightly. Many older people look upon their driver's license as their last vestige of independence. I know that as well as anyone else.

My mother was someone who lived for that driver's license, especially in her declining years. I've shared this story with my listeners many times over the years—it's one of my favorite recollections of my mom. She was diagnosed with breast cancer at a time when her driving skills were at best tenuous. Jan and I flew down to see her at Cedar Sinai Medical Center in Los Angeles. And you know how it is with cancer . . . it's one of those subjects that when you first learn somebody has it, you don't know what to say. But I do remember saying, "Boy, I'm really sorry, Mom."

She looked at me as if I were nuts. "What!?! You lose a breast, you lose a breast. But losing your driver's license . . . *that's a different story.*"

She wasn't kidding, either. Forget cancer. She was more concerned over the possibility of giving up the ability to drive. Like many other older people, she considered her driver's license to be her last link to independence. Take that away and suddenly you're not mobile. You're not free. You have to rely on other people to get around. That's very difficult for anyone to accept.

Believe me, I understand that. But at the same time, what about the rest of us who are on the roads or trying to cross the street?

As I say, it's touchy. Unless you're a complete ogre, the last thing anyone wants to do is remove any semblance of independence from their mom, their dad, the people they grew up with, the people they care about. It's a painful, gut wrenching decision to make. For that reason, a lot of us would rather avoid it altogether.

A voice of reason would say if you want to address the problem with elderly drivers in a fair and balanced manner, don't just focus on the elderly. Come up with a new system where you test all drivers on the same basis, regardless of age.

Let's face it. The written tests in their current form are somewhat meaningless. Sure, you study the driver's handbook if you know you're going to be quizzed on it. But once you pass the written exam, you're liable to forget the rules just as easily as you forgot the facts for the history tests you used to cram for when you were in school.

Common sense would remind us that what really matters is the driving test. So let's develop a new test and make it fair and meaningful for everyone. Drive on a freeway. Change lanes with signal. Drive on a city street. Turn left. Turn right. Park on a hill. Parallel park. And so forth. Sure, it'll probably cost more, but you can easily finance it by charging more for the driver's license if you have to.

Think about it. Depending on the year, model, and number of cars in our household, we pay several hundred dollars a year just to register our cars. Yet, it only costs a few bucks a year for the privilege of driving them. (In California we pay $15 for a driver's license every five years.) There's a certain lapse in logic there that we really ought to address.

IT'S TIME WE HAD A NATIONAL IDENTIFICATION CARD

While we're on the subject of driver's licenses, I think it's ridiculous that you can lose your license in New York yet come out to California and still get one. Or that you can be 14 and drive in one state, but you must be 18 to drive in another.

There's a cliché that goes along with this: If you're old enough to die for your country, you should be old enough to vote, drink, or drive. That makes a certain amount of sense. As it presently stands, though, it's hard to know how old "old enough" is because the age of consent varies from state to state. That's never made sense to me at all.

That's why we should have a universal age of majority: one standardized, agreed-upon age of consent recognized across the country. Once you reach that age—whether it's 16, 18, 19, or 21— you would have the right to drink, drive, vote, marry, join the military, enter into legal contracts, and otherwise make the decisions that impact your everyday life. At that point, you would also become officially responsible for your actions for the rest of your life.

Along the same lines, we also ought to have a national driver's license. Or to make it even simpler, I think we should have one single card that we can use as our driver's license, passport, Social Security card, and all other means of identification. One card with our photo and thumbprint on it that would be recognized as a national ID card for reasons of safety and security is the way to go.

I mean, think about it. Right now, you've got your driver's license. You've got your credit card. Each of these cards has a strip. We don't know what's on that strip. If I'm computer savvy and wanted to find out all about you, I can. So why not make it harder for privacy fiends, hackers and identity thieves (and simplify matters for ourselves at the same time) by making it one single federal card? If you're decent, honest, law-abiding, and have nothing to hide, why would you oppose this?

Now does that sound 1984-ish? Possibly. But let's be real. These are not normal times. Identity theft is a one of the fastest growing crimes today. There are people out there who are malicious and want to mess with our lives simply because they can.

I'll say it again. There are some matters where common sense should prevail.

WOULDN'T YOU WANT TO KNOW IF YOUR CLIENT DID IT?

Speaking of common sense, let's talk about lawyers and legal issues.

At the risk of sounding like an Anglophile, there's another idea from the British that I think we should adopt. This concerns media coverage of high-profile cases. Whether it's the impeachment hearings of Bill Clinton, the assault charges against Kobe Bryant or William Kennedy Smith, or the murders of Laci Peterson or Nicole Simpson, it's common practice for American journalists to effectively "try the case in the media" by reporting and analyzing every single aspect of the investigation as it comes down the pike.

There are practical reasons for this, many of which have to do with the "rush to be first" and constant need on the part of cable networks and Internet news sources to fill content, as we talked about before. But that doesn't necessarily make it right.

That simply isn't done in England. They don't try defendants in the media. The media isn't even allowed to discuss the case until *after* the case is decided in a court of law. I have maintained for years that ought to be the practice in our country as well.

Then again, if that were the case, I might well be out of a job!

There's a certain logic missing in talk shows today because we get so bogged down in reality. It's one thing to say that O. J. Simpson was not convicted of first-degree murder. It's another thing to say that he didn't do it.

Now, is it that unbelievable that O. J. got off the hook? No. I may be outraged by the verdict, but I'm not naïve. I realize that our legal system is not necessarily about seeking justice. It's an adversarial system predicated upon winning. The system is by no means perfect, but it's the only one we have. If the evidence isn't there, or if the evidence *is* there but you're up against a lawyer or team of lawyers crafty enough to convince a judge to throw out the evidence on some obscure technicality or another, there's a very good chance you're going to lose.

I realize that. I realize there are people in prison today who were convicted of crimes they did not commit, just as there are people out on the streets who were acquitted of crimes they actually did.

We may not have had a chance to try the case ourselves, but we still know the facts. We've seen the images. We listened to the testimony and heard all the analysis. Just because the system got it wrong doesn't mean we can't discuss it honestly and directly.

I have a rule of thumb when it comes to certain hot-button, highly charged legal cases. It's an idea I first developed with my listeners as a result of the O. J. case. Whenever we discussed Simpson, I'd start each hour the same way: *This is America, and in America you're presumed innocent until proven guilty in a court of law. But this ain't a court of law, folks—it's a radio talk show. We all know he did it, so let's talk about it and go from there.*

Granted, when I say "We all know he did it," I'm being facetious. My listeners know that. Truthfully, I don't know whether he did it any more than you do. There's always that 0.0001 chance he didn't.

But I know how I feel. And I know how my listeners feel. And I know we need to talk about it because sometimes we just need to vent.

I'll admit, I have a hard time feeling any connection or empathy for criminal defense attorneys. I really do.

I've talked to a lot of different defense lawyers over the years: Johnnie Cochran, Alan Dershowitz, Gerry Spence, John Burris, and many, many others. Invariably, I will ask them: "How can you look at yourself in the mirror? You know your client committed this horrible, horrible crime and yet you're out there defending the guy anyway. How can you possibly live with yourself?"

Invariably their answer is the same: "We don't know if they're guilty or innocent *because we never ask them that.* We don't know, and we don't want to know. The only question we ask our clients is what the charges are, and what their response to those charges will be." Their rationale is this: *Our job is not to "get clients off the hook." Our job is to ensure that our clients receive a fair trial—which is all the more difficult in this day and age when defendants are often tried in the media before they even get to court. Nevertheless, that's our burden. The burden of the state is to prove its case against our clients beyond a reasonable doubt. If the state fails to do so, and our clients are acquitted regardless of whether they may, in fact, have committed the crimes for which they are accused, that's not our problem. That's the state's problem. That's the way the system works in this country.*

I understand their argument intellectually. I would even agree with it on the principle that "Everyone is entitled to a defense." That part is certainly true.

Having said that, on a gut level I find this explanation completely distasteful. Because if what defense lawyers are saying is true, then we're to believe that the "Dream Team" never asked O. J. if he murdered his wife.

There's something inherently wrong with that. You'd like to think we live in a society where someone can say to his lawyer, "Yes, I did the crime. Please get me the best deal you possibly can."

I could accept that from a common sense standpoint. Ours is again an adversarial legal system. As a defense lawyer, knowing that your client is guilty, you then look for extenuating circumstances. You come up with a way of presenting the case so that leniency can be shown. But apparently that's not the case when it comes to defending murderers, rapists, and other violent perpetrators.

Do you really think we're going to think less of you because you know your client committed the crime? *You're a defense attorney. That's your job.* So to suggest that you don't ask because you don't want to know just strikes me as hypocritical.

HOW TO UNCLOG THE COURT SYSTEM: CHANGE THE RULES TO "LOSER PAYS"

We talked before about the importance of taking responsibility for our actions. That means if you go through a Stop sign, and your car gets hit, you're the one that's responsible—not the person who hit you. If you're fat, and you eat at McDonald's every day, it's not McDonald's fault that you've put on all that weight. It's your fault. Own up to it.

Unfortunately, we seem to have reached the point where everyone has forgotten that. Seems the minute anything goes wrong, we look for someone else to blame instead of pointing the finger at ourselves. We've become such a litigious society, it's almost a knee jerk reaction to sue.

Now, the simple solution would be to say, "Let's stop that." Except you can't really do that because in America we have every right to litigate if that's what we choose to do. More to the point, common sense would remind us there are legitimate reasons to sue people. Indeed many lawsuits are not frivolous at all.

The problem is what to do with the frivolous lawsuits that are clogging up our legal system.

There is a way out of this mess. In fact, it's an idea I have advocated for as long as I can remember. Change the rules to "Loser Pays."

"Loser Pays" is a common sense solution that would remind people that there are consequences for our actions, especially in a court of law. Under "Loser Pays," if you sue someone unsuccessfully, you would be required to pay the defendant's legal costs as well as your own.

Think about it. You anger me. I want to make you miserable in return. I decide to sue you for everything you've got just because I can. No matter how baseless, petty or innocuous you think my cause of action is, you still have to respond to my lawsuit. My friend is an attorney. He'll represent me for free. I have nothing to lose and everything to gain.

So unless you already have a lawyer, you have to go out and find one. That will cost you money. That will also cost you time. You still have to plan a defense even though you know by the time the case finally makes its way to court, it will be tossed out immediately for being so patently ridiculous.

Now let's compare results. I get the satisfaction of making you sweat, and it didn't cost me a dime. You, on the other hand, have lost money, lost time, and your life is now a wreck. Exactly how fair is that?

Filing a lawsuit is no different than making a bet. You and I go to a ball game together. Barry Bonds is up. I bet you 50 bucks he hits a home run. We shake on it. Bonds strikes out. I lose the bet. Now it's going to cost me.

Sue someone in court and you're doing the same thing. You're saying, "I bet that the judge or jury will see this my way." All "Loser Pays" would do is hold you to that bet by making it serious. So if I decide to sue you just for the hell of it, only to lose in court, I would be required to cover your legal expenses as the penalty for putting you through such aggravation in the first place.

Not only is "Loser Pays" inherently fair, it would dramatically reduce the number of lawsuits filed in this country, frivolous or otherwise. From a common sense standpoint, are you more likely to sue if you know you might have to pay the other guy's costs . . . or less likely?

I realize opponents to this idea will say, "Nice try, but that would never work. Change the rules to 'Loser Pays' and only the rich can afford to sue."

Except that wouldn't be true at all. Even if you're flat broke, but have solid grounds for a lawsuit, any good lawyer will take your case because he knows he can win. Most attorneys in private practice still do a fair amount of work on a contingency basis, and some pro bono. And if you're a defendant who has truly been wronged but can't afford the costs of litigation, you'll still find representation because your lawyer knows that he'll be paid by the party who initiated the suit. Either way, you're covered.

On top of that, "Loser Pays" would also force some attorneys to tighten up, or at least practice with more discretion. For example, personal injury lawyers—the so-called "ambulance chasers" with dollar signs in their eyes who always seem to pop up every time there's a major accident—might have to think twice before seeking out clients whose claim of whiplash is at best borderline. That's not necessarily a bad thing.

Then again, some would say, "Ronn, isn't there already a mechanism in place that would require the loser to pay?" In employment law, for instance, when a plaintiff's attorney sues a company for intentional infliction of emotional distress (among other causes of action), he'll often ask the court for attorney's fees as part of the original complaint in the event his client wins. Isn't that basically the same thing as "Loser Pays"?

No, it isn't. Just because you ask for attorney's fees does not necessarily mean the court is going to award them to you. Besides, if you're going to ask that the other side pay attorney's fees if you win, you should also be willing to reciprocate in case you lose. When's the last time you ever heard a lawyer offer that?

All I'm saying is that you shouldn't even have to ask for attorneys' fees in the first place. And you wouldn't have to, because that would already be written into the law under the condition of "Loser Pays." In other words, go at it in court. Give it your best shot. But if you lose, be prepared to pick up the tab on both sides.

The only possible snag to a "Loser Pays" system would be in the case of lawsuits that involve large corporations.

Let's say you're a plaintiff with an *Erin Brockovich* type of case. You and your lawyer decide to take on a huge conglomerate like Pacific Gas & Electric. You're confident your case will stand on the merits, but you're going to war with an army of one. PG&E, on the other hand, can throw 100 attorneys at you without blinking an eye.

A lawsuit is stressful enough as it is. It's also a grind. You go up against a PG&E and you can bet they're going to use every resource at their disposal to prolong the case in hopes of discouraging you, wearing you down, and making you go away.

The case drags on for five years, perhaps even longer. After a long, hard, and draining battle, you finally win a verdict in your favor.

On the one hand, PG&E covers your legal costs, as would be required under a "Loser Pays" system. On the other hand, PG&E makes millions of dollars a year. They have to pay their legal counsel anyway. So they dole out an additional six or seven figure amount to you. That's a lot of money to you and me, but it's no big deal to them. They defend themselves against people like you all the time. That's part of the costs of running a large corporation. That's why they have a legal department. Compared to their annual revenue, what they're paying you is merely a drop in the bucket. They'll make back that money in no time.

In the meantime, sure, you may have beaten the big corporation in court. But they made damn sure it wasn't easy. You cost them a lot of zeroes, but they cost you five years of your life and all you'll ever earn. No matter how much money you win in court, you can't get those years back. And guess what? *The big corporation knows that.* Again I ask: How fair is that?

I'll admit that's one question for which I don't have an answer.

Then again, that goes to show the difference between voice-of-reason honesty and the absolute stances of the far left and the far right. The extremes will never admit they're wrong, while a voice of reason will concede there are some problems that not even common sense can solve.

A WIN-WIN SOLUTION FOR THE RIAA

Downloading music from the Internet is another legal matter in desperate need of a compromise.

On the one hand, were I a recording artist who released a CD that sold millions of copies, and I suddenly realize that people are downloading digital copies of my songs from a source that was distributing it without my consent (and for which I receive no additional remuneration), I might be upset. Maybe even a lot upset. That music is my work and my livelihood. I control the rights to that work and should be entitled to earn whatever I can from the fruits of my labor.

Then again, look at it from the consumer's side. You hear a song on the radio you like so much, you want to buy the CD. You pay 20 bucks for the CD. If it's a typical CD, it has that one song you really like, another one that you sort of like, and 10 to 12 others that you will never listen to again. Which means, in essence, that you've just paid 20 bucks for one or two songs.

Why would you want to do that if you knew you could get that same song online for only a fraction of the cost, without being stuck with all those extra songs?

The days of your neighborhood Tower Records, Wherehouse, or Sam Goody selling just CDs and cassettes are rapidly drawing to a close. Virtual music stores are the future. Legally or not, people are downloading. That's the direction this issue is going in.

Why the Recording Industry Association of America (RIAA) refuses to wake up and face this fact is completely mystifying.

If they were smart, the music companies would look at this issue the way politicians responded to term limits. Meaning, instead of fighting reality, find a way to make it work for them. Come up with a solution where everybody wins.

So what does the recording industry do? They insist on resorting to scare tactics and other combative measures when there's no need for that whatsoever. They support Draconian initiatives that call for technology that would blow up your computer if you ever downloaded a song illegally. They throw their weight around by filing lawsuits that target everyone, including 12-year-old honor students and 66-year-old grandmothers.

Rather than be reasonable and practical about this, the RIAA has chosen to act like a bully simply because it can.

Common sense suggests it would behoove the industry to offer a business solution that benefits everyone. Make the music available online. Charge a reasonable downloading fee per song—29 cents, 79 cents, 99 cents, whatever the price happens to be. Make it available digitally, which is how most people get their music today anyway. This way, everyone is happy. You get the songs you want and *only* the songs you want. The recording industry makes their money. The artist gets his share. It's a win-win all around.

That's what you have with virtual music stories such as iTunes, RealNetworks, BuyMusic.com, and MusicMatch Inc. Give people a good product at a good price, and they'll come back again and again.

Such a solution would require the RIAA to utilize common sense and be proactive. So far, that's just not something they've been willing to do.

Now to be fair, Universal Music did announce in the fall of 2003 that it would reduce the prices of most CDs from $20 to $13. That's certainly a step in the right direction.

Then again, if they can slash the price of the same product by as much as 35 percent without even blinking, what exactly does that tell us?

Politics and
Popular Culture

Pop culture lets us all be kids again. Pop culture enables us to talk about things that aren't necessarily important in terms of world events, yet they *are* important in the sense that they provide pleasure and entertainment in our lives. For that reason, pop culture has always been an integral part of my show.

We all work hard. At the end of the day, we look forward to the things that help us unwind: seeing a movie, dining at a restaurant, catching a ball game, spending time at home, or whatever else we enjoy doing. By the end of the week, we're especially ready to relax and recharge for a couple of days before going back to work on Monday.

I know I'm that way. So are my listeners. And my approach to radio reflects that. A typical week of my show tends to start "heavy" in terms of subject matter then gradually becomes "lighter." Some topics have what I call a definite "Friday feel." They may not be earth shattering, but they help us relax and get ready for the weekend. So in addition to discussing politics and the news, we have regular features on movies, television, music, books, wine, restaurants, travel, leisure, electronic gadgets, and celebrity gossip. That's all part of our popular culture.

The great thing about pop culture—whether you're talking about people, movies, music, sports, or TV—is that it opens the door to a forum like no other. That's because when it comes to pop culture there is no right or wrong answer.

You like *The West Wing*. I like *The Sopranos*. You like Leno. I like Letterman.

You like Brad Pitt and Julia Roberts. I like Clint Eastwood and Sharon Stone.

You root for the football Giants. I pull for the baseball Giants. You're a fan of Roger Clemens. I prefer Barry Zito.

You wanted Clay to win on *American Idol*. I voted for Ruben.

You like Fridays at the opera. I like Fridays at the track. Everyone's tastes are different. Everyone's style is uniquely his own. That's part of the fun of pop culture.

In this age of connectivity, we're especially vigilant against viruses that can spread fast and damage our computers. Pop culture, however, is one virus that's always welcome. Little by little pop culture has crept its way into every aspect of our lives. Even the world of politics.

I'm not necessarily talking about celebrities who run for political office, although that *is* a topic we'll get to in a bit. I'm thinking more along the lines of political ads that look so much like regular commercials, you almost forget they're political ads. Not to mention politicians who integrate catch phrases, rock music, or other aspects of pop culture as part of their political campaigns.

Walter Mondale won the 1984 Democratic presidential nomination with an assist from popular culture. At the time, his biggest rival was Gary Hart, a media favorite who promised a lot of "New Ideas" without offering any real specifics. Mondale debated Hart and quickly deflated him when he asked "Where's the beef?"—a simple question that was also an enormously popular slogan that year for Wendy's Hamburgers.

Bill Clinton broke ground in 1992 by using "Don't Stop Thinking About Tomorrow" by Fleetwood Mac as his campaign song, as well as appearing on late night variety shows such as *Arsenio Hall*.

Arnold Schwarzenegger took it a step further by announcing his gubernatorial candidacy to Jay Leno and the rest of the country on *The Tonight Show.* Arnold then attempted to appeal directly to California women voters by appearing on *Oprah* with his wife Maria Shriver at his side.

Then there's the matter of politicians making cameo appearances on popular TV shows. Who can forget Richard Nixon saying "Sock it to me" on *Laugh-In* back in 1968? Or when Rudy Giuliani played himself in the famous "nonfat yogurt" episode of *Seinfeld*?

Speaking of *Seinfeld,* I can't help but think of the one where Jerry first said the line that has since become a classic: "Men don't care what's on TV. They only care *what else* is on TV." When you think about it, that's how most of us view popular culture.

Pop culture is so fluid, we often focus more on what's coming up next than we do on what's going on now. And that's also what makes it fun. Whether it's the latest buzz show, a hot dance craze, or a cool new gadget, by the time a trend finally jumps the shark we've already moved onto the next big thing.

What do I mean by "jump the shark"? Glad you asked. That's a perfect measure of pop culture.

"Jump the shark" is a phrase first made popular by an Internet web site that traces the decline of television shows past and present. The term refers to an episode of *Happy Days* in which someone challenges Fonzie (Henry Winkler) to jump over a shark tank while water-skiing off a ramp—a plot device so preposterous, *Happy Days* went downhill from there. The basic idea of *jumptheshark.com* is that every series likewise has a defining moment where it peaks in terms of quality, popularity, or credibility.

If you followed *Dallas,* for example, that moment came once Bobby Ewing (Patrick Duffy) returned to the show despite having been *fatally struck by a car* the year before. Faced with the task of resurrecting Bobby from the dead, the producers came up with a solution that had *chutzpah* written all over it. In Duffy's first scene, Bobby's wife Pamela (Victoria Principal) wakes up, sees him in the shower and says, "Honey, you won't believe the nightmare I had." Just like that, Bobby's death and every other plot line from the previous season went completely out the window. The audience was now expected to believe the entire year *had all been part of a dream*. From that point on, *Dallas* was never the same. It hit its peak. It lost credibility. It jumped the shark.

And when you think about it, that's the way it is with our kids and pop culture. That's the way it was when *we* were kids. In terms of popularity, everything jumps the shark. There's always another catch phrase, hair style, fashion design, or dance craze waiting in the wings. As a parent, all you can do is try to keep up. Although by the time I finally get around to using whatever new word my daughters are using, it's usually too late. They've already moved on to the next one.

It's interesting how as we grow older our approach to pop culture becomes a little more staid. Not to suggest it's "All Brooks Brothers, All the Time" once you reach a certain age. It's just that there comes a time when all of us realize it doesn't matter if we keep up with absolutely everything that comes down the pike. We form our own opinions. We become our own people. It's no longer important to be like everyone else because we're comfortable being ourselves.

Then again, this is coming from a guy who once bought a Firebird when he was in his thirties simply because Jim Rockford drove one. So maybe some things never change at all.

POP CULTURE REFLECTS WHO WE ARE

There is one constant, though. And that's the fact that popular culture always speaks to who we are. Whether it's jamming as many bodies as we can into a phone booth or VW bug, trying to win stardom on a reality TV show, or slapping a provocative bumper sticker on the back of our car, we latch onto any aspect of pop culture that either appeals to us or otherwise brings attention to ourselves.

Not that there's anything wrong with that. It's part of human nature. All of us crave some kind of recognition. It goes beyond wanting our 15 minutes of fame . . . it's wanting to be noticed, period.

Disagree with that assessment? Then let's look back at most of the fringe candidates who ran in the recent California gubernatorial recall: Larry Flynt, publisher of *Hustler;* Gary Coleman, former child actor and star of *Diff'rent Strokes;* Leo Gallagher, the stage comedian known for smashing watermelons with a sledge hammer; billboard queen Angelyne, the chesty model with the dark glasses whose ubiquitous images appear all over Sunset Boulevard in Los Angeles; Georgy Russell, the 27-year-old software engineer who sold thong underwear on her official campaign web site; Mary Carey, the adult film actress who ran on a platform that would have made lap dances a tax-deductible business expense.

Then there were those whose candidacies were derailed for one reason or another: The 18-year-old high school student who still lived with his parents; the 52-year-old retired police officer whose pet issue, literally, was the legalization of the domestic ferret; the 101-year-old woman whose campaign was underwritten by a 99-cent thrift store; a slew of conservative radio talk show hosts up and down the state; Don Novello, the comedian best known as "Father Guido Sarducci" from *Saturday Night Live;* and others too numerous to mention. In many cases (such as that of Novello), their campaigns were cut short because they did not have enough certified signatures from registered voters to qualify for the replacement ballot. State law requires that in addition to paying a registration fee, prospective gubernatorial candidates must file a petition with valid signatures from at least 65 registered voters. Once the signatures are certified by the secretary of state, the candidate qualifies for the ballot.

Now you can argue that some of these people entered the race as a form of political protest. And in many cases that was certainly true. Gary Coleman, for example, was approached by an Oakland-based alternative weekly newspaper that wanted to express its displeasure with the entire recall process. They offered to pay his registration fee and underwrite his campaign if he agreed to be their candidate. And as I said before, I found a lot to like about Gary as a candidate, even though I did not vote for him.

Now did I take every fringe candidate seriously? No. Did I find them disgraceful? Not at all. Those who ran paid their $3,500 registration fee and got their 65 signatures. Those who announced but didn't run still got their names in the paper.

This is America. Land of opportunity. Anyone in this country is free to take a chance on running for political office. Even a porno actress.

I remember a call from a listener who was particularly irate over the candidacy of Mary Carey. "She's a *porn star*," he said. "How do you explain that to your kids?"

Simple. For one, I'd remind them that the recall was far from a usual election. Beyond paying the filing fee and raising enough valid signatures, potential candidates for governor need only be at least 18 years old and a resident of this state for at least five years prior to the election. Mary Carey qualified on all counts.

Number two, I'd tell them that Mary Carey had little chance of winning . . . and that deep down she probably knew that. But she also knew it would get her all kinds of publicity that could only help her career.

I'll say it again. We're a society that craves attention. Like it or not, that's who we are.

THE CHANGING FACE OF CELEBRITY

Speaking of publicity, we live in interesting times when it comes to celebrities.

When I was a kid, we had movie stars, TV stars, sports stars, music stars . . . and that was pretty much it. Gradually, though, we started getting into other kinds of "stars." For example, Lee Iacocca was one of the first "business" stars. That paved the way for other "celebrity" CEOs such as Bill Gates, Donald Trump, and Rupert Murdoch.

When Charlie Finley ran the Oakland A's, he constantly made headlines by firing managers, alienating his players, and coming up with wacky ideas like the designated hitter, the designated runner, and orange-colored baseballs. That made him the first "celebrity owner" (as opposed to Gene Autry, a celebrity in his own right who for years owned the California/Anaheim Angels). That also opened the door for other spotlight-grabbing sports franchise owners such as George Steinbrenner, Ted Turner, Jerry Jones, and Mark Cuban.

My friend and colleague Dr. Dean Edell was one of the first "medical celebrities," as was psychologist Dr. Joyce Brothers.

Graham Kerr and Julia Child made fame possible for Emeril Lagasse and other TV chefs today.

The O. J. Simpson trials turned legal analysis into a popular form of television. That led to "legal celebrities" such as Greta Van Sustern, Alan Dershowitz, Gloria Allred, Cynthia McFadden, Leslie Abramson, Royal Oakes, and, of course, Johnnie Cochran. Not to mention an entire cable network in Court TV.

And then there are "political celebrities" such as Chris Matthews, Sam Donaldson, Cokie Roberts, Sean Hannity, Bill Press, Pat Buchanan, Arianna Huffington, Wolf Blitzer, and Tim Russert.

Now in this era of instant celebrity and reality TV, we've reached the point where we've come full circle.

I'll bet that half the kids that you talk to these days have either been on television for one reason or another, or at least knows someone who has.

Watch a show like *American Idol* or *American Juniors,* and inevitably you'll hear kids say: "I just want to be famous." They don't know why they want to be famous, and they don't really care. Could be dancing, could be singing, could be acting or telling jokes. Doesn't matter what it is, so long as it gives them a shot at the brass ring.

There's nothing wrong with that. It's a form of competition. Common sense would remind us while competition can sometimes bring out the worst in people, more often than not it brings out the best. Not only that, competition is an extension of capitalism. Capitalism embodies who we are as a people.

Yet at the same time, it's kind of sad. I watch a lot of these shows with my family. As much as I'm fascinated by them, I often wonder about the stability of contestants who are willing to subject themselves to all kinds of humiliation just to be on television. True, for many contestants a reality show is the equivalent of a 13-week audition tape or a live-action 8-x-10 glossy. If they can't win the big prize, they figure maybe some talent agency might notice them and sign them to a contract once the show is over. And in some cases, that happens. Even so, signing a talent contract is no guarantee of fame and fortune. L.A. is brimming with unemployed actors. Before they know it, they've fallen in line with all the other reality contestants, never to be heard from again.

Even if you should win the big prize, that's no guarantee either. No disrespect intended, but beyond posing for *Playboy* what else has Jenna from *Survivor* done?

Celebrities used to be bigger than life. Some will always have staying power: Bill Cosby, Johnny Carson, Larry King, Joe Montana, Willie Mays, Muhammad Ali, Reggie Jackson, Mick Jagger, Sean Connery, Paul Newman, Robert Redford, Jane Fonda, Robin Williams, Billie Jean King. Some have staying power even after death: Frank Sinatra, Bob Hope, Milton Berle, Elvis Presley, Lucille Ball, John Lennon, Clark Gable, John Wayne, Humphrey Bogart, Katharine Hepburn, Marilyn Monroe, John Belushi, James Dean.

Now we seem to have a lot of mediocre stars these days. More and more we see people who are famous just for being famous. Kato Kaelin. Monica Lewinsky. Roger Clinton. Melissa Rivers. Richard Hatch. In this age of reality television, we've gone from celebrities who were larger than life to celebrities who are just like us.

I don't know if that's good or not.

WHO CARES WHAT BARBRA STREISAND THINKS?

What concerns me most about celebrities today is the credence we often give to their views on current affairs. Just because Martin Sheen makes a convincing chief executive in *The West Wing,* doesn't mean he's an expert in presidential politics. So why does it matter whether he opposes Bush's policy in the Middle East or endorses the Democratic candidate in 2004?

Who cares what Pierce Brosnan thinks of the environment, or whether Sean Penn believes there were WMDs in Iraq?

I'd rather hear Madonna talk about her new album (or, for that matter, why she French-kissed Britney Spears at the MTV Movie Awards) than anything she has to say about foreign affairs.

There's a transference here that people are somehow blind to. You may excel in one area, but your expertise doesn't necessarily carry over into others. A newspaper would never hire a politician as a movie critic. That makes about as much sense as having a comedian in the broadcast booth on *Monday Night Football*.

And yet when a celebrity expresses a political opinion, we insist on taking him or her seriously even when common sense would suggest otherwise.

That said, do celebrities have a right to speak out? Sure they do.

Yet, it's been said it is better to remain silent and be thought a fool than to open your mouth and remove all doubt. We've all heard the line, though apparently no one knows exactly who said it. Some cite Voltaire. Some say Samuel Johnson. Others say Abraham Lincoln. Regardless of where it came from, it would behoove some actors to consider the wisdom of this saying before they speak their minds.

Now before you jump on me, let me just say that by no means do I believe that all performers are dim bulbs. I have interviewed countless film and television actors. Many have shown themselves to be quite knowledgeable in their political and world views. Some are even voices of reason.

Let's put it this way: From a business standpoint, speaking out on current events can do an actor more harm than good. You may gain some fans. But you'll probably lose more. Especially if you really don't know what you're talking about. Better to be silent and let everyone project and presume you agree with them.

Case in point: Barbra Streisand. With all due respect to Barbra Streisand's many accomplishments as a singer and actress, her thoughts on the environment and foreign affairs are so preposterous that if anyone else expressed such thoughts they'd be laughed off the planet. And yet when Barbra Streisand talks, people listen.

Or I should say, *some* people listen.

Then again, some celebrities just never quit. No matter what the issue is, we know where Mike Farrell stands. We know where Tim Robbins and Susan Sarandon stand. As we do George Clooney, Janeane Garofalo, or Woody Harrelson. The Hollywood left is alive and well, same as it ever was.

Then again, politics are nowhere near as prominent in movies themselves as they once were. With the notable exception of *The West Wing,* you rarely see films or TV shows with the kind of overt political speeches Jimmy Stewart made in *Mr. Smith Goes to Washington.* And that's partly because most movie companies today tend to be owned by major conglomerates. So you keep politics out of the movies for the same reason—because you know it's bad for business.

Say you're a movie executive. You have a larger, more powerful board of directors to answer to these days, not to mention all those stockholders. Which project gets the green light: the slow-moving yet thought-provoking political drama, or the formulaic blockbuster with big explosions, lots of sex, and Bruce Willis saving the day? One is daring and prestigious but will probably tank at the box office. The other breaks no ground whatsoever but is likely to be a surefire hit. Unless you don't care about losing your job, you really don't have a choice.

Another reason why we don't see politics portrayed as often as before in movies is much more fundamental. In this day and age of 24/7 cable channels, high-speed Internet access, and non-stop media saturation, celebrities have become so ubiquitous they no longer seem important.

Time was, you didn't see celebrities all the time. Now you can turn on *Entertainment Tonight* or the E! cable channel and catch footage of your favorite star arriving at a Hollywood premiere or taking you behind the scenes of a movie or TV show. Or you go online and boom, watch the video stream of the event live in its entirety. We're so accustomed to having the stars delivered to us at our disposal, there's no buildup. There's no payoff. We just take it for granted that they're there.

Which goes back to what we said before. Being famous has lost its luster. There are no more surprises to celebrity itself than there are to celebrity opinions. Barbra Streisand isn't suddenly going to throw her support behind President Bush, any more than Charlton Heston is going to renounce his opposition to gun control.

There's a fundamental hubris at play here. It's excessive pride to presume just because you're a celebrity, people are going to listen to you and automatically take your advice.

Brad Pitt, Jennifer Aniston, and Danny DeVito decide they're going to resolve the conflict in the Middle East. Never mind that they have no experience in international politics. Never mind that they have no experience in conflict resolution. They're Brad Pitt, Jennifer Aniston, and Danny DeVito. They decide they're going to succeed where Bill Clinton, Kofi Annan, the United Nations, and countless others before them have failed.

Talk about calling attention to yourself.

Look, I'm as big a believer in compromise as you'll find. We as Americans tend to believe we can solve just about anything if we just put our heads together and talk. I suspect that's where these three actors are coming from. And I genuinely wish them luck. But if you honestly think you can end centuries of animosity between Israel and the Arab world by sitting down and talking it out between the two sides, you've got another thing coming. Not if you've really paid attention to what's been going on there.

Now you do a talk show long enough and inevitably people will ask for your opinions on politics and current affairs. And while I happen to think a radio talk show host is certainly more qualified to comment on the news than a movie star—after all, keeping abreast of current events is a major part of my job—that doesn't make me right or wrong. It's still just my opinion. In fact, if I've changed my mind on one matter or another, that only goes to show that my opinion isn't always right.

Then again, some celebrities have more substance than others. Ronald Reagan immediately comes to mind. You may not agree with his political views, but he was a bright, dedicated, charismatic leader.

You want an example on the left? How about California State Senator Sheila Kuehl. She began her career in acting. She was Zelda on *Dobie Gillis*. She also graduated from Harvard Law School and taught law at UCLA, USC, and Loyola. Not only is she intelligent, she's a person of integrity. She was the first openly gay person ever elected to the California legislature. She has also been a staunch opponent of domestic violence and an advocate for children, families, and women, first as an Assemblywoman then as a Senator.

Plus what sets apart a Shelia Kuehl, Arnold Schwarzenegger, or Clint Eastwood from other opinionated celebrities is the fact that they've all run for public office. They're not just spouting their political views—they're putting themselves on the line. They're out on the campaign trail, talking to people and trying to make a difference in their city, town, or state.

I have more respect for a celebrity like that than someone who mouths off from the top of their Malibu mansion, only to remain cloistered from the rest of the world.

TWO THUMBS UP FOR INDEPENDENT THOUGHT

The sad part when to comes to political opinions—be they those of a movie star, columnist, or radio talk show host—is that once we find someone whose opinions we admire, more often than not we latch onto them to the point where we let them think for us.

I'm not saying it's wrong to look to others as a benchmark for our opinions. We all do this to some degree. It starts at a young age, usually when it comes to movies. We grow up watching *Siskel & Ebert* (or as the case is now, *Ebert & Roeper*), and we figure if they gave it two thumbs up, the movie must be good. But there also comes a point where we come to realize that the critic's opinion is just that—an opinion. While we may still take that opinion into consideration, hopefully we also learn trust to our own instincts and start thinking for ourselves.

I used to do this myself when I was a kid. I grew up in New York. There was a magazine called *Cue* with a film critic named William Wolf. I was 13 or 14 when I first read him and realized, "You know, this guy looks at movies the way I look at movies." So I started paying attention to his reviews. If he thought a movie was good, I'd go ahead and see it. If he said it was awful, I wouldn't bother.

Well, I'm older now and it's much the same thing. I have an affinity for people who think linearly and come to a logical conclusion, especially one that either teaches me something new or leads me to look at things in a way I may not have considered before. Toward that end, there are certain columnists or commentators whose opinions I particularly like and respect: people such as Chris Matthews, Tom Friedman, Tim Russert, George Will. If they should present a logical conclusion that I happen to disagree with, I won't necessarily switch . . . but I will reexamine my own opinion on the matter and read the article again just to make sure I didn't miss anything.

If I reread it and find that my argument doesn't hold up, I'm willing to change my view and go along with theirs. But if I read the article again and still don't buy the logic, I'll just disagree on that particular issue.

See, that's the beauty of thinking for yourself. You take the time, you look at an issue carefully, and you realize "Okay, we just see this one differently." There's nothing wrong with that at all.

The thing is, we have such a collective Type A/"faster, faster"/ have-to-know-it-right-away mentality, we're too lazy to sit down and decide for ourselves. The voter pamphlet is too long. The issues are too complicated. It's too much time to sort through everything. So we look for the easy way out.

Which accounts for the popularity of cable news shows and certain radio talk shows. Many people will tune in knowing they're liable to vote in the same way as their favorite pundit votes. They're perfectly content with saying, "Hey, I'm in good company. Let somebody else state my position for me."

BUMPER STICKERS: YET ANOTHER WAY OF ATTRACTING ATTENTION TO OURSELVES

One of the funniest things I ever heard on the radio came out of the mouth of my friend Pete Wilson—the talk show host, that is, not the former governor of California. Pete's a longtime Bay Area TV news anchor who also hosts the afternoon drive show on KGO radio. In many respects, he's also a voice of reason when it comes to his political views.

One day I was driving around listening to Pete's show when he somehow got to talking about bumper stickers. Now we all have things that peeve us and Pete is no exception. Bumper stickers happens to be one of Pete's pet peeves.

"What bothers me most about bumper stickers," Pete said, "is that once you see one, there's no way you can talk to whoever put it on the car in the first place. Either the car is parked, and the person is nowhere in sight—or the car is in motion, just as you're in motion. Either way, you can't talk to the driver. There's no room for dialogue. So you see a bumper sticker that expresses an idea you don't happen to agree with, and there's nothing you can do about it."

The minute he said that, I laughed so hard I nearly drove off the road.

I also wonder about bumper stickers but for entirely different reasons. Why anyone would spend $20,000, $40,000, or $50,000 on a brand new car, then immediately slap on a bumper sticker on it is simply beyond me. Especially if it's a political bumper sticker.

Put a political bumper sticker on your car and you're bound to infuriate half the people who see it simply because they disagree with your views.

I think back to the days leading up to the war in Iraq. Seemed like every Volvo you saw in Marin County came with a mandatory "No War on Iraq" bumper sticker. As one of the few people in the Bay Area who strongly supported the decision to invade Iraq, that made it real simple. Whenever I saw one of those bumper stickers, I knew I just wanted to avoid that driver.

Either that, or you'll find that everyone agrees with you. In which case, all you've done is ruin your car.

I'm pro-choice. I'm driving behind you and see that you have "A Woman Has the Right to Choose" slapped on your rear fender. What do you want me to do, honk my horn?

The only bumper stickers that I can conceivably agree with are the ones we see right before an election, where you're demonstrating your support of a particular candidate or proposition.

Then again, how much difference is that bumper sticker really going to make?

Let me get this straight. It's the Sunday before the presidential election. You're still not sure which way you're going to vote, or whether you're even going to bother at all. You and your wife go out for a drive when you see a car with a "Bush" bumper sticker on it. Suddenly you say to your wife, "Gosh, honey, I'm glad we did this. Now that I've seen that Porsche, I'm voting for George W. Bush."

Why do we do this? I go back to what we said before when we talked about celebrity. We want to be noticed. We all just want to be noticed.

The same could be said for "flash mobs," vanity license plates, personal web sites, and Internet web logs (or "blogs," as they're colloquially known).

In some ways you could say that "blogs" are really the bumper stickers of today. People do like to post things on the web.

I have no problem with that. As I say, I spend several hours a day online. I love the instant access to information. You want to buy a new gadget, for example, all you have to do is Google it and you're instantly in touch with other consumers who can help you answer whatever questions you have. I think that's great.

And certainly chat groups, bulletin boards, and the like bring people together, socially as well as professionally, who may otherwise have never met. In that respect, the Internet gives people the opportunity to communicate, to vent, be noticed, or feel as though what they say actually means something.

One thing's for sure. An Internet web log is more effective, reaches considerably more people, and enables you to express your views with many more words than a bumper sticker on the back of your car.

Giving Voice to the Majority: A New Dimension in Politics

The problem with conclusions is that unless the message is clear in the first place, it's hard to know what conclusions to draw.

We talked about this before with the California recall. On the one hand, it's difficult to glean any conclusions from an election in which animosity toward Gray Davis cut through party lines. It didn't matter whether you were Democrat or Republican, politician or private citizen. *Nobody* in California liked Gray Davis. You could certainly argue that even the 45 percent who voted no on the recall were not so much endorsing him as they were voting against a process they felt was wrong in principle.

That said, I think there are some lessons from the recall that apply to politics in general, and presidential politics in particular. One that immediately comes to mind is that if you give people the right ingredients, they will become interested in politics.

Without question, if the recall had been Gray Davis versus Tom McClintock, the interest wouldn't have been the same. With

Arnold Schwarzenegger, you not only had the star power, you had a candidate who was refreshing, someone who gave you "Morning in America" again—the upbeat, positive television campaign dreamed up by advertising guru Hal Riney that is widely credited for helping elect Ronald Reagan president back in 1980.

Whether you're out of work at a time when the national unemployment rate has gone up for the third conservative year, or are concerned about our exit strategy in a war where U.S. military casualties continue to rise, there are times when you need someone to pat you on the shoulder and say, "Don't worry, it's going to be okay." Even if you don't feel that way yourself, whether you're sick in bed with the flu or are worried about making your next mortgage payment, that little bit of encouragement still feels good.

That's basically what Schwarzenegger provided. Multibillion dollar deficit or no, he gave Californians the sense that one way or another, we'll pull through this together.

Say what you will about Schwarzenegger, but he stirred up interest in many different groups of people. He rallied business people behind him not just because he wanted to ease up on regulations for new companies coming into our state, but for the other ideas he proposed to turn the economy around. He pointed out, for example, that California receives just 77 cents for every dollar it spends with the federal government. Arnold wants to improve that figure and the Bush administration said they'd work with him on that. That'll help us with the deficit for sure.

Schwarzenegger got young people who knew him from the movies involved in his campaign. He drew support from men who liked the macho act. He made significant gains with women throughout the campaign, and maintained that support despite the barrage of groping allegations thrown at him just before the election. And he has people across the country paying attention to California politics. Speaking as a person who espouses a middle-of-the-road philosophy, I think that's a good thing.

People will look to Sacramento and see if a Governor Schwarzenegger can work together with a largely Democratic Senate and Assembly and build consensus. At least, they will on a short-term basis. If Schwarzenegger fails, then the interest will wane and nothing will have been accomplished beyond getting rid of a widely unpopular governor.

But if Arnold succeeds, I believe two significant things will happen that will benefit us all in the long run. Number one, we'll see more emphasis on positive accomplishments in political campaigns than perhaps we've ever seen before. And number two, it will trigger a movement away from the politics of the extremes and toward the politics of the middle ground. Political strategists will recognize that the best way to win an election is by coming to the center. Political parties will focus more on the values they have in common with each other than the ideologies which drive them apart. In the long run, that will bring about a new dimension to politics: moderation, if you will, on a national level.

If that should happen, then perhaps those of us in the majority will finally have a voice in mainstream politics that can speak for all of us.

THE MIDDLE GROUND IS A MOUND OF SOUND

The emphasis is on *mainstream*. Certainly the majority has a voice in politics. We just haven't always heard it articulated. Until this book, it's been hip to be square (as my friend Huey Lewis once sang), but it's never been hip to be in the middle. And the reason why is that we live in a society of labels, sound bytes, and instant access. We want our information right away and in terms that are easy to grasp.

Trouble is, the middle doesn't adhere to any one label. That makes us difficult to talk about, let alone understand.

Let's go back to what we said about structure and predictability. In politics as well as in everyday life, we like to know what we're dealing with. That's what you have with the left and the right: Their voices are very clear. You see a person in a Volvo with "No War in Iraq" slapped on their rear fender, or drive past someone holding an "Abortion Is Murder" sign at a rally outside the federal building, you know exactly where these people stand. There are places in radio and on television where they can go if they want their opinions validated.

It's far less predictable if you're in the middle because the middle is much more fluid. There's "movement" in the sense that people in the middle are actively, constantly thinking, weighing each issue on a case-by-case basis instead of strictly along party lines.

The middle doesn't follow any one straight line. The middle doesn't fit into any one pattern—other than perhaps the "pattern" of looking at developments as they come up and keeping an open mind. The pattern of welcoming the other side and seeing what can be gained from it, instead of shunning it reflexively and closing the door. The pattern of valuing independent thought, instead of ridiculing it. The pattern of voting on the basis of what's right, as opposed to what's safe. The pattern of "thinking to win," so to speak, as opposed to "thinking not to lose."

If you're on the far left or the far right, what I did on the recall—voting yes at the last moment after weeks and weeks of agonizing over it—makes zero sense. People on the extremes are too entrenched to agonize over anything.

If you're in that "rational middle" (as I like to call it), what I did makes complete sense. You may disagree with how I voted, but you appreciate the process of weighing everything carefully because you went through it yourself. Not only that, you understand what it means to go against the grain because you've done that yourself.

Fifty-five percent of Californians voted for the recall. Yet, I live in San Francisco. Four out of five people in San Francisco voted *against* the recall. My vote alienated many people. It especially upset some friends and family.

But that's part of being in that rational middle. Sometimes you have to stick your neck out. Sometimes you have to go with what your instinct says is right, no matter how unpopular that may prove to be.

There's also movement in the middle because the middle has many voices. And all of our voices are talking to each other, listening to what we have to say, working to achieve common ground so that we can continue to move forward.

That makes us multidimensional. That doesn't, however, always make us easy to listen to. In a way, we're the noise you hear in the garage when your kids start a band. With all our different voices, we're a cacophony that initially sounds like a terrible racket . . . until we come together in harmony. Then we sound like one.

The extremes, by comparison, are one-dimensional—same song, same note, all the time. You may not like what you hear, but at least you know where they're coming from. Consequently, that makes the extremes easier to deal with than the "mound of sound" (as Phil Spector used to say) you have in the rational middle.

There's nothing wrong with thinking things out. Unless you're clearly pandering for votes, there's nothing wrong with changing your mind. There's no law that says you must always follow the same path on every single issue. There are times to consider the other side because their view may be the right one.

Put them all together and the views of the middle don't always fit in a neat little package. Then again, few things in life do.

COMPROMISE IS NOT A DIRTY WORD

This isn't to say is we're impossible to understand. Everyone has issues that are "slam dunks"—even people in the political middle. But we have many other issues that are not slam dunks. There are problems where the solution does not come about without first a great deal of thought.

Arnold Schwarzenegger becomes governor of California. Despite all the numbers thrown around during the election, no one seems to know the exact size of the deficit. More to the point, now that you're in office what do you do to fix it? You have a lot of options at your disposal. You have to weigh them carefully and make decisions—knowing that in the course of doing so, some of your priorities will get pushed aside.

Say one of your priorities coming into office is repealing the 300 percent vehicle license fee increase—which, in fact, Schwarzenegger did literally within minutes of taking office. On the one hand, you fulfill a campaign promise and make millions of California drivers very happy. On the other hand, the car tax hike was supposed to bring an extra $4 billion into the state. What are you going to do to replace that revenue?

Say another priority is improving education. You want to commit money to the schools. What do you do, cut back on prison funding and start letting people out? Or do you keep pouring money into the jails at the risk of our children's future? These are difficult decisions for which there are no easy answers—certainly none that are neat and clean.

That's why it helps to have a "half-a-loaf" approach, in politics as in life. Sometimes principle has to take a back seat to pragmatism. That's one idea the middle is comfortable with.

Republican State Senator Tom McClintock runs for governor in the California recall. He had a solid political base in the Los Angeles area, but on a statewide or even national level no one had really heard of him. In the course of the campaign, he came off as (1) very right wing—which he is, and (2) a man of integrity. He is just as uncompromising in his views on abortion and gun control as he is in saying the only way to resolve the deficit is to cut, cut, cut.

Give McClintock credit for being honest and direct. The man put his cards on the table. You always knew where he stood.

The problem is, when you're that uncompromising you will always have views that people can't accept. Politically speaking, that makes you the equivalent of the unpopular guy who's always picked last to play stickball. Nobody really wants you. Your approach may play well among your own constituents, but you'll never win on a large scale.

Compromise is not a dirty word. We make compromises every day. You drive to work, and you know you have to be there at a certain time. Well, now the light is yellow. Do you go through it or not? Which is more important: being a few minutes late for work, or zipping through the yellow light and taking the chance that someone might hit you?

Marriage is a compromise. I've come to believe that the secret to a successful marriage is not only understanding everything about each other, but also learning what to ignore—or if you'd rather, learning what to accept.

When you think about it, the same idea applies to politics. You more or less accept some things you don't want in order to achieve the things you do want. That's the difference between people in the middle and the "all-or-nothing" approach of the extremes. If you really want to get anywhere, you have to give a little ground.

I would love to see the Republican party on a national level running more candidates with a Libertarian approach to social issues—which, when you think about it, shouldn't be that difficult to do. As we pointed out before, time was when "Leave me alone, home is my castle, don't tell me what to do" were all at the heart of Republican philosophy. How they deviated from those ideas to telling a woman what she should do with her body with regard to her reproductive rights is beyond me.

Common sense says if that you can get a new Republican party that is more Libertarian in its social views, and more conservative in foreign affairs and economics, you're going to appeal to the middle. Which means you're going to win a lot of elections. Before you know it, we'll see the same change take place among Democrats on a national level—not because they really want to change, but because at some point even partisan liberal Democrats will realize that bringing in Jesse Jackson as a secret weapon is no way to win the White House

Think about it. Who's the last Democrat Jesse Jackson helped elect?

I believe that if people on the far right start to gravitate toward becoming "new Republicans" like Arnold Schwarzenegger, and people on the far left gravitate toward becoming "new Democrats" like Bill Clinton, the day will come when the voice of the middle will finally be heard. Why do I say that? Because the new Republican will find areas of the new Democrat's philosophy *that he believes in, too*. And vice versa.

It's next to impossible for an ultra-liberal Democrat and an arch-conservative Republican to get along. The only thing the extremes have in common is that they're both fanatical about their point of view. But it's very easy for a new Democrat and a new Republican to find common ground. Much like people in the middle, a new Democrat and a new Republican share a much greater capacity than the extremes for seeing the other side. As a consequence, they can work past their differences and find a compromise they're comfortable with, to the benefit of all.

That's why I have confidence in Schwarzenegger, who took office shortly before this book went to press in November 2003. Schwarzenegger understands compromise. He proved that a new Republican can win an election even in a state as far to the left as California.

Bill Clinton was the best and the worst at compromise. Clinton proved that a new Democrat could win the White House because he understood that if you appeal to the center and make yourself attractive to Independents (as well as people who might even be moderate Republicans), you're going to win the office. Which is exactly what Schwarzenegger did in California by appealing to moderate Democrats.

Clinton understood compromise so well on a political level. And yet when it came to his personal life, he didn't understand it at all. He could have applied that same principle of compromise to the Monica Lewinsky scandal had he simply said, "All right, how do I handle this? If I admit the truth, I'm going to look bad in the eyes of my wife and in the eyes of the American people. But at the same time, I might win points with the American people for being upfront about it. That will help me ride this through." Only he couldn't see it that way. His own ego would not allow him to reach the same kind of compromise in terms of disclosing his affair that he had done so many times before in the political arena.

There's no question Schwarzenegger learned from Clinton's mistake when he owned up to the *Oui* interview early in the campaign, as well as when he apologized for "behaving badly toward women sometimes" in the final days of the campaign. He knew it was going to cost him in the short run, but he also knew it would help him win in the long run. And if it didn't . . . at least he was being honest about it.

I get the impression, rightly or wrongly, that that's who Arnold is. I don't think it was a matter of his advisors sitting down and telling him "This is what you have to do." I think when he said "Yeah, I did that" or "I'm sorry that I offended people," that's really the way he is. There's something to be said for that.

LOOKING AHEAD TO THE PRESIDENTIAL RACE

How do the lessons of the recall apply to the 2004 election? On the one hand, it's pretty straightforward. If you want to be president, be positive. Be direct. Have a plan, but be willing to compromise. Deal with people as human beings. Talk to them. Don't be aloof. Don't be smarmy. Don't insult their intelligence. Avoid the puke politics of "Vote for me because the other guy is worse." Tell them why you're good instead. And above all, come to the middle.

Then again, it's a tough road to hoe. Look at what happened to John McCain in the 2000 primaries. McCain certainly ran far to the right on many issues. Yet, he also had the temerity to go against ultra-strict conservative doctrine, much the same as a new Republican would. And as all we know, John McCain walked into South Carolina and got clobbered by George W. Bush. Before long he was out of the race.

If you're running for president, you have to decide what's important to you and push those ideas forward.

Schwarzenegger was resolute in his ideas: "We need leadership. We need to give business more of a break in California." These were direct, basic, almost simplistic points of view . . . and yet they resonated with voters. So did his positive attitude.

Now in fairness, Schwarzenegger is an exceptionally positive candidate. You look over the field running for president and truth be told, the most positive candidate in the race is George W. Bush.

The major Democratic contenders as of this writing were Massachusetts Senator John Kerry, U.S. General Wesley Clark, North Carolina Senator John Edwards, and former Vermont Governor Howard Dean, with Dean regarded by most political observers as the front runner for the nomination. With that in mind, I talked to some of the top political analysts in the country and asked for their predictions as we head into the primary season:

John Kerry. Tucker Carlson, the conservative co-host of CNN's *Crossfire,* thinks Kerry will end up getting the Democratic nod, "even though he's run a terrible campaign thus far. But ultimately I think he's the best candidate the Democrats have to offer and that he'll win the nomination. But we will have to see."

Chris Matthews of *Hardball* thinks Kerry will ultimately run a better campaign, but that it won't be enough for the nomination. "Most things in life are yes or no: Are you getting married, or not? Are you going to take that vacation, or not? One of the burning issues of this campaign is *are you for this war, or not?* So far Kerry won't answer the question."

General Wesley Clark, the anointed candidate of Bill and Hillary Clinton. "Clark is learning the hard way that politics is a tough business," said Wolf Blitzer of CNN. "He knows a great deal about national security and military matters, but he doesn't necessarily know a great deal about domestic and economic issues, health issues, social issues. He's going to have it tough. What he has going for him, though, is that he's brilliant. He graduated top of his class at West Point, which is not easy to do. He's a Rhodes Scholar from Arkansas who didn't dodge the draft, if you know what I mean. He has brought in a lot of Clinton people who are working with him. He has put together a solid political team who will help him."

Obviously, Wolf knows Clark very well from their work together on CNN, and I certainly respect Wolf's opinion. But I have a problem with Wesley Clark.

On the day he announced his candidacy, Clark told the American people that if he were in Congress at the time he would have supported the resolution that authorized the United States to invade Iraq. As one of the few people in the Bay Area who supported the war, that piqued my interest. I already respected Clark's military record and career in public service. Now he seemed to come across as an independent thinker. I respected that about him, too.

Trouble is, Clark's advisors went ballistic: "Look, you're running for president on the Democratic ticket. Coming out in support of the war is no way to win the nomination. You have to pull back on your remarks. And this is how you do it."

Sure enough, the next day Clark did a flip-flop: "Forget what I said yesterday. I would have voted against the war."

That's part of the problem with our two-party system. To win the nomination, you have to run to the left if you're a Democrat, run to the right if you're Republican. To win the general election, you have to move to the center. How is the voter supposed to know who you really are?

I think Clark's initial statement spoke to who he really is. But I have no way of knowing that. As it stands, it looks like he's fudging one way or the other. That's no way to start a campaign. And I think that will haunt him in the end.

I'll remain open to Clark, because I think he can bring stability to the Democratic ticket. But I'd have a lot more respect for the man had he stayed true to his original feelings. Right now he's coming off like Gray Davis in the California recall: "What do I say in order to get the right number of votes?"

Howard Dean and **John Edwards.** That's who Chris Matthews believes the Democratic race will boil down to as of October 2003. "The nomination will come down between an anti-war candidate and a pro-war candidate. At this point, that will be Dean against Edwards. Dean will do well in Iowa and New Hampshire. Edwards will pick up steam late in the game—he may finish third or a close fourth in New Hampshire, then he'll do well in South Carolina. He'll be the Southern candidate, pro-war. Dean will be the Northern candidate, anti-war. That will be the battle all the way to California. And if that holds up, California will go to the anti-war candidate."

"That being the case," I said to Chris, "then Howard Dean is your Democratic nominee. Which means George W. Bush wins reelection."

"That may be," countered Chris, "but let me say this: *events matter.* The American people love to pick as their president the man with the sun in his face, the eternal optimist who comes in from the outside and challenges the system. That was Reagan. That was Ike. That was Truman. That was JFK. That was Clinton. At this point in the primary season, that's Howard Dean. Maybe he's peaked too early. By the time we get to the general election, Dean may look too left wing, too civil union. But right now he seems just right. I don't see Bush picking up any of the liberal states that voted for Gore in 2000. Not New Hampshire. Not Pennsylvania. Not Michigan. Not Wisconsin. Not Washington. Not Oregon. Not Iowa. Not California—not even with Arnold.

"I think the country is looking for hope and deliverance, and that many issues will drive this election. If the economy is about what it is now (which is bad, but not terrible), Bush will probably squeak by. But if the unemployment rate goes down to 5 percent, Bush wins big. If it goes up to 7 percent, Bush loses—or at least, he *should* lose. And as far as Iraq is concerned . . . over 100 U.S. soldiers have been killed, and over a thousand more badly wounded, since Bush declared victory in May. If we continue on with another 13 months of casualties in the field, or GIs getting knocked off by Iraqi soldiers, then look out George Bush."

It's hard to argue with Chris's analysis because he understands politics so well. And I certainly agree that a Democrat who runs as an optimist stands a much better chance of winning than a Democrat who whines and complains.

Howard Dean is uncompromisingly liberal on so many issues, many of which I happen to support. Like Wesley Clark he may be too irascible for his own good, but he seems like a man of integrity. But unless the economy goes completely in the tank I don't see him galvanizing the country. Not with 60 percent of the country still believing that the United States taking action in Iraq was the right thing to do. And even if Americans are in a feisty mood by the time of the general election, I don't see Dean coming to the middle and appealing to the people whose votes he needs in order to win the White House. A man that far to the left has as good a chance of becoming president as a Republican like Tom McClintock has of becoming governor of California.

Then again, there's always the chance **Hillary Rodham Clinton** will surprise everyone and enter the race, notwithstanding her previous statements to the contrary. That's what Sam Donaldson of *ABC News* believes. "If she calculates that Bush can be taken in 2004, she's coming in and I think she'll get the nomination," according to Sam. "But if she calculates that if Bush can't be taken, then she won't enter the race—in which case, it won't matter who the Democrats put up because they will lose."

SIGNING OFF

We talked before about how the middle is fluid. For that matter, so are opinion polls. President Bush reacts to 9/11. His approval rating goes off the charts. The United States goes into Iraq. His numbers go up. We topple Saddam. His numbers go up.

As this book goes to press, Bush's numbers are favorable. Not what they were at the beginning of the war, but still on the positive side. That said—and without knowing the Democratic candidate, or the future course of events in Iraq, or how bad the economy will be at election time—I still say he's the favorite at this point because Bush, like Arnold, makes people feel good about themselves. He makes them feel good about this country. And I think he's genuine in that. He's a man of substance, certainly more so than people give him credit for. But absent that, he has a love of this country, he believes in this country, and he believes in the goodness of people in general.

That's what I'd advise the Democrats to do in 2004. Take what you believe in and find the best way of presenting it to the American people. Remind us of what a good country we have, and above all, tell us what you're going to do to make it even better.

Let's face it. That's what people want to hear. No matter how dour things may be, people want a sense of hope.

It's hard to energize people when you're negative. Somehow you have to balance that by being positive.

Not only is there nothing wrong with that, it's only common sense.

Index